SMALL TOWN,
STRANGE WORLD

SMALL TOWN, STRANGE WORLD

An Unofficial and Unauthorised
Guide to *Smallville*

Mark Clapham

First published in Great Britain in 2003 by
Virgin Books Ltd
Thames Wharf Studios
Rainville Road
London
W6 9HA

A catalogue record for this book is available from the British
Library.

ISBN 0 7535 0778 1

Typeset by TW Typesetting, Plymouth, Devon
Printed and bound in Great Britain by
Mackays of Chatham PLC

Contents

For Davina

About the Author

Mark Clapham lives in his Fortress of Arrogance, hidden away in the wild mountain steppes of North London. Ever since he was bitten by a copy of the *Radio Times*, he has led a mysterious double life. By day, he's a civil servant. By night, he writes about television, among other topics. As part of his ongoing crusade for justice, he has written *Doctor Who* spin-off novels, half of *Soul Searching: The Unofficial Guide to the Life and Trials of Ally McBeal* (also published by Virgin), and reviews for genre magazines. He is currently editor and writer for www.shinyshelf.com, a website devoted to films, television and comics. He'd love to hear from readers of this book, whether it be in the form of comments, suggestions or criticisms – email him at mark@shinyshelf.com.

Introduction

I can't remember there ever being a time when I didn't know who Clark Kent was.

Clark and his alter ego, Superman, have been culturally prevalent since long before I was born; in comics, in movies, on television, and in every other medium you can think of. Very few symbols are as recognisable as that red 'S' on the yellow background, and with over fifty years of pop-culture supremacy under his belt, Superman's position as a twentieth-century icon is unassailable.

But the twentieth century is behind us, and even an icon can do with a little reinvention now and again. Although only the latest in a long line of reinventions for the 'Man of Steel', the TV show *Smallville*, which launched in the USA in October 2001, is certainly one of the most radical overhauls the Superman myth has ever seen. The series' producers have summed up their approach in one short motto: 'No flights, no tights'. *Smallville* is set before Clark Kent became Superman, before he could fly, before he hid behind thick glasses and a secret identity, and long before he put on that iconic red and blue costume. So no cheesy Lycra costumes, no hard-to-pull-off flying effects, and no need to try and stage monumental battles with universe-eating supervillains on a TV budget. Instead the producers have reinvented the myth in the teenage action-fantasy genre popularised by *Buffy the Vampire Slayer* and inhabited by the likes of *Roswell* and *Charmed*, throwing in the wholesome small-town appeal of *Dawson's Creek* for good measure.

The result is a heady pop-culture cocktail, an enduring icon reinvigorated for a new century. *Smallville* boasts a talented and attractive young cast, intriguing ongoing storylines, top-notch special effects, a cool soundtrack and a neat line in the kind of small-town unease that has been a television staple since *Twin Peaks*. *Smallville* is clever, well made, witty and in general the kind of show that appeals to an intelligent and lively audience.

That, by the way, means *you*. And if *Smallville* is your kind of show, this should be your kind of book. Within its pages you'll find a guide to the episodes of *Smallville* broadcast so far, as well as information on the characters' previous existence in comic books and on the big and small screens. At the end of the book you'll find a few words on *Smallville*'s life in other media as well as some speculation on what the show's future might bring.

Welcome to a small town in Kansas, and the strange world of Clark Kent . . .

Before *Smallville*

To fully understand *Smallville* the series, you really need to look at the decades of Superman history that inspired it. Although it would take a book three times this size to chronicle the full history of the character both in fiction and as a real-world phenomenon, it is worth going over the basics in this chapter, while the next one goes into the background of the characters in the show, as well as giving a little production background to the series.

But first, a little history lesson. The character of Superman debuted in the first issue of *Action Comics* in June 1938. The brainchild of struggling comic-strip creators Jerry Siegel and Joe Shuster, he was an alien infant who escaped the destruction of his home world to land on Earth, where he developed amazing powers and lived a double life as both reporter Clark Kent and the heroic Superman.

The concept was a runaway success, and while the comic-book adventures continued to emerge from the publisher that would become DC Comics, the character quickly spread into other media. Most successful of these was a radio show, which created many of the trappings of the Superman legend that we know today, but there were also newspaper strips and a series of short cinematic cartoons beautifully animated by Fleischer Studios, one of the few serious rivals to Disney. In 1948 the first live-action Superman emerged in the cinematic serial *Superman*, but it was in 1953, when the *Superman* TV series starring the avuncular George Reeves began in syndication, that the character really became flesh. Reeves was a Superman people were happy to invite into their homes, warm and charming, and the series was a huge success.

No incarnation would match Reeves' efforts until almost twenty years after the actor's untimely death in 1959, when director Richard Donner's *Superman: The Movie* emerged on to cinema screens in 1978. Donner's film is a strange, dysfunctional epic, boasting a gaggle of screenwriters and conflicting styles of storytelling, but it was a huge success. Christopher Reeve's boyish, chiselled superhero redefined the character for a new generation. The producers of the film, Alexander and Ilya Salkind, went on to produce the film's first two sequels, *Superman II* and *Superman III*, the spin-off *Supergirl* movie and a poorly regarded *Superboy* television show, all of which ably demonstrated the principle of diminishing returns. However, one achievement cannot be taken away from them: in Christopher Reeve they found a Superman to rival George Reeves in the public mindset – no mean feat.

At the same time as the sequels to Donner's film became weaker and weaker through the early 1980s, the comicbook series had backed itself into a corner. DC Comics had been producing stories solidly featuring Superman, Batman and other characters for over forty years and the histories of these characters had become painfully convoluted. In reaction to the backlash against horror comics of the 1950s, comics had gone through a phase of anodyne whimsy, the legacy of this being that there were many stories involving DC's superheroes that they would do well to forget. Superman himself had become insanely powerful, making it almost impossible to create threats strong enough to take him on. Elsewhere, parallel worlds and other inaccessible bits of comics' lore made the books hard to read for newcomers. A spring-clean was needed.

In 1985 DC Comics blew up their universe and started again from scratch. Marv Wolfman and George Perez's seminal *Crisis on Infinite Earths* destroyed all the parallel universes and started the story of the DC Comics' characters again from the beginning. Writer/artist John Byrne re-launched Superman with his 1986 mini-series *The Man of Steel*, which made radical alterations to the character's background and abilities. Many of the ideas Byrne introduced have influenced every subsequent adaptation of the source material, making him the most influential comicbook creator to work on the character since Siegel and

Shuster. Although many other writers and artists contributed to the myth, for the purposes of simplicity in divining the inspiration for *Smallville* I will divide the comics into *historic* (i.e. pre-Byrne, pre-*Crisis*) and *modern* (post-Byrne) eras. That modern, post-Byrne era of Superman is still going on today, with the comics functioning as a continuous narrative since 1986. While the historic Superman had suffered from a stagnant status quo, the modern character has seen tumultuous changes in his life, most noticeably the epic 'Death of Superman' storyline, and his marriage to Lois Lane.

Although Richard Donner's 1978 movie was a definite adaptation of the historic Superman (albeit a radical, post-*Star Wars* vision), there have been important screen adaptations since that have taken their cue from the modern comics. *Lois & Clark: The New Adventures of Superman*, starring Dean Cain as the Man of Steel and Teri Hatcher as Lois, may not have defined the character in the public imagination to the same extent as Reeves or Reeve did, but it was a huge popular hit nonetheless. Aside from Teri Hatcher's position as one of the early sex symbols of the Internet age, the series brought a soapy, character-based version of Superman to the screen for the first time. Producer Deborah Joy Levine seems to have taken a lot of her cues from Byrne's work, but brought a lightness of touch to the series that made it almost a proto-*Ally McBeal*, a workplace fantasy romance show.

Although *Lois & Clark* took the character aspects of Byrne's work and put them on-screen, the animated series produced by Alan Burnett, Paul Dini and Bruce Timm took the more fantastical aspects of modern Superman comics as their inspiration, mixing in a dose of Fleischer for good retro measure. Slick, iconic and entertaining, the cartoon ran for 54 episodes, and this incarnation of Superman lives on in the *Justice League* cartoon produced by Timm.

Unfortunately, while these television versions of the character have prospered, and *Smallville* has demonstrated the ongoing success of Superman in that medium, a big-screen revival has proven more elusive. To list the current status of the movie project being developed by Warner Bros. would merely date this book, as no doubt by the time it is published the writer, director and stars will have changed all over again. Attempts to revive the series as a cinematic franchise have been ongoing since the mid-1990s, and millions in development money have been invested. So far, not a frame has been shot. Hopefully these plans will bear fruit.

Back in the world of comic books, Clark Kent still appears in the pages of *Superman*, *Action Comics*, *The Adventures of Superman* and numerous other titles from DC Comics. Of late, the comics have been throwing in occasional flashbacks to Clark's youth in Smallville, a sure sign of the TV series' influence. There's a beautiful logic to this – *Smallville* is an ingenious synthesis of many variations of the Superman story, adding a few unique twists of its own, so to see its influence feed back into the comics is a post-modern joy. The next chapter will untangle some of these influences and provide a concise guide to the world of *Smallville*.

Secret Origin: A History of the Characters and World seen in *Smallville*

Many of the characters and concepts in *Smallville* have been around for over half a decade – see **Before** *Smallville*. The creators of the series, Alfred Gough and Miles Millar, have effectively taken various seams of inspiration for this revisionist version of Superman, giving each element their own twist along the way.

Clark Kent

Strange as it may seem from watching *Smallville*, Clark Kent has, for many of the years of his fictional life, been a bit of a joke. In the historic Superman comics, Clark Kent was a disguise, the fumbling, slightly bland alter ego behind which the almost perfect persona of Superman was concealed from the world. This is certainly the impression given in *Superman: The Movie*, in which Christopher Reeve came as close as is humanly possible to making Kent and Superman two completely different people. The movie Clark is a façade, a series of theatrical tics that Superman rather smugly drops when he can. One of John Byrne's greatest contributions to the character was the idea that *Clark* was the real man, and that Superman was the face he put on for the world; this made for a more human character, one who could be more sympathetic. It's this Clark Kent whom Dean Cain plays in *Lois & Clark: The New Adventures of Superman*, for instance: a charming and straightforward man who becomes Superman out of a sense of honesty and decency, rather than an *Übermensch* pretending to be human.

Stories of Clark Kent's youth are not new. In 1945 the first *Superboy* story appeared, telling a tale of Clark Kent's costumed adventures as a boy. Superboy had his own comic book from 1949 to 1960, substantially adding to the history of the Superman character. Although there are many innovations from later comics in *Smallville*, the basic concept of a young Clark Kent and his friends having adventures in his home town dates back to those *Superboy* comics. With *Man of Steel*, Byrne changed all that, showing Clark's powers grow through his youth, and not having him wear the costume until he reached Metropolis as an adult. It is this version of the story that *Smallville* most closely follows, as Clark's powers become stronger over time. While Byrne loosely skips over Clark's adolescence in a few pages of his *Man of Steel* mini-series, Gough and Millar have managed to make these years into a whole TV series.

Visually, the *Smallville* Clark Kent seems inspired by the forgettable Jeff East (as the young Clark Kent) from *Superman: The Movie*. From his mop of dark hair to his red plaid shirts, East looks a lot like the *Smallville* incarnation of the character, although even with Christopher Reeve's voice dubbed over his own he has little charisma. While East is a put-upon outsider, the *Smallville* Clark Kent is a straightforward guy who has good friends and family, but also has to put up with growing pains of a kind no other kid has to deal with.

Much of Clark's charm in the series comes from his portrayal by model-turned-actor Tom Welling. A native of New York, Welling made several appearances as Rob Meltzer in the TV show *Judging Amy*, as well as guest shots in *Special Unit 2* and *Undeclared*, before landing this role.

Lana Lang

Historically, Lana Lang has never been the most interesting character. A creation of the *Superboy* comics, she fulfilled a similar role to Lois Lane in the Superman stories, that of pseudo-girlfriend and comic female foil. Superboy's adventures leaned towards the whimsical, and Lana found herself undergoing several magical and weird transformations, briefly, for example, gaining superpowers. In the Metropolis-set stories, the adult Lana simply functioned as a love rival for Lois. Byrne altered the character, making her the one person outside the Kent family that Clark shares his secret with, telling her on the night before he leaves town altogether. This disrupts Lana's life, leaving her rather sadly as the one who was left behind. Tortured by Lex Luthor in an attempt to learn Superman's secrets, Lana finally found happiness in the comics, marrying Pete Ross. Lana's main on-screen appearance has been in the Salkind-produced *Superman III*, where *Smallville*'s own Martha Kent, Annette O'Toole, takes the role. While O'Toole does a good job, she has very thin material to work with, and the film as a whole is poor.

The notable connection between all these versions of Lana is her red hair, one thing that Kristin Kreuk noticeably does not have! Kreuk's Lana is not the lovelorn country girl swooning after the oblivious Clark – quite the opposite in fact; in *Smallville* it's Clark who has to do the chasing, as Lana is attached to school football hero Whitney Fordman. Kreuk brings an innocent charm to the role of Lana, as well as undoubted good looks. One of the stars of Canadian teen soap *Edgemont*, she has also played the title role in a TV movie version of *Snow White*.

Lex Luthor

Introduced in *Action Comics #23*, Lex Luthor was a generic supervillain for hire. A redhead at first, he soon adopted the bald look favoured by his predecessor in the role of Superman's nemesis, the Ultra-Humanite. Through most of the historic comics, Luthor was a scientist and evil genius, and it's this exuberant, pantomime version of Lex that Gene Hackman plays in the Salkind-produced movies. Lex even had a historic connection to Smallville, his antipathy towards the Man of Steel coming from one of Superboy's experiments accidentally blasting Luthor's hair off! Thankfully, this teenage bitterness was abandoned by John Byrne, who on the suggestion of fellow writer Marv Wolfman made Lex Luthor a corporate raider. Byrne's Luthor is bulky and threatening, a redhead once more, and the head of the all-powerful LexCorp. He doesn't meet Superman until Clark is an adult.

Although the business background of Byrne's Luthor is similar to that of the *Smallville* version, other details are different. The modern comics' Lex is a self-made man rather than the product of a wealthy background, and much of his animosity towards Superman comes from the fact that while Luthor clawed his way up from poverty and an abusive childhood to become king of Metropolis, Superman simply flies in and eclipses his position as the most powerful man in the city. The comic-book Luthor is also decades older than Clark, a contemporary of *Daily Planet* editor Perry White (although the rigours of ageing have somewhat been dispelled by a brain transplant into a younger, cloned body). As well as being cloned (after a fatal case of cancer) Luthor has also had a child and successfully run for President of the United States. As on-screen, so in the comics: Lex is one of the most fascinating characters in the Superman canon in any medium you can think of.

Michael Rosenbaum plays Alexander 'Lex' Luthor with a dangerous charm. The most experienced actor among the younger members of the cast, New Yorker Rosenbaum starred as Jack in the sitcom *Zoe, Duncan, Jack and Jane* (latterly known simply as *Zoe*). His film appearances include *Urban Legend*, *Midnight in the Garden of Good and Evil* and *Sweet November*. Rosenbaum has prior experience of TV adaptations of comic books, having played numerous characters in *Batman Beyond* (*Batman of the Future* in the UK). He now plays the role of Wally West, a.k.a. the Flash, in the animated *Justice League* series. His latest films are *Sorority Boys* and *G-S.P.O.T.*

Whitney Fordman

A new creation, headstrong football captain Whitney Fordman is something of a small-town hero, and has a beautiful girlfriend in the form of Lana Lang. While created for *Smallville*, Whitney has a precedent in Superman lore – Lana has a similar jock boyfriend, Brad, in the Smallville sequence of 1978's *Superman: The Movie*. Whitney is Clark's love rival, and they soon find themselves clashing over her. Although arrogant and impetuous, Whitney is self-aware enough to know that his school sports career will only take him so far in life. Thus he's constantly on the lookout for the chance to try out for major teams like the Metropolis Sharks and Kansas State, and hopes to gain a football scholarship.

Canadian actor Eric Johnson appeared as a young Brad Pitt in the movie *Legends of the Fall*, and has had roles in the TV show *Texas Rangers* and the TV movie *Atomic Train*. Johnson's most recent role is in the TV movie *Bang, Bang, You're Dead*.

Pete Ross

Another character from the *Superboy* comics, Pete Ross has always been, and is in *Smallville*, Clark's oldest school friend. The *Smallville* Pete has many of the qualities of his comic counterpart, in that he's wisecracking, a little shady at times and not entirely reliable. Historically, Pete knew that Clark was also Superboy, and secretly helped him in his adventures. In the modern comics, Pete never found out. The modern Pete went into politics, becoming Senator for Kansas and, later, Vice President under President Lex Luthor. This puts his wife, Lana Lang, in a difficult position, as she knows Lex's true nature while her husband does not. Although Pete's political intentions have been touched upon in *Smallville*, the idea of an alliance with Lex seems unlikely, as the series' Pete dislikes and distrusts the Luthors. One notable difference is that in the comics Pete has always been white, while in *Smallville* he is black.

Boston-born Sam Jones III made two appearances in the hugely successful crime drama *CSI: Crime Scene Investigation* as James Moore before landing the role of Pete. He has also appeared in a TV movie version of Twain's *The Prince and the Pauper*, and played the lead in the movie *Snipes*. He co-starred with Allison Mack (Chloe Sullivan in *Smallville*) in the 'Camp Nightmare' episodes of *The Nightmare Room*, based on the book by teen-horror writer RL Stine. He recently played the title role of an autistic teenager in the movie *Zigzag*.

Chloe Sullivan

Student journalist Chloe Sullivan is an entirely new character, but has an obvious heritage as a junior version of the adult Superman's love interest, journalist Lois Lane. Chloe isn't just a clone though, as her character also exhibits a dash of post *X-Files* paranoia and the geek chic that is fashionable among secondary female characters in US teen soaps these days. Creator of the 'Wall of Weird', which chronicles local strangeness, Chloe can find whatever information the plot requires of her, computer hacking being a particular speciality. Chloe is the daughter of Gabe Sullivan, Lex's plant manager, and moved to Smallville from Metropolis with her family. Chloe has a cousin who is a student in Metropolis – fan rumour has it that this may be one Lois Lane . . .

Having made her debut as a child actor in the late 80s, German-born, LA-raised Allison Mack has appeared in projects as diverse as the movie *Police Academy 6: City Under Siege*, the sitcom *Opposite Sex* and the straight-to-video *Honey, We Shrunk Ourselves*. Her TV guest appearances include *7th Heaven* and *Providence*.

The Kents

In the historic comics, Clark Kent's adopted parents always died before he reached adulthood. Indeed, in the very first origin story Clark was brought up in an orphanage, before the later introduction of the aged Kents. Ma and Pa – Martha and Jonathan – Kent have always been portrayed as elderly rural folk, so it's no surprise perhaps that they didn't survive to see Clark become a man. *Superman: The Movie* broke this pattern, with Jonathan Kent dying from a heart attack, while Martha is still alive when Clark joins the *Daily Planet*. This could be inspired by Spider-Man, for whom the death of his Uncle Ben proves that 'with great power comes great responsibility'. The message of Jonathan's death in Richard Donner's film is rather different, as it demonstrates that even Clark's powers have limits. Unfortunately this useful limitation is totally belied by the movie's time-bending ending.

It was John Byrne who decided to allow the Kents to live, as part of his campaign to deepen Clark Kent as a character and give him human roots. The Kents have provided a sounding board for Clark's feelings ever since, helping to keep the man in Superman. Although adaptations since Byrne have followed his model, *Smallville* makes the most radical amendment to Clark's family since *Man of Steel*, making his parents considerably younger. In a story about a teenage Clark Kent, it makes sense that there is only a gap of a generation between parents and adopted child. As a result the Kents are far less the picture of rural conservatism they were in the historic comics.

Clark's adoptive mother, Martha, isn't a native of Smallville. In fact, she grew up in Metropolis, but moved out to the farm after falling in love with Jonathan Kent. By the time of the meteor shower Martha had become increasingly distressed by their inability to have a child. The arrival of Clark, his spaceship crashing in the path of the Kents' truck, was seen by Martha as destiny.

Texas-born Annette O'Toole has a pre-existing connection to the Superman story, having played Lana Lang to Christopher Reeve's Clark in *Superman III*. Her other film roles include Walter Hill's *48 Hours*, the ill-advised 80s remake of *Cat People* and the romantic comedy *Cross My Heart*. Her television work includes the Stephen King mini-series *It*, the crime series *Nash Bridges* and a starring role as a bounty hunter in *The Huntress*.

Jonathan Kent may not be Clark's biological father, but he is a pivotal influence on the man Clark is becoming. The latest of generations of men to work the Kent Farm, Jonathan considers the land his family's legacy, and fiercely protects the farm's independence in the face of severe financial pressures. Jonathan's other main concern is the preservation of Clark's secret – at all costs. He has a quick temper that occasionally gets him into trouble.

John Schneider is still famous for playing Bo Duke in the early 80s action show *The Dukes of Hazzard*. Since then he's made numerous TV appearances, both as an actor and as a presenter. He recently played the voice of Rick O'Connell in the animated spin-off from *The Mummy*.

Lionel Luthor

Ruthless, venal and self-serving, billionaire Lionel Luthor is a new creation, but close to John Byrne's vision of Lex. A recurring presence throughout Season One, Lionel becomes a regular cast member in the second season.

John Glover brings his usual malevolent exuberance to the part of Lionel. He previously played the Devil in TV's *Brimstone*, Dr Jason Woodrue (known in the comics as The Floronic Man) in the disastrous *Batman & Robin*, and provided the voice for The Riddler in *Batman: The Animated Series*. His other films include *Payback*, *In The Mouth of Madness* and *Gremlins 2: The New Batch*. Recent roles include playing Bill Gates in the movie *Mid-Century*.

Smallville, Kansas

The town of Smallville, as portrayed in the comic books, is a sleepy and pleasant place, where Superman can return for some peace and quiet. The town wasn't firmly located in Kansas until the Salkind-produced movies, a change incorporated into the comics in *Man of Steel*. Although occasionally hit by the odd tornado, or the side effects of some world-shattering comic-book crossover, the modern comics' version of Smallville isn't the 'source of all weirdness' it seems to be on TV. It's the meteor shower that accompanies the arrival of Clark's spaceship in 1989 that changes the town forever, turning it from the creamed corn capital to the meteor capital of the world. It's on that same day that the Luthors buy the creamed corn factory, turning it into the fertiliser plant that employs most of the townspeople. While in the comics Smallville still relies on agriculture, in the series farming is a marginal business, as shown by the Kents' perilous finances.

Metropolis

One of America's great fictional cities, Metropolis has, like DC Comics' other prominent city, Gotham, always been a reflection of a mythical idea of New York. *Smallville* relocates the city, making it one of the closest major cities to Smallville itself, and therefore in Kansas. The comic-book skyline of Metropolis was originally based on the artist and Superman creator Joe Shuster's home town of Toronto, Canada. *Smallville* brings the city back to its Canadian roots, filming in Vancouver.

The Meteors

In all previous versions of the Superman story, Clark's capsule fell to Earth alone. Introduced in a 1943 episode of the long-running *Superman* radio show, kryptonite was a mineral deposit from Superman's devastated home planet, which fell to Earth in meteors. Gough and Millar devised the use of a meteor shower to deliver both Clark and the (so far unnamed within the series) kryptonite meteor rocks to Earth in one devastating event. This serves a threefold purpose within the format of *Smallville*. Firstly, it explains how a spaceship could land on Earth in the satellite age without being noticed – the meteors covered its arrival.

Secondly, the unearthly effects of the meteors cause mutations and other strangeness in the local population, acting as a catalyst for many of the show's stories. Thirdly, the link between Clark's arrival and the incredible destruction caused by the meteor shower gives Clark a motivating guilt behind his heroic actions: Clark knows that he is linked to the event that killed Lana's parents, lost Lex his hair and caused untold damage to the people of his home town. Arguably the largest alteration to the Superman myth, the meteor shower in *Smallville*, is a brilliant, multipurpose plot device.

In the comics, kryptonite is a green mineral that weakens Superman, and can kill him. The green mineral rocks have a similar effect. Red kryptonite, a variation that causes personality alterations, appears in Season Two. Over the course of Superman's historic comic-book adventures he has encountered many other types of kryptonite, so the possibilities for future meteor variants are almost endless.

Production Team

Personnel change across the course of a television series, with many behind-the-scenes staff only working on one episode. However, four men came together to bring *Smallville* to the screen, and they deserve separate attention:

Mike Tollin and Brian Robbins – Executive Producers

Between them the multi-talented duo of Mike Tollin and Brian Robbins (of Tollin/Robbins Productions) have produced the movies *Hardball* (which Robbins also directed), *Big Fat Liar* and *Varsity Blues*, and the TV series *The Nightmare Room*, *What I Like About You* and *Birds of Prey*. Tollin also directed the films *Radio* and *Summer Catch*, while Robbins has made a number of acting appearances in shows such as *Knight Rider* and *Charles in*

Charge. It was after their proposal for a television series based around the young man who would become Batman, *Bruce Wayne*, had failed to take off, that it was suggested to Tollin/Robbins that a better bet would be a series based on the early life of Superman. The producers brought in a pair of writers to create the show ...

Alfred Gough & Miles Millar, Series Creators and Executive Producers

The team of Gough and Millar are responsible for the screen story for *Lethal Weapon 4* as well as the screenplays for *Showtime*, *Made Men* and Jackie Chan/Owen Wilson period buddy flicks *Shanghai Noon* and *Shanghai Knights*. Their TV credits include the television version of *Timecop*, Sammo Hung-vehicle *Martial Law* and *The Strip*. Since *Smallville* began, they were also involved in the screenplay for Sam Raimi's big-budget movie *The Amazing Spider-Man*.

How This Book Works

This book covers each episode of *Smallville* broadcast so far, including all of the first season and about half of the second. To bring out the key points of each episode, the reviews of each individual show are divided into categories. Each entry starts with some basic information – the **Episode Title**, **Production Number**, **Transmission Dates** (for the US on all episodes, and for the UK for Season One), **Writer** and **Director** credits, and details of the **Cast**. There then follows a brief **Synopsis** of the episode's story, divided into individual storylines. This is not intended as a comprehensive, beat-by-beat account of the plot, more as a summary and aide-memoire. Under the heading **Speech Bubbles** you'll find a few choice dialogue quotes.

The first few categories refer to characters within the show, tracking their development through the episodes. These will be in a different order depending on the level of involvement that character has in the episode in question:

Small Town Boy: The story of Clark Kent, his personal development and growing superpowers.

Girl Next Door: The love of Clark's life, Lana Lang.

Not an Evil Genius: Clark's newest friend, the youthful billionaire Lex Luthor. Just as Clark is destined to become Superman, so Lex is eventually going to become a villain. This category notes when he seems to be drifting towards evil, and when he shows his good side.

Bad Dad: Lex's father, Lionel Luthor, a pivotal and often malignant influence on his life.

Torch Bearer: Chloe Sullivan is editor of the Smallville High school newspaper, the *Torch*, and one of Clark's closest friends.

Just the Funny Guy: Pete Ross, Clark's lovable best friend.

The Quarterback: Whitney Fordman, Lana's football-playing boyfriend and all-round jock.

Down at the Farm: Jonathan and Martha Kent, Clark's adoptive parents. This category also follows any developments on the Kent family farm, a key backdrop to Clark's life.

Mad Scientist: Dr Hamilton, a recurring character obsessed with researching the meteor rocks.

Other categories cover recurring elements of the show, following trends within the series and commenting on ongoing themes:

Strange Visitors: The villains who menace Clark, most of whom have some unusual ability that makes them a challenge. This section covers their personalities, origins and abilities.

Love's Young Dream: The romantic entanglements between the characters.

Mild-mannered Reporters: Just as he's destined to become a superhero, so Clark is also heading for a future in journalism. Examples of journalistic practice, both conventional and unorthodox, will be noted here.

Man or Superman?: As in much American fiction, the theme of what kind of man a boy will become is prevalent in *Smallville*. This is particularly relevant in relation to the various father figures who influence the characters.

Another Planet: A very occasional category tracing any revelations regarding Clark's alien origins. While these are rare in early episodes, the background mythology of a series like this will grow.

Go Crows!: The Smallville High football team, the Smallville Crows, play an important part in school and town life. References to them appear here.

Ad hoc categories and special box-outs will note any other important details that don't fit in with the usual categories. Each episode entry ends with a few categories wrapping things up:

Secret Identities: Notes on the previous careers of the guest cast and, where appropriate, the writer and director. Recurring performers and crew will get a write-up for their first appearance only.

Music: The songs heard in each episode.

From the Pages of: This is a comic-book based show, and there are many nods to the DC Comics' universe in the show, as well as sly references to Superman mythology and cliché. These references will be carefully tracked here.

Loose Ends: Gaping plot-holes and inconsistencies. Not everything can be cleanly resolved in 44 minutes of screen time, and this is the place to find the exceptionally glaring examples.

Trivia: Occasional bits of behind the scenes info, small details of on-screen action that you might have missed, and any other fun bits that don't fit anywhere else.

The Last Word: A brief review of the episode.

Season One

Superman created by Jerry Siegel & Joe Shuster
Developed for television by Alfred Gough and Miles Millar
Executive Producers: Alfred Gough, Miles Millar, Mike Tollin,
Brian Robbins, Joe Daviola
Music by Mark Snow

Regular Cast:
Tom Welling (Clark Kent)
Kristin Kreuk (Lana Lang)
Michael Rosenbaum (Lex Luthor)
Eric Johnson (Whitney Fordman)
Sam Jones III (Pete Ross)
Allison Mack (Chloe Sullivan)
Annette O'Toole (Martha Kent)
John Schneider (Jonathan Kent)

The Episodes

1
Pilot (Smallville)

Production #475165
1st US Transmission Date: 16 October 2001
1st UK Transmission Date: 31 December 2001

Writers: Alfred Gough and Miles Millar
Director: David Nutter
Special Guest Star: John Glover (Lionel Luthor)
Guest Starring: Sarah-Jane Redmond (Aunt Nell)
Co-starring: Adrian McMorran (Jeremy Creek), Jade Unterman,
Malkolm Alburquenque (Baby Clark), Matthew Munn (Lex, aged 9),
Dee Jay Jackson, Alvin Sanders, Steve Bacic, Justin Chatwin,
Wendy Chmelauskas, Ben Odberg, Amy Esterle

Synopsis: It's October 1989 in Smallville, Kansas, and a group of meteorites and a small spacecraft head towards Earth. As the meteors hit, several people are affected by the devastation: Jeremy Creek, hung up in a cornfield with an 'S' painted on his chest, is caught in the blast; industrialist Lionel Luthor's young son Lex is in the same cornfield, and after seeing Jeremy he too gets caught in the impact, losing his hair; Lana Lang sees her parents killed by one of the meteors hitting the high street; and childless couple Jonathan and Martha Kent find the young boy who came to Earth in the spacecraft.

Today. The alien baby has grown into Clark Kent, Jonathan and Martha's adopted teenage son. He's a boy with very special abilities, and some unusual vulnerabilities. Clark's parents don't want him playing football for fear of him injuring someone with his abilities. When Clark survives a car accident (see below), Jonathan tells him about his unearthly origins, which further causes him to feel alienated.

Clark attends Smallville High alongside his friends, the witty Pete Ross and student journalist Chloe Sullivan. Clark has a crush on Lana Lang, but two things keep him away from her: her boyfriend, school football captain Whitney Fordman, and Lana's meteor-rock necklace, which has a debilitating effect on Clark. Lana lends her

necklace to Whitney for good luck, and later the same day
she and Clark have their longest-ever conversation, discussing their loneliness as orphans. Unfortunately, Whitney sees them together.

When Lex Luthor arrives in town, he soon encounters
Clark in the most violent way possible, accidentally driving
his sports car into him, crashing straight off a bridge and
sinking to the bottom of a river. Clark, surviving the
impact without a scratch, pulls Lex out of the car and
rescues him, and the two become friends.

Elsewhere in town, Jeremy Creek has emerged from the
coma he has been in since the meteor shower. The alien
meteors have given Creek the power to manipulate electricity, an ability he uses to take revenge on the former
football players who 'scarecrowed' him, stringing him up
in the cornfield all those years ago.

Matters come to a head on the day of the homecoming
dance. Whitney takes his revenge on Clark, 'scarecrowing'
him in the cornfield, leaving Lana's necklace around
Clark's neck. Creek finds Clark and tells him that nothing
ever changes – he's going to the homecoming dance to
make them pay. Lex rescues Clark, who stops Creek from
killing the students at the dance. Lex finds Lana's necklace,
lost in the cornfield. Clark watches Lana from a distance
as she arrives home from the dance.

Speech Bubbles: Lionel Luthor (to a young, scared Lex):
'You have a destiny, Lex. You're never going to get
anywhere with your eyes closed.'

Chloe: 'OK, just because everyone else chooses to ignore
the strange things that happen in this leafy little hamlet; it
doesn't mean that they don't happen.'

Lex: 'Clark, do you believe a man can fly?'

Small Town Boy: Clark Kent seems a happy, well-adjusted
teenager living in a loving home. But there are problems –
his abilities mean that he can't play football for fear of
losing control and hurting someone, and he's in love with
Lana Lang, who is already dating school football captain
Whitney Fordman. His daydream of using his powers to
win a football game and charm Lana is wonderfully

innocent, and certainly modest compared to the rampant ambition Lex exudes. Clark even seems innocent when watching Lana through his telescope – that this seems romantic rather than voyeuristic is a testament to the charm Tom Welling brings to the character.

Clark is upset when he finds out that he's from another planet – but if his alien origins are such a surprise, where did he think all that strength and speed came from? And why did he keep his abilities a secret if he wasn't aware of his own unusual nature? (Some explanation of Clark's thinking is given in the *Smallville* novel *Strange Visitors* by Roger Stern. According to the novel, Clark believed himself to be an anomaly of nature, gifted rather than super-powered. See **Smallville on the Page**).

Although Clark's first reaction to finding out his origins is to feel isolated and aware of how separated from the world he is, it's only when he finds a picture of a distraught young Lana on Chloe's 'Wall of Weird' that Clark realises that the event which brought him to Earth has caused so much misery, and he begins to feel responsibility for all the results of the meteor shower. When he confronts Creek outside the homecoming dance, he talks about having a destiny, presumably to help people. However, Clark isn't entirely too good to be true – not only does he daydream about stealing Lana from Whitney, but he gets his revenge on Whitney and his other tormentors by stacking their trucks in the parking lot.

Clark's powers are limited at this stage – he's very strong, almost invulnerable (he doesn't have a scratch after being knocked through a crash barrier by Lex's Porsche or a wall by a truck) and can run at superspeed (is the skateboard strapped to his rucksack a cover story for how fast he gets everywhere?). At this point in his life he has none of the more exotic powers Superman will be known for, and he certainly can't fly. Clark's only noticeable weakness is the green meteors that accompanied him to Earth, which leave him weak and powerless. Ironically, one of the meteor rocks is permanently installed around Lana's neck so Clark can't get near Lana without stumbling (possibly a reference to the lead character in Robert Mayer's 1977 novel *Super-Folks*, who becomes clumsy whenever he tries to use his powers for lecherous reasons, thereby making his human alter ego seem incredibly inept). Although his powers seem to be growing as he gets older, so does his susceptibility to the meteors.

Along with his tendency towards impetuousness, Clark is some way from becoming the physically and morally perfect Superman of later life. In fact, the only mention of Superman is in reference to Clark's current reading material – *The Portable Nietzsche*. Nietzsche's 'superman' is a superior being who does not sublimate his power drive but 'becomes himself', creating his own value system – a far from heroic use of power.

Not an Evil Genius: When Lex Luthor is first seen in 1989 he is a young boy with a vast head of (unconvincing!) red hair. Even at this early stage he is being bullied by his overbearing father, Lionel, who seems disgusted with his son's fear of flying. Lionel tells the young Lex that the Luthors do not have the luxury of being afraid – they're leaders, and as such Lex has a destiny he must face. Lex is far from being a strong man at this point; he's rather nervous, easily distracted and uses an inhaler when he gets out of breath. The meteor impact he's caught in causes his hair to fall out, and it never grows back. The older Lex is far more confident, even reckless, especially when driving. He's extravagant with his money, buying Clark a new truck as a gift after Clark saves his life. Lex has a personal fencing trainer and gets sufficiently angry, when he loses, to throw his foil into the wall.

Lex tells Clark that he's been bald since he was nine, and has become used to people judging him on appearances. He also tells Clark that he had an out-of-body experience during the period when his heart stopped after the accident, and that he flew over Smallville and saw a new beginning in his life. He believes that Clark has given him a second chance at life and doesn't want anything to come between them – he believes they have a destiny. This Lex Luthor is not yet evil, but is certainly impulsive, fairly aggressive and definitely arrogant. However, he does have many redeeming factors: he's charming, generous (albeit only to those he decides are his friends) and shows no signs of snobbishness towards the locals of Smallville, in spite of his wealthy background. At this stage in his life, Lex is a young man torn between the conflicting influences of his venal father and his honest new friend, Clark Kent.

Girl Next Door: Ironically, the first glimpse of Lana is as a little girl in a fairy princess dress, the image that will immortalise her as a front-page image of the meteor shower, an image which the teenage Lana will be desperate to try and escape. In her fairy costume Lana grants Martha a wish, and afterwards it's clear that Martha wished for a child. In another layer of irony, that wish is granted by the meteor shower delivering Clark to the Kents – the same event that takes Lana's own parents away from her. The scene of a young Lana witnessing the death of Lewis and Laura Lang in an explosion is exceptionally brutal, a small child watching as her smiling family is suddenly consumed by a fireball. In later life Lana wears a necklace containing a piece of the meteor that killed her parents, the logic being that it caused so many bad things that it can 'only have good luck left'. Lana constantly feels alone and talks to her dead parents at the graveyard. She sometimes dreams of being picked up from school by them and being taken away to a life with them in Metropolis. The dream leaves her happy for a minute when she wakes up – until she remembers it isn't real.

It's this tragic past and overwhelming sense of loss that makes Lana more than the cheerleader and homecoming-queen stereotype of the girl-who-has-everything. As such she's more than just a school beauty for Clark to be attracted to. Lana is someone Clark shares a bond with, both in the mutual loss of their parents, and the link that Lana doesn't yet know about – that they are tied together by the events of the meteor shower.

Lana is adopted by her Aunt Nell, who runs the flower shop in Smallville, and who seems to have some past connection to Jonathan Kent judging by her conversation with the Kents in 1989. Nell also knows the Luthors socially (see **2**, 'Metamorphosis').

The Quarterback: Lana's boyfriend is Whitney Fordman, captain of the football team and all-round local hero. Although Whitney is seen primarily in a bad light in this episode – he's the typical high-school jock – loud, arrogant and aggressive, and is responsible for 'scarecrowing' Clark – he's a fully developed character. Whitney does what he does to Clark because he sees him with Lana; anger, fear and jealousy rather than malice motivate his actions. There's a touching scene with Lana where Whitney demonstrates a degree of self-awareness – he knows that there are plenty of washed-up former school sports heroes in every small town, and he's determined not to be one of them. However, leaving Lana's necklace – a memento of her dead parents – hanging around her friend's neck after hanging him up in the middle of a field is fairly unforgivable bad boyfriend behaviour.

Just the Funny Guy: Pete Ross is Clark's best friend, although that doesn't stop him from making a bet with Chloe that Clark will miss the bus. This slightly shady and comic side to Pete's character sets him apart from his rather earnest friends. Pete knows that Chloe has a crush on Clark, but his carefully worded suggestion that he and Chloe should go to the dance 'as friends' suggests that he may be interested in her himself. Pete is understandably terrified of becoming this year's 'scarecrow', and wants Clark to join the football team with him because the jocks won't pick on 'one of their own'. Pete and Chloe function as a great double act in the early school scenes, acting as the audience's guide to the world of Smallville High as they comment on Clark and his relationship with Lana.

Torch Bearer: Chloe Sullivan is instantly established as being more than a little paranoid. She jumps out of her skin when something rattles the school bus, and is instantly suspicious of Clark's impossibly fast arrival at school: her reference to Clark travelling through 'a black hole' instantly marks Chloe out as the nerd-identification figure among the group. While Pete mocks Chloe's belief that strange things happen in Smallville, comparing her to a character from *Scooby-Doo*, Chloe herself is sure that there is weirdness at work. As editor of the Smallville High school newspaper, the *Torch*, Chloe has an investigative streak, and her obsession with the weird effects of the meteor shower is demonstrated by her collage to it, the 'Wall of Weird' in the *Torch*'s office. Chloe is incredibly defensive when Pete asks her whether she wants Clark to invite her to the dance, strongly denying any feelings for their mutual friend – a sure sign that those feelings *do* exist.

Mild-mannered Reporters: Both Chloe and Pete work on the *Torch*. We get a brief introduction to their journalistic skills when they attend a crime scene and pick Jeremy Creek out of a crowd as a suspect (a leap of plot logic that defies any sense, but which helps the story keep moving). One scene takes place in the *Torch*'s office, where Chloe and Pete bombard Clark with information found on that great tool for plot short cuts, the Internet. The most notable part of the office is the 'Wall of Weird', a pinned-up collection of news clippings covering every strange or unexplained event to happen in Smallville since the meteor shower. Interestingly, the *Torch*'s office seems to physically move between episodes. In this episode it's an open, gym-type space, while in future episodes it is based in smaller rooms. One can only presume the school nudges the paper around depending on their space priorities at the time.

Down at the Farm: The Kents are first seen in Nell's florist's shop, and there's a tension between Nell, Jonathan and Martha. There's an implicit sexuality to Nell's suggestion that they partake of an exotic tiger orchid. Jonathan supports his wife's desire for tulips, which Nell describes as an 'uncomplicated' flower. Martha doesn't seem threatened by this interplay, more amused than anything, so it's clear that the Kents are a very solid couple. The fact that Jonathan doesn't attend the Smallville Crows' big game – and doesn't even remember it – may tie into his reservations about Clark playing football later on, although he is noticeably pleased when he realises they've won (he was on the team himself in his youth).

When they find the young Clark, Martha instantly bonds with the child and clearly wants to keep him. Jonathan isn't sure, and doesn't know what they're going to tell people – but by the present day Clark is their adopted son. (There's a story to be told here, one that will become significant in **14**, 'Zero'.)

Jonathan has an instant contempt for Lex, and not just because of his careless driving; he resents the Luthors and how they cheated local farmers out of their property. He tells Clark that he can't accept Lex's gift of a shiny new truck, as the money that bought it is tainted by association with the Luthors. This tension will run through most of the season. Jonathan is very protective of Clark, not just in terms of trying to shield him from the Luthors' baleful influence but by trying to keep Clark's secret hidden. Jonathan is adamant that Clark shouldn't play football, fearful of what he could do in the heat of a game, and doesn't even tell Clark about how he came to Earth until the events of this episode. When Clark tells his father that he's glad it was the Kents who found him, Jonathan replies that they didn't – Clark found them.

Bad Dad: Lex's father Lionel Luthor is a pivotal influence in his life, shipping Lex out to Smallville in disgrace. Lionel also had the Luthor mansion – their supposed ancestral home – shipped over from Scotland stone by stone, although Lionel has never visited it himself. In 1989 Lionel bought the Creamed Corn Factory from the Ross family, and subsequently developed it into the Fertiliser Plant which Lex now manages, latterly named LuthorCorp Fertiliser Plant No. 3. According to Whitney, the Luthors own the football team the Metropolis Sharks.

Love's Young Dream: Clark's infatuation with Lana seems to be at a distance, both because of Whitney and because of the debilitating effect Lana's meteor necklace has on him. Their chat in the graveyard about the loneliness they both feel is the longest conversation they have ever had. Lana gives Clark a kiss afterwards, but only on the cheek. Lana and Whitney are very cosy at the homecoming dance, leaving Clark under no illusions of how far he has to go to get the girl.

Strange Visitors: Jeremy Creek, caught up in a meteor impact in 1989. After twelve years in a coma he wakes up, not a day older but with lightning-throwing powers, and sets off to avenge himself on the jocks who strung him up in that cornfield over a decade before. Creek won't be the last person to have their ageing process interfered with by the meteorites – Harry Volk in **6**, 'Hourglass' has his ageing reversed, although Creek's ageless appearance seems to be down to an 'electrolyte imbalance', whatever that may mean. Creek finds himself unsatisfied with taking revenge on the jocks who strung him up: when Clark becomes the most recent 'scarecrow', Creek decides to extend his vengeance to all the attendees at the homecoming dance. He sees himself as acting to defend everyone who was ever bullied by a jock in Smallville. Creek's powers – and his memories of everything since coming out of the coma – seemingly disappear when he uses his powers while covered in water, giving himself a severe shock.

Man or Superman?: Father and son tensions run throughout the pilot. Clark is a hot-headed young man whose responsible, caring father wants him to be careful with his powers. Lex's father Lionel casts him out, exiling him from Metropolis to Smallville in the hope that he'll learn to take responsibility. The contrast couldn't be stronger: Jonathan's approach to his son is to care for the safety of others, and is motivated by compassion, while Lionel's attitude to Lex is far colder, trying to teach him a harsh lesson in a harsh way. Both upbringings reflect how the sons are beginning to grow up: while Clark is honest, open and caring, Lex is secretive and ruthless. Interestingly, while Lionel spouts on about the importance of the Luthor bloodline, Clark follows his father just as much even though he's adopted; in *Smallville* it's a running theme that nurture, upbringing and environment make a child the person they become rather than nature – their biological traits. The differences between the two approaches are illustrated by the gifts both fathers give to their sons. Lex gets Luthor-Corp Fertiliser Plant No. 3, a heavy responsibility, while Clark is given a telescope passed down through the Kent family from father to son, so that he can look at the stars.

Another Planet: The first fragments of knowledge about Clark's background become clear. He came to Earth in a spaceship, under cover of a meteor shower. However, at this stage no direct connection is made between the meteors and Clark's home planet. The only other alien artefact the Kents possess apart from the spaceship, which they keep in the storm cellar, is a flat piece of metal engraved with alien symbols.

Go Crows!: The local high-school football team, the Smallville Crows, win a big homecoming game the day of the meteor shower in 1989. The team have a rather unsavoury tradition around this time of year, that of abducting a non-player, stripping him, painting a red 'S' on his chest and hanging him up in a cornfield as a 'scarecrow'. Whitney is interested in playing for two major teams – the Metropolis Sharks and Kansas State. The Crows' mascot, briefly glimpsed in this episode, is a cartoon crow wearing a cape with a red 'S' logo on its chest.

Loose Ends: Quite a few loose ends are left hanging from this packed, multi-layered introduction to the series: Is Whitney left trying to retrieve his truck after the dance, or is he in the cars that drop Lana off at her home? What happens to Jeremy Creek after being in a coma for twelve years? Creek just wanders off in an amnesiac state, his powers seemingly gone – is he really going to step back into normal life just like that? Isn't Chloe, the ever-inquisitive journalist, going to follow her story up? And if not, why does her involvement end after telling Clark? She doesn't know about his powers, or that he's going to do anything about it, so why tell him then consider the matter closed?

The audience is also left wondering about Lex, and some of the questions *will* be answered in weeks to come: What is Lex going to do with Lana's necklace? Why was he exiled from Metropolis? How does he reconcile his memory of hitting Clark with his Porsche?

And most intriguingly of all the questions left open by the pilot, how did Jonathan and Martha explain the sudden appearance of Clark after the meteor shower? There are some answers in **14**, 'Zero', but this is a plot that's set to run and run . . .

Secret Identities: The pilot is directed by David Nutter who, after a stint on the late 80s *Superboy* series, came to prominence directing some of the strongest episodes of *The X-Files*, including the Emmy-winning 'Clyde Bruckman's Final Repose'. Nutter went on to become something of a serial pilot-director, shooting the first episodes of *Millennium*, *Space: Above and Beyond*, *Roswell*, *Sleepwalkers* and *Dark Angel*. Nutter has also worked on such prominent series as *ER* and *Band of Brothers*, as well as directing the teen horror flick *Disturbing Behavior* and a couple of entries into the straight-to-video *Trancers* series of cult SF movies.

Sarah-Jane Redmond (Nell) had a recurring role in *Millennium* as Lucy Butler, as well as parts in the movie *Disturbing Behavior* and the television series *The X-Files*, (in which she controlled killer trees) *Harsh Realm* and *Dark Angel*. She can be seen in the Clive Barker-derived horror film *Hellraiser VI: Hellseeker*.

Matthew Munn, who plays the nine-year-old Lex, also played a younger version of Byers from the *X-Files* spin-off *The Lone Gunmen* in the episode 'Like Water For Octane'. Malkolm Alburquenque, who plays the baby Clark, has appeared in *Dark Angel*. Steve Bacic appeared in the movies *The 6th Day* and *Another Stakeout*. His recurring TV roles include the treacherous Gaheris Rhade in *Andromeda* (as well as his more honourable descendant, Telemachus Rhade), and Colonel/Major Coburn in *Stargate SG-1*.

From the Pages of: In 1989 Luthor senior is reading a copy of the *Daily Planet* – the newspaper that Clark Kent famously works for as an adult in virtually every version of the *Superman* myth. The headline of the paper is QUEEN INDUSTRIES CEO MISSING, PRESUMED DEAD, a reference to DC Comics' superhero Oliver Queen, a.k.a. 'Green Arrow',

Canadian Casting: In the last decade Canada, in particular the cities of Toronto and Vancouver, has become the thriving production base for US TV shows. Of particular note are the large-scale fantasy and science-fiction shows which base themselves across the border, Canada's relatively low overheads (certainly compared to LA) and wide variety of available locations, allowing it to double for most of the US in the first five seasons of *The X-Files* and the full run of Chris Carter's other show *Millennium*, a dystopian future in *Dark Angel*, and now, of course, Kansas in *Smallville*. Shooting out of Vancouver allows for bigger set pieces than more traditional locations may allow, and generally stretches the budget further. This ongoing trend in US drama series has resulted in a thriving Canadian acting community who make appearances in numerous Canadian-lensed shows. *Smallville* pilot director David Nutter praised Vancouver as a casting location in an interview with Frank Garcia for *DreamWatch*: 'I think outside of Los Angeles, Vancouver probably has the largest, best talent of young actors in the world.' Regardless of the budget and talent considerations, there's a lot of fun to be had from spotting regular faces from this unofficial rep company as they appear in show after show. So don't be surprised next time you're watching *Smallville* and you recognise someone from Mulder and Scully's case files . . .

who gained his tremendous archery and survival skills after going missing at sea and fending for himself on a desert island. The bright-red blanket draped around Clark's shoulders on the river bank echoes the Superman costume, as does the red plaid shirt and blue jeans combo he wears later – he sports these colours in every episode of Season One. Other elements of the Superman costume appear elsewhere, from the red and yellow shields on the Smallville Crows' jackets, to the red 'S' painted on to Clark when he's 'scarecrowed', not forgetting the team's Crow mascot.

Music: It's clear it's the 1980s in the first scene – they're playing Bruce Hornsby's 'The Way It Is'. In the present day there's 'Long Way Around' by Eagle Eye Cherry,

'Eight Half Letters' by Stereoblis, 'Wonder' by Embrace, 'Unstoppable' by The Calling (see **Music** for 2, 'Metamorphosis'), 'Inside the Memories' by the superbly named Fear the Clown and 'Let's Go' by Capitol Eye. At the school dance they play 'Maybe' by rock outfit Stereophonics (in the unaired version they used Coldplay) and 'Everything I Own' by Jude. The memorable closing song to this episode is called 'Everything', performed by Lifehouse.

Trivia: The version of the pilot used to pitch the series featured Cynthia Ettinger as Martha Kent, the role being recast with Annette O'Toole – and the appropriate scenes reshot – before the series went into full production and hit the air. Watching that original pilot, it's obvious why the part was recast – although Ettinger is a good actress, she doesn't have the presence or sophistication of Annette O'Toole. Ettinger's Martha would have been a less interesting, more obviously maternal and innocuous character. Other details worth noting from the unseen pilot are the 'temp' soundtrack, which features a totally different (and inferior) score and a number of different songs. The reshooting of all the scenes which include Martha, in many cases results in tighter, more fluid scenes in the broadcast episode.

When broadcast in the UK, the pilot has one scene cut. This scene comes immediately after Jonathan tells Clark why he can't keep the truck, and shows Clark demonstrating to Jonathan how far from 'normal' he is by shoving his hand into the woodchipper, then removing it unscathed. Clark then tells Jonathan that he didn't dive into the river to save Lex, but was hit by the Porsche at sixty miles an hour, leading into the scene where Jonathan tells Clark his origins. The 'woodchipper' scene was almost certainly cut because it shows extremely dangerous behaviour that could be imitated by younger viewers.

Like many pilot episodes on US TV, the broadcast episode has no title sequence, with the main cast and creator credits running as captions over the first few present-day scenes. On its first UK broadcast the pilot was shown along with the second episode, 'Metamorphosis', to create a feature-length pilot film, leading to some complaints that the two episodes had been spliced together far too crudely. In fact this version was prepared in the US to be sold as a TV movie or video release in international markets. It has been released on DVD in Canada.

Thanks to the DVD, fans have access to some more deleted scenes from the pilot episode. These cut scenes include the original first appearances of Pete's (unnamed) father and uncle, Principal Kwan, and Chloe's father, Gabe Sullivan. Although the Ross family have yet to be seen in the series as broadcast, the cut scene establishes that they owned the Creamed Corn Factory before being cheated out of it by Lionel Luthor, a detail that will seem to come out of nowhere when revealed later in the season. Principal Kwan doesn't appear in the series proper until **3**, 'Hothead'. The scene featuring Gabe is interesting because of the actor playing the role, who is very different from Robert Wisden, who plays Gabe when he makes his first broadcast appearance in **8**, Jitters. The actor playing Gabe in the cut scene is overweight, and a more obvious comic relief than the Gabe we eventually get to see. Other scenes add nice little character touches, including Lionel hectoring Lex even further in the helicopter in 1989, Chloe waiting outside the homecoming dance to see if Clark will show, and a scene showing the jocks driving up in the trucks Clark stacks at the end of the show.

In 1989 Smallville is the 'creamed corn capital of the world' and has a population of 25,001 according to a roadside sign. In the present day the same sign says the town is the *meteor* capital of the world and has a population of 45,001 – so if nothing else the meteors haven't adversely affected fertility in the region. It's never explained whether this huge rise in population owes something to the LuthorCorp plant and its employees, or whether there is some other explanation. According to Clark's application to join the football team, the Kent Farm is on Hickory Lane, Smallville, and their phone number is 5550145.

The Last Word: 'So, what are you – man or superman?' Take a sixty-year-old pop-culture myth, reinvent with themes of adolescent romance and responsibility culled from recent hits like *Buffy the Vampire Slayer*, add a touch of rural American gothic, then try and put the whole concept on screen as a comprehensible, entertaining 44-minute pilot episode. An impossible task? You might think so, but that's exactly what writer/creators Alfred Gough and Miles Millar, along with director/executive producer David Nutter, manage to pull off in this exhilarating introduction to their vision of a twenty-first century Superman. There's not a single main character that we're not properly introduced to in this pilot, and all the character dynamics are sketched in neatly, along with vital plot elements such as the strange effects of the meteor rocks. Although a pre-knowledge of the Superman story and its traditions adds to an appreciation of some of the story points and in-jokes, a training in comics' continuity is unnecessary to enjoy and be involved in this very new, very fresh version of the story. Production values are high, and the special effects sequence that opens the pilot is spectacular and disturbing, as the meteorite shower rains destruction upon the town. Kansas is also wonderfully recreated in Canada, with a real sense of rural isolation in the cornfield scenes. *X-Files* alumnus David Nutter, a veteran of a number of movies and pilots, brings his considerable directorial talents to bear, keeping the action moving and squeezing the budget for every last drop of visual gloss. There are some lovely directorial touches – Clark standing in front of a statue in the graveyard, an angel's wings seemingly his own, being one notable moment – and a cinematic quality throughout.

However, while the pilot works well as an introduction to the series, it does fall down slightly as a story in its own right. Although the incorporation of Jeremy Creek into the 1989 sequences, and the tying in of his story into Clark's arrival and Lex's childhood is seamless, his activities in the present day are choppily presented. Creek is never very well defined, and his scenes are fitted in around our introductions to the main characters. Clark finding out about Creek is also unconvincing – Chloe and Pete take a huge, sudden

interest in Creek at a crime scene, then spit his life story at
Clark for very little reason. However, all this dramatic
shorthand is a necessary evil to give Clark a solid
confrontation to demonstrate his powers and to show the
kind of adversaries he's going to face in the series proper.
The lack of resolution for Creek's story – he loses his
powers and his memories, then just wanders off – is the
first example of a lack of closure that afflicts many
episodes.

But what matters is that by the end of the episode we
want to know more: more about Clark and Lana, about
Lex and his ambitions, and about the effects the meteors
have had on this small Kansas town.

2
Metamorphosis

Production #227601
1st US Transmission Date: 23 October 2001
1st UK Transmission Date: 31 December 2001

Writers: Alfred Gough and Miles Millar
Directors: Michael Watkins, Philip Sgriccia
Guest Starring: Chad E Donella (Greg Arkin),
Gabrielle Rose (Greg's Mother)
Co-starring: Jay Kirby

Synopsis: Nerdy insect obsessive Greg Arkin is stalking
Lana, leaving presents for her and videotaping her from a
distance. After an argument with his mother, Greg crashes
his car and is attacked by meteor-infected bugs. He
emerges after the attack with insectlike powers, and
proceeds to go on a crime spree to get what he wants. Greg
kills his own mother and tries to put Whitney out of the
picture by causing his car to crash. When Greg kidnaps
Lana, Clark confronts him in an old foundry. Though
Clark has to fight while weakened by meteors, he defeats
Greg, who is crushed by falling machinery.

Lana wants her necklace back and is upset with Whitney
when he doesn't have it. She's even more upset when hints

dropped by Lex lead her to find out about the scarecrowing incident. Lex gives the necklace to Clark, but Clark refuses to use it to win Lana over, instead leaving it on her porch – which means she doesn't realise it's from him.

Speech Bubbles: Lex: 'You were tied to a stake in the middle of a field. Even the Romans saved that for special occasions.'

Jonathan: 'Soon as you start breaking the law of gravity, we're definitely in uncharted territory.'

Greg's mother: 'What the hell has gotten into you?' Greg: 'About two million years of intelligence and instinct.'

Small Town Boy: Another of Clark's possible powers is previewed with his dream of flying. When he wakes up he's floating, and falls on to his bed from some height, suggesting perhaps that he already has the ability to fly but can only access it subconsciously. Clark tells Jonathan that he's scared by the changes in him, which are more extreme than the usual teenage growing pains. At one point Clark uses his strength to slyly push a long nail into wood with his thumb. Clark's superspeed allows him to move at a pace where everything else seems to slow down, allowing him to cross the barn and catch Jonathan in the time it takes him to fall from the balcony. After the rather underwhelming electrical powers of the pilot episode's main villain, it's good to see Clark using his powers in a full-on superhero fight scene at the episode's finale.

The meteor stone in the necklace still makes Clark weak, but he also finds out that its power can't reach through the lead of a box Lex gives him to keep the necklace in. Clark experiments with its effects, indicated by a horrid rippling of the veins on the back of Clark's hands, which wears off within seconds of the box being closed.

Of course, Clark saves Whitney even though they hate each other, but a more tempting opportunity is the chance for Clark to give Lana her necklace and tell her about the 'scarecrowing'. The fact that the necklace is a threat to Clark, and a barrier between him and Lana when she wears it, gives Clark good reason to keep it. When she talks about the importance of her necklace Clark is visibly guilty, glancing at the box which contains it. When Lana visits Clark in his barn loft den, he tells her his father, who calls it Clark's 'Fortress of Solitude', built it. Clark is understandably embarrassed when Lana points out that his telescope can be used to watch her house, and quickly redirects it into the sky.

It's the comparison with Greg – a man who takes whatever he wants, regardless of rules, morality or the wishes of others – that reminds Clark that we can't just take what we want. In the end he gives Lana her necklace back – but in a way that ensures he doesn't take the credit and Whitney probably does.

Not an Evil Genius: Lex's dabbling in Clark's life begins in earnest here. He's clearly fascinated by this altruistic farm boy who seems to spend his time saving people's lives in dangerous situations, and quickly gets an insight into the Clark–Lana–Whitney triangle. Lex begins to lobby Lana on Clark's behalf, tipping her off to the 'scarecrowing' incident, and giving Clark his 'Trojan horse' – Lana's necklace. The fact that Lex gives Clark the lead box – apart from being a plot device to allow Clark to carry the necklace – is interesting, as the box was a gift from his mother. (Lex's mother bought it from a market trader in Morocco who claimed it was made from the armour of St George, one of the noblest of saints.) That Lex should give Clark something connected to his late mother, and also representative of a shining knight, demonstrates the extent to which he is trying to repay Clark for saving his life. Lex's 'Trojan war' metaphor for the conflict between Clark and Whitney over Lana comes from the war game his father gave him when he was nine. Lex tells Clark that if he hadn't rescued Whitney from the truck, his problem would be gone. Lex claims that he is joking, but there's a lingering sense that under similar circumstances that's how he would see it.

The scenes where Lex tempts Clark into playing dirty to win Lana's heart have a Faustian quality to them: Lex gives Clark the power to destroy Whitney in Lana's eyes, a temptation even Clark finds hard to resist. Michael

Rosenbaum is wonderfully ambiguous in these scenes, as is Tom Welling as a heroic figure severely tempted to get some payback.

Lex himself definitely registers how attractive Lana is; he compliments Clark on his taste, and later tells Lana how much she's grown compared to when they first met. This encounter shows that Lex is not entirely without shame – he seems embarrassed when Lana tells him that they've already met, and recounts the anecdote of a ten-year-old Lana finding Lex skinny-dipping with a girl in the Luthor family pool. Lex is impressed by Lana's riding trophies and gives her advice on reshoeing her horse, so he clearly knows a little about horses.

In a stylishly casual act, Lex swipes an apple from the crate Clark is carrying, takes a bite, then chucks the rest back into the Kents' truck!

Girl Next Door: Lana, although not unkind to Greg, seems aware of his infatuation, and is smart enough to insist their study date should take place at the school library rather than at Greg's house. Just as we're never sure how far Clark can drift towards misbehaving, or exactly how far Lex will go to get what he wants, so Lana has her own ambiguity about her. Exactly to what extent is Lana innocent, and when is she being coy? She seems aware of Greg's interest in her but never acknowledges it, and one has to wonder to what extent she knows Clark's feelings, especially when she innocently points out that his telescope can be aimed at her house. It may not occur to her, though, that Clark is a romantic possibility until Lex spells it out for her in the stables.

Finding out about Whitney 'scarecrowing' Clark shakes Lana's faith in her boyfriend – if she doesn't know Whitney as well as she thought she did, what else might she not have realised? This theme will be built on in **4**, 'X-Ray', when she finds out more about her mother's youth. Aunt Nell presented Lana's necklace to her on the day her adoption was confirmed, and its loss distresses her.

The Quarterback: Whitney begins to show some remorse for his actions, claiming to both Clark and Lana that the 'scarecrowing' was 'just a prank', and fretting about having lost Lana's necklace. Whitney gets his inaugural battering in this episode, when his truck is turned over by another super-powered rival for Lana's affections, Greg. (As he's just got into trouble for beating up on Clark, should Whitney really be so aggressive with Greg anyway?) Whitney apologises to Lana for what he did to Clark but, as she points out, he should be apologising to Clark. Then he gets *another* beating, knocked out cold for the second time in twenty-four hours. Whitney tries to apologise to Clark, only to find he ran away when he was not looking, and wins the girl back by rescuing Lana with Clark's information while Clark is off doing the fighting. At this stage Whitney is more than the thug he may initially seem to be – but he's still too arrogant for his own good.

Love's Young Dream: In spite of Lex playing a particularly Machiavellian cupid for Clark and Lana, the pieces in the game don't shift around that much. Lana may be more aware of how dodgy Whitney can be, and is increasingly shown Clark's nobility, but the status quo is intact at the episode's end. Lana and Clark have lived a mile apart for most of their lives, but this episode sees the first time that Lana has visited Clark at home.

Torch Bearer: At the market, Chloe mocks the 'homecoming king and queen', i.e. Whitney and Lana. She seems genuinely hurt when Clark tries to walk away without telling her why he's interested in Greg, and wants to know whether Clark is 'outgrowing' her as a friend. Chloe still can't resist the 'Kent charm', forgiving Clark as soon as he relents. Chloe makes one of her amazing leaps of deduction, guessing that as Greg didn't move to Smallville until after the meteor shower, the meteors couldn't have infected him first-hand – it must have been his insects which were infected, and they passed the mutation to him through a bite. She also tells Clark that it would take a large amount of toxin to cause mutation, which is why not everyone in town who got bitten by a bug has mutated.

Down at the Farm: In a nice irony, Jonathan – who can't *stand* Lex, Clark's closest ally – is quite chummy with Whitney, his son's archrival. When Clark and Whitney are caught in a fireball as Whitney's truck explodes, Jonathan and Martha are terrified, and Martha is in shock for some time afterwards – although Jonathan tells Clark that she's also proud of what he did. When Clark tells Jonathan about his feelings of guilt over the meteor shower, and the death of Lana's parents, Jonathan tells him that no matter how many powers Clark gets he will never be able to change that, and the fact that he has that guilt and regret is what makes him human. Jonathan thinks that Greg's insect powers sound unlikely – until Martha reminds him he's the man with a spaceship in his storm cellar! The Kents sell their produce at the farmers' market, where the sign shows that it's all organic food. (It seems unlikely the food can be truly described as organic, as during the course of the series the Kents use fertiliser. What's more, the area has been bombarded by meteorites, and the farm is near a pollution-spewing fertiliser plant. The Kents might consider relabelling their produce.)

Strange Visitors: Greg the insect geek, who gains insectlike powers after being mauled by meteor-tainted insects. Greg's eyesight and skin condition improve, and he becomes more confident, throwing out his geeky clothes in favour of bad-boy all-black gear – but he's still a creepy stalker who talks about insects all the time. His insect powers allow him to cling to sheer surfaces, scamper along quite fast, jump far and have increased strength. Or, to put it another way, he can do pretty much everything a spider can, but on a human scale. This includes vomiting webs – which is pretty disgusting, but better than the more obvious way of him excreting them. Greg also begins to adopt insect psychology, living patterns and so forth, living in webs, eating his mother and trying to mate with Lana. How much of this is related to his physical changes and how much is the wish fulfilment of an insect-obsessed outcast is anyone's guess. In many ways Greg fits Nietzsche's idea of the 'superman', rejecting what he sees as society's 'false values' when he talks to Clark in the treehouse. As Greg says: 'I have no rules, Clark. I eat what I want. I go where I want. I take what I want.' Greg has created his own world view,

rejecting the rules of civilisation in favour of an assertion
of his own will. Clark's counter-position is that he believes
that Greg is nothing more than a slave to his instincts.

Like Lex, the bugged-up incarnation of Greg displays
his villainous potential by wearing the shorthand colour
scheme for those inclined towards transgression – lots of
black, in his case including a slick leather jacket.

Mild-mannered Reporters: Although Chloe and Pete are
barely present in the first half of the episode, Lana does a
little off-screen investigation of her own, following Lex's
clues to find out about the 'scarecrowing' incident. Before
his change, Greg did some work on the *Torch*, although
Chloe hasn't seen him lately. Clark and Chloe do some
varied research: Clark looks up Greg's personal history,
while Chloe digs up some wacky facts about Amazonian
tribesmen!

Man or Superman?: Greg's father is gone, his parents
having divorced when he was in the seventh grade. He
therefore lacks a strong male influence. In the cod psychology of *Smallville* (in which father figures are vitally
important) this could go some way to explaining why Greg
is such a creep even before he becomes bug-boy. Clark and
Pete – who used to be friends with Greg at a young age –
refer to Greg having stopped calling them once his parents
divorced, which lends credence to the idea that he became
socially introverted and hostile once his father left.

Teenage Kicks: . . . or in this case the lack of. The regular
characters must be *very* well behaved, as the morning after
the big school dance none of them seem even slightly the
worse for wear.

Go Crows: Jonathan congratulates Whitney on the previous day's game, and says he hasn't seen the Crows play so
well since he was on the team.

Loose Ends: How did Whitney get his truck back on the
road after it got stacked the previous night? Whose car is
he driving after the truck gets totalled? Do those insects
crawl out of Greg's body, or does he split into them?

From the Pages of: Lead as a barrier to the effects of
'kryptonite' – the comic-book name for the meteorites –

has been a staple of the Superman myth for many years. In the comics the 'Fortress of Solitude' was traditionally a vast space Superman carves out of the ice in the Antarctic. The first person to use the gag about the 'Fortress' being the name of a childhood lair of Clark's was writer/artist John Byrne in his 80s reinvention of the character, *Man of Steel*. The joke has been picked up and used on TV before – in *Lois & Clark: The New Adventures of Superman* it was used to describe Clark's boyhood treehouse. Greg's powers seem similar to those of the Marvel Comics hero, *Spider-Man*. This episode seems particularly influenced by the recent *Ultimate Spider-Man* comic's retelling of the character's origins, in which nerdy Peter Parker doesn't just gain superpowers when he gets bitten by that spider, but also stops wearing glasses and becomes generally more socially capable – this is also similar to what happens to Parker in the Sam Raimi *Spider-Man* movie released in 2002. Using a version of a rival superhero is more than a little cheeky, but, judging by Gough and Millar's involvement in the forthcoming movie *The Amazing Spider-Man*, there were, presumably, no hard feelings. Ironically, the lesson Clark wrestles with throughout the episode is that there cannot be power without responsibility – the key moral associated with Spider-Man.

One part of the Superman costume has disappeared from the show. After the pilot the Crows' football jackets were clearly rethought, as the 'S' logo is more generic without the Superman-esque triangle background. Quite a sudden change, considering it takes place overnight!

Secret Identities: Chad E Donella (Greg) made two appearances in David E Kelley's legal series *The Practice*, playing Kevin Peete. He's also been in *The X-Files*, *ER*, *Taken* and the movies *Final Destination*, *Disturbing Behavior* and *The Long Kiss Goodnight*. Gabrielle Rose is also in *Taken* and appeared in the movies *The Sweet Hereafter*, *Double Jeopardy* and *Timecop*. Her TV credits include a couple of appearances in *The X-Files* and roles in *Millennium* and *Dark Angel*.

Directors Michael Watkins and Philip Sgriccia have both directed episodes of the previous Superman series

Lois & Clark. Sgriccia has also worked on *Hercules: The Legendary Journeys*, *Xena: Warrior Princess* and *The Agency* as a director, while Watkins has directed episodes of *Chicago Hope*, *NYPD Blue*, *The X-Files* (on which he was also a co-executive producer), *Millennium*, *CSI* and many episodes of *Quantum Leap*.

Music: 'Island in the Sun' by Weezer plays during the market scene. Other tracks played in the episode are 'Last Resort' by Papa Roach, 'I Do' by Better Than Ezra, 'Underdog (Save Me)' by Turin Brakes, 'Love You Madly' by Cake and 'Damaged' by Aeon Spoke. The closing music is 'Wherever You Will Go' by The Calling, who had great success with this song as a single after performing it in the movie *Coyote Ugly*. 'Save Me' by Remy Zero, the title song for the show, is also first heard in this episode.

Trivia: Chloe's reference to Greg having 'gone Kafka' refers to Franz Kafka's 1915 novel *Metamorphosis*, in which a man wakes up to find he has become an insect.

The feature-length version of this episode (spliced with **1**, 'Pilot') is available in Canada as a Region 1 DVD, featuring a couple of deleted scenes from this episode. The first cut scene features Pete having breakfast at the Kent Farm, and restates that the events of the pilot were only the previous night. The second scene is a good character piece with Jonathan and Martha, where they discuss their fears for Clark's future and whether he'll ever be able to have a normal life.

On the UK broadcast, the scene where Greg moults in the shower was cut heavily to remove any images of his skin being scraped away. The line where Greg says that the Pharoah Spider 'eats its mother' was also cut, although Greg spewing webs over his mother was not.

Creators Alfred Gough and Miles Millar on the DVD commentary for this episode recount how many problems they had with Tom Welling's hair having been cut during shooting. The most obvious example of this is in the scene outside Greg's house with Clark, Pete and Chloe, where Clark's hair is noticeably an inch shorter than in the surrounding scenes.

The Last Word: 'It's amazing how far that Kent charm will get you.' An episode about the extent to which you should take what you want, 'Metamorphosis' builds on the work done in the pilot episode and establishes a workable formula for the series. Following on from the end of the pilot, the story picks up certain threads and clarifies some plot points while telling a story all of its own. The direction is fine, although a couple of effects shots are less than stellar, and Gough and Millar display the same eye for sharp characterisation that they did in the previous episode. There are some character tensions building, not just between Clark, Lana and Whitney, but also between Lex and Jonathan. The entire regular cast demonstrate great range and charisma, especially Michael Rosenbaum as Lex, wandering around whispering in the ears of both Clark and Lana, attempting to move them closer together. Chad E Donella makes a great villain as the increasingly nasty Greg, and the effects team show they can pull off superpowers on a television budget as Greg convincingly bounces around like a grasshopper. The final fight scene is convincingly executed and there's a poignant emotional kick to Clark's constant distance from Lana. Good stuff, and signs of a series that's developing nicely.

3
Hothead

Production #227603
1st US Transmission Date: 30 October 2001
1st UK Transmission Date: 2 January 2002

Writer: Greg Walker
Director: Greg Beeman
Special Guest Star: John Glover (Lionel Luthor)
Guest Starring: Jason Connery (Dominic),
Sarah-Jane Redmond (Aunt Nell), Hiro Kanagawa (Principal Kwan),
David Paetkau (Trevor Chapel), Dan Lauria (Coach Walt Arnold)
Co-starring: Allan Franz, Jada Stark

Synopsis: Walt Arnold is coach for the Smallville Crows, and a man with a temper. In his personal steam room, Walt inhales steam from meteor rocks and develops a power to direct fire against his enemies. When Smallville High's Principal, Kwan, finds out that members of the football team have cheated in a maths test, he wants the cheaters suspended from the team, which will endanger Walt achieving the 200th win of his career.

Clark gets drawn into Walt's world when he joins the football team, actively defying his father. When Principal Kwan uncovers Walt's role in the cheating scandal, he threatens to expose him. Walt uses his power over fire to try and kill Kwan by setting his car on fire. Walt threatens the cheating jocks with his powers if they tell – he makes the sprinklers on the field spit fire rather than water – and when Chloe investigates she finds her own life in danger, trapped in the *Torch*'s office as Walt sets it aflame. Clark, having rescued both Kwan and Chloe, confronts Walt, who traps him with the meteor rocks in the steam room. Clark is rescued by Jonathan and confronts Walt, who is consumed by his own flames. Jonathan and Clark are reconciled, but Clark has decided he doesn't intend to keep playing football anyway.

The same day Clark joins the football team, Lana is moving in the opposite direction, quitting cheerleading when she becomes disillusioned with the Crows after the cheating scandal. To Nell's disappointment, Lana determines to get a job and takes a waitressing gig at the Beanery. However, she isn't a very good waitress.

Lex is also trying to defy a parental figure, as Lionel tells Lex that the plant is unproductive and he must cut his workforce. Lex disagrees. Lex and Lionel have a fencing match to determine the outcome, and when Lex loses he is obliged to cut his workforce by 20 per cent. Lex cheats his way out of the impasse, cutting the operating budget by the required 20 per cent while still keeping the full workforce.

Speech Bubbles: Chloe (on Lana): 'There's something you don't see every day – a pom-pom meltdown!'

Lex: 'You both stood your ground and are doing what you want. I caved. You two have inspired me.' Clark: 'Oh yeah, joining the football team and pouring some coffee. We're a couple of real rebels.'

Lionel: 'Empires aren't built on clever book-keeping.'

Small Town Boy: Clark is stuck between a rock and a hard place when Coach Walt pressurises him into trying out for the team – especially when he accuses him of being in his father's shadow, challenging his masculinity in front of Lana. When Walt tells him football is in his genes, Clark replies that he's adopted, slightly deflating the coach's argument. Clark just wants the opportunity to play and take advantage of his powers rather than have to be punished for having them, and believes he has enough self-control to play without anyone getting hurt. Clark is understandably disappointed to find that the day he joins the football team is the same day Lana quits cheerleading. By the end of the episode Clark has quit football, having realised it isn't all it's cracked up to be and that he doesn't need to challenge Jonathan and thus has no reason to play.

In terms of using his powers, football is a cinch for Clark, and the reason Walt spots him is that he plucks a fast-moving ball out of the air when it's thrown at Chloe. During practice he charges through and leaps over the opposition to score, much to Jonathan's disappointment.

Not an Evil Genius: Lex's anger at his 'exile' and at his father's latest attempt to intervene in the running of the plant, burns through his scenes. While Luthor senior wants cuts made to improve results, Lex insists on pushing up productivity – a risky strategy – in an attempt to capitalise at the expense of their opponents when the market recovers. In his meeting with Dominic, one of Lionel's representatives, Lex not only refers to Lionel's underlings as 'drones', but he asks Dominic to give his regards to his sister, presumably another of Lex's conquests. Lex tells Lana and Clark that they have inspired him by standing up to their parents while he caved in. He tells Clark that he understands his currently frosty relationship with Jonathan – the Luthors could have written a book on uncomfortable silences. Lex chivalrously says his coffee is perfect after Lana has given him completely the wrong drink. When Lex fences with Lionel he loses because he's too emotional and rash – something his father berates him for – but in their later confrontation it's Lionel who begins to lose his cool, annoyed that Lex defied his explicit instructions. Lionel tells Lex that he only gets one chance to defy him like this, but Lex believes Lionel is just annoyed that he didn't think of his idea first.

Girl Next Door: Lana is genuinely offended that Whitney doesn't consider his team-mates' cheating important. Although Clark agrees to try out for the team at least partially because he's being challenged in front of Lana, she seems disappointed by the way he caves in under peer pressure. Lana's increasing disillusionment with the football team causes her to break away from being the meek, supportive cheerleader and strike out on her own, quitting the cheerleading squad and getting a job waitressing at the Beanery. Lana gets a waitress uniform that Clark says makes her look very 'waitress-like'. She describes it as breaking a vicious cycle, as both her mother and Nell were cheerleaders. So, like Clark and Lex, Lana is trying to move out of the shadows of her parents. Unfortunately, she isn't a very good waitress – she can't remember the difference between various types of coffee, she's far too slow, and at one point she drops a tray loaded with drinks. Later she claims to hold the record for most dishes broken in a single day and says that she just wants to scream, before giving Clark and Lex completely the wrong drinks. By the end of the episode she's been fired but still doesn't want to go back to her old routine.

The Quarterback: In spite of this being an episode about football, Whitney gets surprisingly little to do. He isn't too concerned about his friends cheating, which causes a micro-rift between him and Lana. When asked by Coach Walt if Clark would be any good in the team, Whitney is grudgingly positive about his chances.

Torch Bearer: Clark thinks Chloe's caffeine addiction is driving her aggressive articles. Her article about the football team has the headline: FOOTBALL: SPORT OR ABUSE?! Chloe has been getting hate mail – which she is rather proud of – and thinks that it's coming from the football team as the standard of literacy is poor. She is less pleased when one of the team tries to take her head off with a well-thrown football. Chloe's contempt for the football team and their attendant cheerleaders is shown in her constant jockstrap and pom-pom jokes, and shows the extent to which Chloe considers herself the rebellious outsider journalist, commenting on a dumb school elite. When Clark gets involved in the team Chloe finds it hard to believe, and Lana's quitting to become a waitress baffles her equally. After the fire in the *Torch*'s office, Chloe believes Coach Walt has been controlling the fires some-how – another huge leap, but having seen the burning sprinklers she at least has some evidence this time.

Just the Funny Guy: Walt coached Pete's father when he was at school and used to watch the Super Bowl at the Ross household. Chloe considers this a 'Hallmark mo-ment' – in reference to the slogan of the Hallmark greeting card company. The coach says that Pete has no talent, but has a lot of heart, a backhanded compliment Pete is less than pleased with. He finds Chloe's use of the word 'jockstrap' as a name for the football players rather wearing.

Down at the Farm: Jonathan is described by Walt as one of the best athletes he ever coached. Jonathan's picture remains in the Crows' trophy cabinet. Jonathan still doesn't want Clark playing football (see 1, 'Pilot'). He seems equally concerned that Clark's abilities should not get found out – even checking that he wasn't seen while rescuing Kwan. As Martha says, Jonathan wasn't exactly the obedient son himself, as he once ran away from home to try out for the Metropolis Sharks. Martha stays neutral, considering both Jonathan and Clark to be stubborn, but encouraging them to give each other a chance.

Strange Visitors: Walt Arnold has coached the Crows for over twenty years and is a local legend. As he approaches his 200th win, the coach becomes more ruthless in his attempts to make that record, bullying his team and helping them cheat at academic tests so they don't get thrown out of school. An angry man already, a lungful of meteor-tainted steam gives him the ability to express his rage with actual flame, allowing him to terrorise his team even further and attempt to eliminate both Chloe and Kwan. Although Dan Lauria is suitably aggressive and frightening as Walt, he isn't the most psychologically intriguing villain as his insistence that he cannot be stopped comes not from his power, but from his inflated social standing. Unfortunately this slight undercurrent of social commentary can't stop the coach from being little more than a caricature of that nightmare PE teacher everyone has at some point in their schooldays.

Man or Superman?: Coach Walt constantly challenges Clark's ability to be his own man, pushing him into defying his father. When the coach gives Clark the position Jonathan used to play in, the symbolism is even more blatant – the son taking on the mantle of the father (indeed, Trevor, the player who has spoken to Chloe about what's going on, says that the coach acts as if he's the father of his players). Elsewhere, Lex is breaking free of his own parental restraints, insisting on using his own business methods.

Interestingly, there is also the feminine mirror of these conflicts in this episode, as Lana breaks away from being a cheerleader like her mother and aunt before her and strikes out on her own. So *Smallville* isn't quite as concerned with purely guy's stuff as it might have appeared.

Go Crows!: The Crows have been coached by Walt Arnold for going-on 25 years. Whole generations of young men owe their careers to the team and its coach, having got into college on the back of good school football careers.

Loose Ends: What exactly happens to the coach? Does he burn to nothing, does he die, is he just badly scorched to end up in hospital with all the other *Smallville* mutant-of-the-week characters who get stretchered away at the end of subsequent episodes?

Secret Identities: Making his first appearance as Principal Kwan is Hiro Kanagawa, an actor with diverse credits including *Josie and the Pussycats*, *The 6th Day* and TV shows including *The X-Files* and *Millennium*. Jason Connery is best known as the son of Sean Connery, but has carved out a career of his own including the title role in *Spymaker: the Secret Life of Ian Fleming*, as well as playing the second Robin Hood in the British TV series *Robin of Sherwood*, and a role in the Jackie Chan western *Shanghai Noon*. Dan Lauria is best known for his role in *The Wonder Years* (where his character's surname was also Arnold), and has made numerous appearances in many other TV shows, including *ER*, *NYPD Blue*, a voice-over role in *Batman Beyond*, and a regular role as another Coach in teen soap *Party of Five*. He also appeared in both *Stakeout* movies and the 1996 blockbuster *Independence Day*. Writer Greg Walker is one of the show's co-producers, and was previously a writer and story editor on *The X-Files*. This is the first episode by recurring *Smallville* director Greg Beeman, who has previously shot episodes of *The Wonder Years* as well as directing the 'comedy' sequel *Problem Child 3*.

Music: Gorillaz' 'Clint Eastwood' plays over the initial school scene, while Sum 41's 'Motivation' is used to back Clark's first football practice. Other tracks include 'Renegade Fighter' by Zen Silencer, 'Bad Day' by Fuel, 'Never Let You Go' by Third Eye Blind and the closing 'You' by Binocular.

From the Pages of: In John Byrne's revised Superman origin story, *Man of Steel*, Clark is the local football hero, much to the discomfort of his father. It's Clark using his powers for sporting fame that leads Jonathan Kent to tell him about his arrival on Earth, encouraging Clark to use those powers for more heroic purposes.

The Last Word: 'Just because you win doesn't make you right.' 'Hothead' is an episode about challenging your parents and finding yourself, as Clark, Lana and Lex all run up against parental opposition to their ways of living. While the nemesis-of-the-week follows an already strict formula – someone getting powers from the meteor rocks, then beating up Clark when the rocks leave him vulnerable – Dan Lauria plays Coach Walt for every ounce of malevolent, bullying rage, providing an alternative, abusive father figure for Clark.

It's good to see Clark's football-related daydreams from the pilot get a pay-off, and it says a lot about the show that it's evolving beyond the characters as portrayed when the series began. Lana's growth from living the cheerleading dream to attempting to grow as a person is just one welcome character development.

Not a spectacular episode by any means, but this is still rock-solid. It's also very reminiscent of *The X-Files* – unsurprising, perhaps, given writer Greg Walker's CV . . .

4
X-Ray

Production #227604
1st US Transmission Date: 6 November 2001
1st UK Transmission Date: 16 January 2002

Writer: Mark Verheiden
Director: James Frawley
Guest Starring: Lizzy Caplan (Tina Greer), Tom O'Brien (Roger Nixon),
Beverley Breuer (Rose Greer), Sarah-Jane Redmond (Aunt Nell)
Co-starring: Annabel Kershaw, Mark McConchie (Mr Ellis),
Brian Jensen, Mitch Kosterman (Deputy Ethan Talbot)

Synopsis: Clark develops a new ability: X-ray vision. Initially, he can't control the power and it disorientates him, but soon he manages to bring it under his control.

Clark's new ability first manifests itself when he sees Lex robbing the Smallville Savings & Loan, only to get a glimpse of Lex's skeleton, which is tainted green. Although Clark doesn't know this, the thief isn't the real Lex, but is instead Tina Greer, daughter of antique-shop owner Rose Greer. Tina has the power to change her shape, as well as super-strength. When Tina's mother isn't happy about the stolen money, Tina and Rose fight, and Rose falls down the stairs, breaking her neck. After deciding not to call for help, Tina conceals her mother's death and impersonates her, using her abilities to try to protect her secret. When

Martha finds a roll of stolen money in the antique shop, Tina impersonates Clark and tries to run Martha down in the Kents' truck. When Clark gets close to the truth, Tina impersonates Lana and visits Clark, kissing him before using her meteor-enhanced strength to throw him out of a window. Tina tries to persuade Lana that Nell should let Tina live with them. When Lana tells Tina that she can't live with her and Nell, Tina tries to steal Lana's life. Tina impersonates Lana to borrow Whitney's jacket, then impersonates Whitney and assaults Lana by her parents' grave. Tina traps Lana in a nearby tomb, but Clark finds her using his new power. Tina impersonates Whitney, but Clark punches her out and she reverts to her normal form. Clark rescues Lana.

While Tina is wreaking havoc, Lana is more concerned with her mother, after finding her teenage diaries. Lana begins to discover that Laura Lang wasn't as happy with her life as Lana had believed. Nell tells Lana that Laura gave a speech at their graduation which summed up her feelings about life in Smallville. With Chloe's help, Lana manages to get a recording of the speech.

Journalist Roger Nixon comes to Smallville, intending to blackmail Lex with documents relating to his wild past. Lex threatens to delete all record of Nixon's existence, and Nixon is cowed into working on a job for Lex – investigating Lex's car crash (see **1**, 'Pilot').

Speech Bubbles: Lex (to Nixon): 'I've read comic books with less fiction than your rag!'

Tina (impersonating Lana): 'It's like having a dual identity. There's the person that everybody sees, and the person that you want to be.' Clark: 'I know the feeling.'

Lana (on her mother's diary): '[It's] like she could see right through me. Do you ever feel like that?' Clark: 'More than you know.'

Small Town Boy: Clark's new power – X-ray vision – can peel back layers of things, or act as an actual X-ray showing only bones, superstructures of buildings and so on. Clark has problems taking control of this ability: at first the flashes of vision are completely out of his control, but by the end of the episode he seems to have mastered it. In later episodes he manages to use the ability with ease (see the scenes where he uses it to rescue Martha in **6**, 'Hourglass' and **17**, 'Reaper'). Clark is shown trying to look into the box Lex gave him, which suggests that he might not be able to see through the lead lining. The most notable of Clark's uses for his new gift is his peek through the walls of the girl's changing room, just as Lana emerges from the shower. Clark grins broadly as he looks in, proving he isn't yet completely the chivalrous hero.

After Lana has told him about her mother's diary, Clark tells her that she is lucky to at least have her mother's words. When Lana asks if Clark has ever tried to contact his biological parents, he replies that their lives are probably 'a million years' from his. He tells Lana he wants to know what happened, why his parents let him go and how to explain how strange his life is.

Not an Evil Genius: Lex can't resist needling Jonathan about his low opinion of him. When he arrives at the Kent farm he promises he's 'not packing heat', nor is he a criminal mastermind. Lionel Luthor is apparently obsessed with the *Daily Planet*, but Lex thinks the *Metropolis Inquisitor* is the paper people really read, and recruits blackmailing *Inquisitor* journo Roger Nixon to run stories for him. Lex keeps his wrecked Porsche and is determined to unravel the mystery of how he survived a car accident that should have killed him. Lex's approach to Nixon's blackmail attempt is ruthless and brilliant – he gives him the money, but then explains exactly how he's going to destroy Nixon's life with one phone call, arranging to have all Nixon's personal details deleted.

Girl Next Door: After finding out that Whitney wasn't as clean-cut as she thought, and that her football team friends were up to their neck in cheating, Lana now finds that her mother wasn't the person she's been told about. When Lana reads the diary her mother kept when she was seventeen she finds out that Laura Lang wasn't the happy cheerleader who loved everything about her life. This cuts into Lana deeply, as up to this point she's tried to live up to the image of her mother that Nell told her about. Lana says that when she reads the diary it's like her mother is talking to her, and afterwards she's gone.

There's something self-effacing about Lana which people find hard to dislike, as seen in the scene where Lana charms Chloe. That said, in **2**, 'Metamorphosis' Lana was being kind to a geek and in return he tried to make her the mother of his insect spawn, and this week Tina, Lana's 'unpopular' friend, is trying to kill Lana and steal her life. Lana's kindness and openness with others might be admirable, but it's a dangerous quality to have in a town full of super-powered lunatics.

Lana's pink rollneck sweater is worth a mention – it's so chunky it nearly swallows her head!

The Quarterback: Whitney responds strongly to Tina's flirtatious version of Lana. Sucker.

Love's Young Dream: After the false start of Clark being kissed by a fake Lana, he gets a visit from the real Lana and they have another heart-to-heart about their lost parents. However, in spite of their closeness as friends, Clark sees Whitney and Lana all over each other inside the Lang household at the end of the episode and realises he still has a long way to go.

Torch Bearer: Chloe is initially dismissive of Lana when she comes to the *Torch* asking for help, and makes another crack about pom-poms, although she does quickly apologise. Chloe is writing her bi-annual 'Where Are Our Priorities?' rant, and that apparently makes it difficult for her to switch off from taking no prisoners. She's intrigued by the suppression of Laura Lang's speech, presuming that if it was the only graduation speech never to be printed, it must also be the only one worth reading. By the end of the episode she's clearly beginning to feel affection and sympathy for Lana, having been forced to see her in a new light.

Just the Funny Guy: When Clark tells Pete his theory about Tina, Pete replies that that's Chloe's department, whereas he's there to talk about the general guy stuff. At this stage in the series Pete is still largely a running source of witty asides and hasn't been deepened as a character yet. When someone enters the *Torch*'s office Chloe refers to Pete throwing a rubber spider at her all day – well, it passes the time.

Strange Visitors: Shape-shifting Tina, who starts her criminal career with a vengeance by committing a bank robbery and matricide on the same day. Like so many characters in the show, Tina is raised by a single parent, only to become another of the show's orphans when she kills her mother. Tina hates her own life and wants Lana's, which Tina regards as perfect. Tina and Lana have clearly been friends for some time, but not so close that Lana wants her as a sister. Tina claims to be unpopular, while Lana says that Tina used to be the one who didn't care what people thought of her. Tina claims that her mother is still alive, using her abilities to impersonate her mother. She's worried about being taken to a foster home and tries to insinuate herself into the Lang household before deciding to just cut to the chase and take Lana's place. While impersonating Lana, Tina takes full advantage of Lana's opportunities by pouncing on both Clark and Whitney.

Secret Identities: Lizzy Caplan played Sara in the short-lived sitcom *Freaks and Geeks* and appeared in the movie *Orange County*. Tom O'Brien, making his first appearance as journalist Roger Nixon, appeared in the movies *The Big Easy* and *The Astronaut's Wife*, as well as making notable guest appearances in *The X-Files* two-parter 'Tempus Fugit/Max' and the *Timecop* TV series. Mitchell Kosterman, making his *Smallville* debut here as the deputy, has appeared in a checklist of fantasy shows: *The X-Files*, *Millennium*, *Stargate SG-1*, and *MacGyver*. Beverley Breuer has appeared in *The Lone Gunmen* and *The New Addams Family*.

Writer and supervising producer Mark Verheiden is a former writer of comics, including a notable trilogy of *Aliens* miniseries as well as *The Mask*, and has since gone on to write for *Timecop* (the film and the short-lived spin-off TV series, both of which were based on his own comic), *Freaky Links* and *Martial Law*. James Frawley has directed episodes of *Ally McBeal*, *Ed* and *Columbo* as well as *The Muppet Movie*, *The Big Bus* and *Nancy Drew*.

Loose Ends: In the UK version at least there seems to be a nonsensical cut, with Whitney's jacket disappearing off the Whitney-ised Tina's back for no reason at all. Clark can't have pulled it off her at superspeed to throw it away, as Tina is holding a shovel with both hands at the time, and the necklace in the jacket pocket should prevent Clark from tearing it off. Presumably there's a missing scene where the jacket is discarded.

Tina's powers are based around a shifting bone structure – and Clark's X-rays show that her skeleton is irradiated by the meteors – but how does that allow her to change her hair, voice, eye colour and so forth? At the end of the episode the viewer sees an ambulance, and Martha says Tina won't be hurting anyone again, but what actually happened to her? Presumably she's not dead, so did Tina lose her powers, or slip into a coma, or is she simply restrained by the authorities?

One dangling loose end that does get resolved is the reference to something that happened to Lex at a place called 'Club Zero' – in **14**, 'Zero'.

Music: Alien Ant Farm's 'Movies' plays at the very start of the pre-title sequence. 'Ooh La La' by the Wiseguys plays when Clark's X-ray vision strikes in the gym. Other tracks heard are 'Breathe You In' by Stabbing Westward, 'Analyse' by mawkish Irish rockers The Cranberries, 'Unbroken' by Todd Thibaud, 'Up All Night' by Unwritten Law and 'Wall in Your Heart' by Shelby Lynne.

Trivia: In the school gym Clark is told to climb a rope hanging from the ceiling, even though he's showing signs of disorientation. This is probably not a sensible approach to taking care of young people. Even worse, when Clark falls over ten feet to the floor, the coach's response isn't to call for a nurse but rather to ask if he is all right. I fear for Smallville High's legal bills with this kind of treatment.

The Last Word: 'I never wanted this life, it just kind of happened.' A story about perceptions, preconceptions and masks, 'X-Ray' has its characters struggling to separate surface impressions from the truth, and trying to uncover something real. The hugely embittered Tina feels that orphaned Lana is better off than she is and tries to steal her life, while Lana is trying to find out something solid about a mother she's realising she never really knew. Nixon jumps to conclusions about Lex and finds himself sorely mistaken, while Clark gets to look beneath the surface of things and doesn't like a lot of what he sees. Even Chloe gets her perceptions corrected, as she begins to realise there's far more to Lana than just beauty and cheerleading. Although in many ways it fits the increasingly prevalent 'meteor-powered psycho-of-the-week' formula, 'X-Ray' is executed with tremendous skill by all concerned and provides some good character insights. The entire cast have fun playing Tina as she impersonates their regular characters. Kristin Kreuk in particular excels as a far more bitter and snappish young woman pretending to be the mild-mannered Lana Lang, while Michael Rosenbaum plays Tina-as-Lex with a few girly mannerisms that are hilariously camp. 'Don't trust first impressions', the moral of the story, isn't the deepest message in the world, but at least it's delivered in an entertaining way.

5
Cool

Production #227605
1st US Transmission Date: 13 November 2001
1st UK Transmission Date: 23 January 2002

Writer: Michael Green
Director: Jim Contner
Guest Starring: Michael Coristine (Sean Kelvin)
Co-starring: Tania Saulnier (Jenna), Elizabeth McLaughlin,
Ted Garcia (News Anchor)

Synopsis: At a party near the frozen Crater Lake, school football player and womaniser Sean Kelvin chats up Chloe. However, after falling into a frozen lake full of meteor rocks, Sean finds himself permanently cold, with the ability to drain heat from any source around him. But the only thing that really warms Sean up is draining human body heat, leaving the victim a frozen corpse. Sean kills his ex, Jenna, this way, then seeks to charm Chloe.

Lana is feeling neglected by Whitney, leaving her open to Clark's invite to a concert in Metropolis. Although they're going as friends, both seem to be treating it as a date.

Lex's interest in the Kents continues. Not only does he manipulate Clark into asking Lana out on a date by offering him concert tickets and a limo for the night, he also invites Clark's parents to the Luthor mansion to discuss investing in the farm.

On the same night Lana and Clark are going to the city, and Jonathan and Martha are going to see Lex, Chloe and Sean are set to meet at the school. Clark sees a news report on Jenna's death and deserts Lana to rescue Chloe. Clark saves Chloe from Sean, who then drains electricity from a junction box, causing a town-wide powercut. Whitney picks Lana up, and crashes his truck when Sean walks into their path. As Whitney and Lana head towards the Luthor mansion, Sean is going the same way, with Clark close behind. At the Luthor house, Sean threatens Martha, but Clark manages to throw him into the lake, where ice forms around him.

Neither of Lex's plans for the Kents pay off – Lana is comfortably back with Whitney, while Jonathan refuses Lex's offer of a partnership.

Speech Bubbles: Lex: 'If this town ever had connections they wouldn't have named it Smallville.'

Lex: 'A High School boyfriend isn't a husband, he's an obstacle.'

Small Town Boy: The main focus of the episode is Clark rising to Lex's challenge to take Lana on a date after Whitney cancels her big day out (see **Girl Next Door**). In this Clark is acting cold himself, adopting Lex's ruthless attitude to getting what he wants. Clark gets carried away by the possibilities of this just-friends, non-date turning into something more, but has to leave Lana in the lurch to save Chloe, thus reverting to putting the needs of others above his own desires. Later he asks Lana for another non-date, but by then the moment has been lost – Whitney has reasserted his position in Lana's affections and Lana is making it quite clear that she and Clark are just friends. Clark is left high and dry, standing on his own under a huge banner reading 'achievement' – an ironic comparison if ever there was one.

Clark jokes about taking up a pro-sports career to raise money for the farm – with his abilities he could make a fortune in endorsements alone. Clark has never been in a limousine before his date with Lana, and endearingly plays around with the fittings. Clark uses astronomy as an escape mechanism, looking at the stars, wondering if his life would be better if he lived on another planet. Of course, Lana doesn't realise how much of a possibility that really is. Clark shows Lana a card trick, using his X-ray vision to see the card she's holding. Clark's abilities allow him to thaw out after having his heat drained by Sean.

Girl Next Door: Lana is being taken to Metropolis by Whitney to see an exhibition. When Lex suggests she's trying to educate the quarterback, Lana says it was Whitney's idea. Lex's sarcasm is proven correct when Whitney backs out of the trip in favour of watching a fight on TV. She's reading Boris Pasternak's *Doctor Zhivago*, a book in which a long unrequited love is finally fulfilled, but with disastrous consequences for all concerned. Lex says he saw the exhibition Lana wanted to see in St Petersburg, so presumably she has an interest in all things Russian. She accepts Clark's invitation to the concert once he says they'll be going as friends. Clark notes that Lana has always practised defensive reading – disappearing into a book at the first sign of trouble – ever since they were kids. Lana feels that she has to explain her night out with Clark to Nell, but she doesn't tell Whitney. Lana later lets Pete take a spin in the limo, even though Whitney is present at the time.

When Lana does tell Whitney about her planned evening with Clark, she insists that it wasn't a date and that Clark is just a friend, and claims she didn't tell Whitney about it because she knew he would overreact. Lana tells Clark that she told Whitney the truth about her and Clark, but says that she goes out with Whitney because he's always there when she needs him. That's the shift that Lana's feelings go through – being disappointed with Whitney when he lets her down, taking an interest in Clark but realising that he's not there for her in the way that Whitney is.

Not an Evil Genius: Lex tells Martha that he wants to invest in local farms to help Smallville to become the big hitter in Kansas agriculture that it once was, allowing farmers to invest in new equipment and modernise. This is all a front, of course, to allow him to try and pay the Kents' way out of financial hardship. Even when Jonathan rejects the offer, Lex still leaves it open, his desire to help Clark's family undimmed.

Lex is also still lobbying Lana on Clark's behalf, mocking Whitney's trip to the museum and telling Lana she's with the wrong guy. When Whitney cancels, Lex tips Clark off that Lana is free that night, then offers him the tickets to the big Radiohead concert in Metropolis – *if* Clark can get Lana to go with him. As extra incentive he tells Clark that if he asks Lana in sixty seconds, Lex will throw in a round-trip ride in a limousine. Laying on this kind of pressure is a very manipulative tactic, showing how Lex is willing to jerk people around like puppets, even if, in Clark's case, it may be for his own good.

Lex tells Clark he's like 'the younger brother I never had'. He doesn't miss a trick to destabilise Lana and Whitney's relationship, referring to Lana and Clark's aborted evening out as a date in front of Whitney. Lex is not too keen on physical confrontation – he's quite happy to hide behind his security system, only half-heartedly offering to help the Kents check on the generator and the gates when Sean is nearby.

Torch Bearer: Yet again Chloe proves to be easily flattered by anyone who compliments her on her writing, as Sean gets mileage out of having read and liked her columns. Although she claims to only have given Sean her number to get rid of him, she's positively glowing with the attention. When Sean asks her if she's busy, and Chloe has to finish the paper first, Sean moves straight on to approaching his ex, Jenna, which leaves Chloe less than happy. After arranging to meet Sean the next day, Chloe admits to Clark that she quite likes Sean, because he's hot. After Sean attacks her and she's rescued by Clark, Chloe promises that it wasn't 'a passive/aggressive attempt' to ruin his date. Chloe berates herself for having nearly been killed due to falling over herself when a guy took an interest in her, and unhappily drags Pete away so that Clark can talk to Lana alone.

Chloe asks if Clark is from an ice planet when he doesn't find it cold by Crater Lake. When Pete jokingly tells Clark to ask Chloe out, she puts them straight, saying she isn't a crash-test dummy for them to test their dating skills on, and telling them both to treat her better. She says Clark should ask Lana out but is visibly disappointed when he does so.

As well as still being the show's resident Mulder character – coming up with the insane but strangely accurate theories as to the villain-of-the-week's powers – Chloe is also getting a severe case of the Scullys, managing to never quite see Clark using his powers. She's amazingly trusting when it comes to Clark: she doesn't question how he survived his run-in with Sean near the swimming pool, or why he insists on calling for help himself rather than letting her phone the authorities (Clark, of course, is intent on pursuing Sean himself).

The Quarterback: Whitney foolishly forgets a cultural trip to Metropolis he's planned with Lana, instead committing himself to a night with the guys. Luckily for him, he turns up at the right time when Lana is stranded at the Beanery by Clark's desertion. The threat of Clark and Lana's non-date gives Whitney the impetus to plan a day out in the city for him and Lana. Whitney crashes another truck in this episode – either the Fordmans have an entire fleet of the things or they have very good insurance. It's never explained which.

Just the Funny Guy: Pete is seen with a date, although she doesn't actually get any dialogue, and he claims that she's just a friend. When Lana offers him the chance to take his non-date in the limo, he reluctantly accepts. Later it's clear the limo worked and Pete got a promise of another date for the following weekend. Pete tells Lana about his friendship with Clark and how sometimes his friend can seem entirely normal, while at other times he seems more enigmatic. Pete refers to Clark as an 'International Man of Mystery' – the subtitle to the 1997 first *Austin Powers* film.

Love's Young Dream: When Whitney cancels their date, Lana is left disillusioned and vulnerable to advances from Clark. They go out on a just-friends date, which is in danger of becoming more when their hands touch. Unfortunately, having seen a news report, Clark has to run off and save Chloe from Sean (Chloe and Lana's positions here are almost precisely reversed in **21**, 'Tempest'). Whitney then gets to play the shining knight, picking up Lana from the Beanery and helping her to walk to the Luthor mansion after the crash.

Pete's anecdote about his sister not being called by a guy because of a family illness doesn't apply to Sean not calling Chloe, but it is remarkably similar to Lana's problems with Whitney later in the season (see **10**, 'Shimmer' through to **19**, 'Crush').

Down at the Farm: The Kent farm is in serious financial trouble and a bank loan may be required to keep it afloat. The audience gets a little insight into the economics of having a son with superpowers, as the farm has been saved the cost of several farm hands by having Clark there. Martha explains to Lex that Jonathan doesn't hate him personally, but that he's wary of the Luthors due to their local track record, and she tells Jonathan that they should hear out Lex's offer of investment in the farm, just so that they have some financial options. At the Luthor mansion Jonathan tells Lex that his father managed the farm without financial help, but Lex produces the paperwork showing the government subsidies handed out to the farm during that period. This means the Kent Farm has been in debt for two generations at least. Under the circumstances, Lex's opinion that he can make a profit from investing in the farm would be overly optimistic if it weren't a cover for an act of charity.

Strange Visitors: Sean Kelvin, who spends a night trapped underwater with meteor rocks, bursting out from beneath the ice the following morning. He has an incredibly low body temperature, and can only get warm by draining heat from elsewhere (his surname is, of course, the same as the basic unit of thermodynamic temperature). Sean explains to Chloe why he can't just stay by a fire – it's only a quick fix, while body heat replenishes him for longer. Chloe compares Sean's condition to when the thermosensitive cells of the brain are damaged. Sean can use his ability in various handy ways, like freezing the swimming pool to capture Chloe or freezing a padlock and shattering it. He can drain considerable amounts of electricity into his body without any ill effects, although the charge doesn't alleviate his cold for very long compared to human body heat.

Like many of the meteor mutants, the nature of Sean's mutation reflects some element of his personality. In this case Sean's cold and predatory attitude to women becomes more literal, as he uses them for their body heat then leaves them for dead.

Music: 'Rescue' by Eve 6 plays over the beach-party scene at the start of the episode, while 'Top of the World' by the Juliana Theory plays during Jenna's shower. 'Let Your Shoulder Fall' by Matthew Jay and 'On Your Side' by Pete Yorn are played in the Beanery at different points in the episode. The final track played as Lana leaves Clark in the corridor is 'Standing Still' by Jewel.

Secret Identities: Michael Coristine appeared in *Taken* as well as the film *Get Over It*. Tania Saulnier is in the movie *Cheaters* and has appeared in *Special Unit 2*. Ted Garcia has presented the news in a number of other shows, including *The West Wing* and *Six Feet Under*. Director Jim Contner, sometimes known as James A Contner, has a long string of directorial credits including episodes of *Buffy the Vampire Slayer*, *Angel*, *Roswell*, *Enterprise*, *The X-Files* and previous Superman show *Lois & Clark*. Michael Green has written for *Snoops*, *Cupid* and *Sex and the City*.

From the Pages of: Chloe's line that guys find her attractive 'even though I don't have raven hair and the initials LL' is an in-joke, the 'raven hair' description being usually applied to Lois Lane in the comics, not the traditionally ginger Lana Lang. In the comics, Clark also has a habit of involving himself with women with the initials LL – he also had a thing with one Lori Lemaris, a mermaid. *Smallville* probably has many seasons to go before things get that silly.

Chloe tells Clark that blue is a good colour on him, the writers yet again riffing on the Superman costume.

Trivia: The sign by Crater Lake prohibits swimming, fishing and skating, 'By order of Kansas State Parks Department'. One fears what the fish living in that crater might be like with all those meteor rocks – presumably they're psychic time-travelling fish that can fire flame from their gills and kill people with a fishy glance.

Loose Ends: There is absolutely no explanation as to what happens to Sean after Clark throws him into the water – the next scene takes place at least a couple of days later.

The Last Word: 'I finally find a guy I like and he turns out to be homicidal.' At this point, the series' formula is becoming a little too tight for comfort: we meet a character with a personality quirk (bad temper, insect obsession or, in this case, a cold attitude to women), they come into contact with the meteors and they gain a power relating to that personality quirk. While Sean Kelvin is a suitably nasty threat, treating Chloe first as a potential sexual conquest and later as a heat source to be tapped and left for dead, we've seen this a couple of times too many. Fortunately the character threads help the rest of the episode along, with Lex trying to help Clark with Lana and the Kents with their financial difficulties. Although both these attempts fail – Lana remains with Whitney and the Kents reject Lex's partnership offer – there's still a feeling that these stories are developing, and that plot resets aren't quite as total as they may seem.

6
Hourglass

Production #227606
1st US Transmission Date: 20 November 2001
1st UK Transmission Date: 23 January 2002

Writer: Doris Egan
Director: Chris Long
Guest Starring: George Murdock (Old Harry), Eric Christian Olsen
(Young Harry), Jackie Burroughs (Cassandra Carver)
Co-starring: Mitchell Kosterman (Deputy Ethan Talbot), Lisa Calder, Alf
Humphreys, Reg Tupper, Lois Dellar

Synopsis: Clark and Lana are doing community work in an
old people's home and come into contact with two unusual
residents: Harry Bollsten, a cantankerous old man under
Lana's care, falls into a meteor-filled pond in the grounds
and, unbeknownst to her, re-emerges as a younger man;
Clark meets Cassandra Carver, who was blinded in the
meteor shower of 1989, but gained an ability to see the
future. When Cassandra touches Clark, she tells him that
someone close to him is going to die.

As the police search for the missing Harry Bollsten, it is
revealed that he is Harry Volk, a convicted murderer who
had served his time and been released under a new name.
Harry poses as a nurse at the home, while hunting down
and killing the descendants of the jurors who convicted
him. Zoe Garfield, a local waitress, is one of those
descendants, but Clark manages to stop Harry and hand
him over to the authorities. When the mysterious young
man caught attempting to kill Zoe disappears, to be
replaced by the aged Harry Volk, the police have nothing
to hold him on and release him back to the old people's
home. Harry throws himself into the pond and becomes
young again, seeking out the descendants of Hiram Kent,
Jonathan's father. With Jonathan out of the house, Harry
tries to kill Martha, but Clark comes to the rescue, and
Harry re-ages while trapped under tonnes of grain.

After her first vision, Clark returns to Cassandra for
more information. She is shocked when Clark proves able

to share the visions. Cassandra has visions of Clark's future: of him outliving everyone around him, and of him helping people in times of need. Lex takes an interest in Cassandra's abilities, wanting her to tell him what she has found out about Clark. Cassandra refuses, but offers to tell Lex his future. Lex initially refuses to believe in fate, but eventually allows Cassandra to take his hand. She sees a horrific vision of things to come (see **Lex's Future**), and the shock kills her. Clark realises that Cassandra's prediction of death had been about herself.

Speech Bubbles: Lex: 'Life's a journey, Clark. I don't want to go through it following a roadmap.'

Clark: 'What if it is my destiny to outlive everyone I love? I don't want to be alone.'

Lex: 'I come bearing gifts.' Cassandra: 'So did the Greeks!'

Small Town Boy: Clark's thoughts during this episode turn to mortality – the mortality of those around him, and the possibility that he might not be mortal himself. Early on in the episode, after Cassandra's prediction, Clark becomes paranoid about the safety of those around him, including his parents and Lex. The visions Clark shares with Cassandra give a wonderful insight into his personal nightmares; more than anything he fears outliving everyone he loves. The endless graveyard is a bleak image and is echoed by the fields of bone in Cassandra's vision of Lex's future. Once more Clark is reminded of the meteor shower he arrived with and the devastating effect it had on the residents of Smallville, with Cassandra having lost her sight due to the meteors. When Clark tells Cassandra he's sorry (Tom Welling playing Clark's guilt and discomfort to perfection), Cassandra replies that it wasn't his fault. Clark shows similar remorse when Lana describes her own feelings about being overshadowed by the death of her parents on that day, telling her that if he could go back in time and stop that day from ever happening, he would (this is of course exactly what Superman does in the nonsensical ending to *Superman: The Movie*). By the end of the episode, judging by his calm reaction to Cassandra's death, Clark seems to be more accepting of death as part of life.

Clark gets to use his superpowers a great deal in this episode. As well as zooming around town at superspeed, and putting his X-ray vision to good use, Clark also gets a new power, that of sharing in Cassandra's visions (although obviously the ending of the show precludes *that* gift being utilised again). Clark's invulnerability comes in handy; not only is he run over by a truck, the friction leaving another perfectly good jacket in tatters, but when Harry tries to stab Clark the knife shatters, fragments drifting across the screen in slow motion. The slowed-down sequences in other episodes (especially **9**, 'Rogue') suggest that this might be how Clark perceives the world while moving at superspeed.

Cassandra's reference to having seen Clark in the futures of others, saving people from burning buildings and so forth is, of course, a positive thing even though it sounds gloomy in the context of the episode. It gently hints at his future as Superman without spelling it out. Like her other visions, there is a balance between the literal and the metaphorical.

Not an Evil Genius: The Luthors are completely obsessed with ideas of fate, self-determination and their own great destinies and, although Lex may like to think he's different from Lionel, it's just that his fixation comes from a slightly different angle. From driving like a maniac to initially turning down Cassandra's offer to look into his future, Lex seems determined to prove that he makes his own destiny and won't be confined by misfortune or superstition. This belief in his control over his fate leads Lex to question the lway that he was saved from certain death by Clark. While to Clark's face Lex is almost taunting, treating Clark like a good-luck charm, it's clear that Lex is disturbed, and increasingly obsessed, by Clark's ability to intervene in his fate. Lex seems especially riled when Cassandra suggests that Lex's father has his life already planned out for him, and it's the ever-difficult relationship between Lionel and Lex that probably lies behind Lex's insecurities. There's a tension in Lex in these scenes, between his belief in his ability to shape his own destiny, and his fear that his power and influence might not grant him any freedom at all.

Could it be not fate that Lex fears, but genetics? That whatever he may try to do, he will end up being his father?

Lex's long black jacket is particularly stylish, and his shoes are apparently expensive, although, as it's the blind Cassandra who mentions this, they must *sound* or *smell* pricey for her to know.

> **Lex's Future:** Cassandra's vision of Lex's future kills her stone dead, so she never gets to fill Lex in on his destiny. But the audience gets to see it, and it's a mouthwatering, terrifying vision.
>
> Lex is in the Oval Office, standing behind the presidential desk. He is dressed in a glowing, unreal white suit, and wearing a black glove on one hand. He walks to the window and looks out. Cut to Lex, still dressed in white, standing in a vast field of sunflowers. He sniffs one, then touches it with his black-gloved hand. Where he touches decay sets in, a decay which spreads through the entire field until Lex is left alone in a never-ending landscape of bones, under a storm-strewn sky. He smiles. The sky turns red, and Lex looks up as blood begins to rain down, staining his pure white suit.

The Girl Next Door: When Harry disappears, Lana is aghast, unable to believe that she could lose a whole person. Lana sees the 'Wall of Weird' for the first time and is offended that the *Time* magazine cover of her as a little girl is among the odder results of the meteor shower 'in between the three-headed calf and the monster from Crater Lake'. Like Clark and Lex, Lana also fears being trapped, frozen in time as the little girl in the fairy princess costume who lost her parents in the meteor shower.

Just the Funny Guy: Pete would rather be the lifeguard for the girls' swimming class than work at the old people's home. Fair enough.

Torch Bearer: Chloe comes up with another of her increasingly deranged (and eventually accurate) ideas about what is going on. When Harry first disappears, Chloe suggests that one of the koi carp may have turned into a piranha and eaten him. When the first murder occurs, Chloe is first to believe that Harry has somehow started killing again, even before they discover his rejuvenation. As the curator of the 'Wall of Weird', it's perhaps unsurprising that Chloe correctly guesses the role of the ever-present meteors in that rejuvenation.

Strange Visitors: The murderous Harry Volk, who finds himself young again after falling into a meteorite-strewn pond. There's also Cassandra Carver (appropriately named – Cassandra being a mythical seer), who lost her sight but gained the power to see the future on the day of the meteor shower.

Down at the Farm: After being told that someone close to him is going to die, Clark becomes paranoid about his parents' safety, unplugging the buzzsaw they're using and asking them to leave jobs like that to him. Jonathan reminds Clark that it's a farm, and jobs like sawing go with the territory.

Jonathan and Martha are constantly suspicious of Cassandra and nervous about the possibility of the truth about Clark getting out. When Clark tells his parents about the vision he and Cassandra shared, Jonathan tells him that Cassandra doesn't have all the answers, and that Clark controls his own destiny. This is reaffirmed by Martha at the end of the episode, after Clark rescues her from the grain silo – as far as the Kents are concerned, people make their own destiny. This is one of the few matters on which Lex Luthor and Jonathan Kent agree.

Love's Young Dream: Much to Pete's disgust, Clark takes on community service at the retirement home just because Lana works there. There's a weirdly intimate moment between Clark and Lana as they discuss the loss of her parents, in the softly lit office of the *Torch*. When Lana tells Clark he's the only person who doesn't define her by the tragedy that befell her parents, it feels like an important breakthrough for them, even though, for his own reasons, Clark is one of the people *most* conscious of her loss.

Teenage Kicks: The young Harry flirts slightly with Lana early on, and charms Zoe the waitress.

Mild-mannered Reporters: We see Lana visiting the *Torch*'s office for the first time. Chloe and Pete dig up information on Harry's past, with the *Torch* appearing to have a remarkable level of access to local newspaper records.

Secret Identities: George Murdock (the older Harry) is one of the many *X-Files* alumni to appear in *Smallville*, having played 'Second Elder' (a recurring villain) on that show in several 'conspiracy' episodes. Murdock also appeared as God in *Star Trek V: The Final Frontier*, as well as appearing in other *Trek* guest roles. Eric Christian Olsen, who plays the younger Harry, had a role in the Jerry Bruckheimer epic *Pearl Harbor*. The two actors in the same role are remarkably convincing, although the *huge* age gap between the two Harrys allows them a lot of leeway.

Jackie Burroughs, whose waspish performance saves Cassandra from being the twee old lady she might easily have been, has had a long and varied career, including playing Mona Ramsey in *Tales of the City*, as well as voice parts in TV series *Ewoks* and *Angela Anaconda*. Director Chris Long has worked on a number of fantasy shows, including *Hercules: The Legendary Journeys*, *Roswell* and previous Superman show *Lois & Clark: The New Adventures of Superman*. Writer and co-producer Doris Egan has written for *Dark Angel* and *Profiler* and wrote the Clive Barker-inspired TV movie *Saint Sinner*.

Music: Another track from Gorillaz' eponymous album is used here – '5/4' plays over the café scene introducing Zoe. The young Harry plays Chopin on the piano (Piano Sonata No. 3 in B Minor, Op. 59 and Piano Sonata No. 1): the performance is actually by Idil Beret rather than actor Eric Christian Olsen. 'Time Served' by Dispatch and 'Crush' by Kevin Clay are also heard.

From the Pages of: Cassandra's vision of Lex has him in the Oval Office – Luthor had been President of the USA in the 'Superman' comics for about a year when the episode was broadcast. Lex's gloved hand in the vision ties into another comics' story, in which Luthor wore a glove to disguise the cancerous effects of the radioactive kryptonite ring he wore to ward off Superman.

Trivia: In a story which has already become *Smallville* folklore, one of the production team had a friend on the staff of *The West Wing*, allowing them to borrow that show's Oval Office set for the vision of Lex's future.

Loose Ends: What happens to Harry? Surely Clark didn't let him die under the grain, so what happened to him after his attempt to kill Martha? Could the police prove his involvement in the murder of Jim Gage? How could the Kents convince anyone that an old, disabled man could try and murder Martha? One can only presume that Harry, after going missing twice, was moved to a different retirement centre, away from the rejuvenating meteors, and was therefore rendered harmless.

More importantly, how literal or metaphorical are Cassandra's visions of Clark and Lex's futures? Will Lex really possess a Touch of Death, or is that just symbolic?

The Last Word: 'I've got so many questions in my life, I just want some answers.' Such potentially heavy themes as mortality, destiny, free will, youth and old age all blend together seamlessly in this clever, thrilling episode, by far the best of the series so far. Although the dual paranormal aspects of Cassandra's visions and Harry's rejuvenations are already a break from the 'meteor mutant of the week' formula that dominates the early episodes, there's also growing hints of more long-term storytelling going on, as Lex's obsession with the mysteries surrounding Clark deepens. Great character moments abound – Clark's concern for his parents, Jonathan and Martha wanting to protect Clark's secret, Lana and the magazine cover, Lex staggering away from the dead Cassandra ... all great moments, albeit overshadowed by the episode's abiding image – who could forget that vision of Lex standing under a reddened sky, blood raining down on his brilliant white suit? A benchmark moment in the development of *Smallville*, 'Hourglass' is both an entertaining, thought-provoking hour of TV in its own right, and an early indication of the ambition of the show's producers.

7
Craving

Production #227607
1st US Transmission Date: 27 November 2001
1st UK Transmission Date: 30 January 2002

Writer: Michael Green
Director: Philip Sgriccia
Guest Starring: Amy Adams (Jodi), Sarah-Jane Redmond (Aunt Nell),
Malcolm Stewart (Jodi's Dad), Joe Morton (Dr Hamilton)
Co-starring: Alex Rae, Damonde Tschritter, Jeff Seymour (Lex's Doctor)

Synopsis: Jodi, an overweight girl, is trying to lose weight by drinking vegetable shakes. The vegetables were grown in meteor-strewn soil in her family's greenhouse and cause her to lose weight at an incredible speed. However, this gift comes with a downside: an insatiable hunger. When Jodi hits a deer with her car, she gorges herself on the animal, draining its body fat. She similarly drains the body fat of an obnoxious jock at school, Dustin, leaving him in a coma.

Lana's birthday is approaching, but her party clashes with a tryout Whitney has with Kansas State, so he can't attend. Clark volunteers to be chaperone, and Lana doesn't want him to let her down. Jodi has a date with Pete for Lana's birthday party, but doesn't want to hurt him. He refuses to back off and has to be rescued from Jodi by Clark, who deserts Lana once more to save a friend. Clark and Jodi fight in her greenhouse, with Clark weakened by the meteor rocks around him. Jodi is knocked out and wounded when the greenhouse explodes owing to a gas leak. Clark returns to Lana's birthday too late, but wins back his position with her by arranging a special gift (see **Girl Next Door**).

Lex discovers that he has an unusually high number of white blood cells, which may be related to the meteor shower. His investigation into the meteors leads him to Dr Steven Hamilton, a disgraced scientist obsessed with the meteor rocks and their effects.

Speech Bubbles: Hamilton: 'Mineralogists don't have fans.'
 Clark: 'Gotta fly.'

Small Town Boy: Clark manages to arrange to be Lana's escort for her birthday party in Whitney's absence and has to insist to everyone that they're going just as friends. He frets over her birthday present but eventually strikes gold by re-creating the last good birthday Lana can remember (see **Girl Next Door**), which makes up for him having stood her up to rescue a friend from an evil date *again*.

Clark tells Lex that he can't remember where he was the day of the meteor shower, as it was before the Kents adopted him. He gets another reason to feel guilty about the meteor shower when Lex tells him that it was then that he lost his hair. When Chloe isn't looking he opens a locked door by poking out the lock with his finger, and later on he twists a pipe in the boiler room.

Girl Next Door: Lana's birthday approaches, and Nell has organised a party at the Luthor mansion. Lana feels alienated from Nell's party plans; she would prefer pizza and music with her friends. Lana is nervous about accepting Clark's offer to escort her to the party – obviously aware of the subtext – but then seems more worried that he'll stand her up again. When he fails to show at the party, Lana is left tearful and alone.

Lana's happiest birthday memory is her parents taking her to a drive-in movie, an event which she cites as the last time she felt completely safe. She's delighted with Clark's present – a re-creation of that moment on an ad hoc screen hung from the Kent's barn.

Not an Evil Genius: Lex had asthma as a child (seen in **1**, 'Pilot'), but hasn't had it since the day of the meteor shower. He doesn't get ill, have any allergies or require any medications. His doctor tells him he has a higher than normal white cell count in his blood, apparently a quite common condition in Smallville. Lex passes his medical exam easily and considers it a waste of time. However, the phenomena of the white cell count in Smallville does lead him to take an interest in the strange events in town, and Chloe's theory tracing them back to the meteor shower.

Lex is sufficiently impressed by Chloe's theory to offer to arrange her a summer job on the *Inquisitor*. His conversation with Chloe and Clark leads him to find disgraced scientist Hamilton, who sells meteor rocks to tourists to fund his work. Lex offers to fund Hamilton's research.

Lex tells Clark about being in Smallville on the day of the meteor shower; characteristically for the Luthors, Lionel was supposed to be spending quality time with his son but ended up dragging him along to a business meeting. (When asked by Hamilton why he's so interested in the meteors, Lex refuses to answer, saying he saves that story for the people he trusts.) Lex sees his baldness as a gift, something that defines him and sets him apart. Another example of his isolated childhood is that he spent all the Luthor Christmas parties hiding in the cloakroom (or so he claims to Lana).

Lex continues to lobby Lana in Clark's favour, telling her that he prefers her escort for the party, Clark, to Whitney. There's a hint that Lex might have arranged for Whitney to get through to the football scholarship tryouts for Kansas State so that he wouldn't be at the party.

Just the Funny Guy: After Clark's failed attempts to get together with Lana, and Chloe's impromptu dip in the pool with the iceman, it's about time Pete had a date ruined by a mutant. Pete, endearingly, is attracted to Jodi when she's still slightly overweight, so he isn't as shallow as this story could have made him.

Torch Bearer: Chloe's father, Gabe Sullivan, is Lex's Plant Manager, and she instinctively calls Lex Mr Luthor. She's flattered by Lex believing her meteor theory. But Chloe's usually amazing journalistic skills fail her – she discusses with Clark why anyone would drain body fat, but then doesn't put two and two together while sitting with the ravenous, mysteriously weight-losing Jodi.

The Quarterback: Whitney's early birthday gift to Lana is a first edition of *A Confederacy of Dunces* by John Kennedy Toole, which was published in 1980 and won the Pulitzer prize. Lana tells Clark that it's an indication of how Whitney can, just when she thinks he isn't there for her, suddenly surprise her. Whitney has a tryout for Kansas State which clashes with Lana's birthday party, which he only goes to once Lana has said she doesn't mind.

Down at the Farm: The Kents are a very cosmopolitan farming family: Jonathan offers Lana a latte. Martha tells Clark that she doesn't want to see him get hurt over Lana and advises him to get her a gift that comes 'from the heart' – advice Martha's mother gave to her.

Mad Scientist: Introducing Dr Hamilton, the obnoxious, meteor-obsessed recluse who was kicked out of his academic career for dubious involvement with a student. He works from a barn converted into a lab, and supports his researches by selling meteor rocks to tourists. By the end of the episode Hamilton is on Lex's payroll, an addition to the growing cadre of semi-regular characters with whom Lex can show his darker side.

Love's Young Dream: Contrary to the opinion of most viewers, closer examination reveals that, from Lana's perspective, Whitney is by far the better bet of her two suitors. Whereas Whitney gives her a thoughtful gift then asks for permission to go to the audition of his life, Clark fails to turn up to her birthday party, standing her up for the second time in a matter of weeks. Clark regains ground with his heartfelt present, but that only really brings him back to where he started, and he's not much closer to winning her over.

Strange Visitors: Jodi is an overweight girl who drinks gloopy vegetable shakes to try and lose weight. Unfortunately the ingredients were grown in meteor-rich soil, her house being near to a major meteor site, and Jodi develops a condition where she gets thinner and thinner, but needs to feed constantly. Normal food isn't enough, and she ends up snacking on an injured deer in the road, draining it of body fat. She then does the same to Dustin the obnoxious jock, and would have – reluctantly – done the same to Pete if Clark hadn't arrived in time. Jodi isn't evil as such, just confused and driven by a hunger she can't control. Like so many characters in *Smallville*, she lost a parent, being raised by her father.

Secret Identities: Joe Morton, making his first appearance here as Dr Steven Hamilton, is best known for his role as Dyson in *Terminator 2: Judgment Day*. His other roles include the Kevin Costner movie *Dragonfly*, and providing voices for the documentary series *Jazz*. Amy Adams starred in the pilot for the *Cruel Intentions* spin-off show *Manchester Prep* as Kathryn Merteuil. Her other roles include the part of Tara's cousin Beth in the *Buffy the Vampire Slayer* episode 'Family', as well as appearances in *Zoe, Duncan, Jack and Jane* (which co-starred Michael Rosenbaum), *Charmed*, *Providence* and *That '70s Show* as well as the movie *Drop Dead Gorgeous*. Malcolm Stewart was in the movies *Best In Show* and *Jumanji* as well as numerous TV roles, including appearances in *The X-Files*, *Millennium* and a recurring role as a director in *Dark Angel*.

Music: 'Slide' from Dido's huge-selling album *No Angel* plays while Jodi is weighing herself. Fuel and Third Eye Blind, two bands heard in **3**, 'Hothead', reappear here with the tracks 'Innocent' and 'Invisible' respectively. Also on the soundtrack are 'The Fool' by Call and Response and Enrique Iglesias' massive hit 'Hero'.

Loose Ends: Jodi gets taken to Metropolis General, where she's going to meet her father. There's no explanation as to how her condition will be treated, or whether the fat-drained Dustin will ever fully recover. Yet again Chloe tenaciously investigates a case, then loses interest the moment she's handed it over to Clark to resolve.

From the Pages of: There's a Professor Hamilton in the Superman comics, but he's a good guy rather than the shady character played by Joe Morton. Lex's assertion that the loss of his hair was a gift that set him apart from others is a direct inversion of the old *Superboy* comics, where Lex lost his hair as a boy when one of Superboy's experiments went wrong, causing Luthor to despise the Man of Steel for the rest of their lives.

The Last Word: 'Funny how one day can change your whole life.' Like his script for **5**, 'Cool', this is another solid but unspectacular episode from writer Michael Green, leaning heavily on the show's formula but at least playing each metaphor for all it's worth. Green's dialogue doesn't exactly set the world on fire, but he has a solid grip on the regular characters. Interestingly, apart from the unfortunate deer, this is an episode with no fatalities, although Dustin doesn't end too well. Notch up another efficient steal from a big-budget movie – Jodi's extending jaw is taken straight from *The Mummy* (see also Greg's extending mouth in **2**, 'Metamorphosis') and works just as well as its blockbuster counterpart.

Yet again, high production values, a good cast and a healthy development of the regular characters enliven potentially mediocre material. Lex in particular gets to reiterate his back story, while developing a new obsession with the meteor rocks. Joe Morton gets a good introduction as new Luthor foil Hamilton, a shady and dubious figure to whom Lex can demonstrate his darker inclinations. The Clark and Lana plotline is a (deliberate) partial replay of the ruined date in **5**, 'Cool', with Clark almost burying his chances with Lana before coming through with the perfect birthday gift. It's well-observed character arcs like this that make 'Craving' more than the pedestrian affair it occasionally threatens to become.

8
Jitters

Production #227602
1st US Transmission Date: 11 December 2001
1st UK Transmission Date: 6 February 2002

Writers: Cherie Bennett and Jeff Gottesfeld
Director: Michael Watkins
Special Guest Star: John Glover (Lionel Luthor)
Guest Starring: Robert Wisden (Gabe Sullivan), Tony Todd (Earl)
Co-starring: Michael Eklund, Andrew Johnston, Michelle Goh,
Mitchell Kosterman (Deputy Ethan Talbot), Terry O'Sullivan,
Yvonne Myers, Jessica Amlee, Ken Kirby, Mark Gibbon,
Marke Driesschen, Claudine Grant, Lucia Walters, Kendall Cross

Synopsis: Earl Jenkins, a former janitor for LuthorCorp, has a serious problem with the jitters, suffering from violent shaking so severe it can kill anyone near him. Earl's problem has alienated him from his family and lost him his job. When he accidentally kills another LuthorCorp janitor, Earl goes to Smallville. Before working for Luthor-Corp, Earl had been a farm hand for the Kents, and he hopes they will help him find the truth of what happened. Earl is sure that his problems stem from tests that took place in Level 3 of the LuthorCorp plant in Smallville, but there are no signs of that level on the plans of the factory.

On the same day that Clark's High School class is being given a tour of the plant, Earl breaks in with the intention of getting answers. Earl holds the kids hostage, but Lex goes in and swaps himself for the students, though Clark secretly goes looking for the hidden level. Lex thinks there is no Level 3 – his father has sworn it doesn't exist – but Clark's X-ray vision locates it. Clark leads Earl and Lex down a secret elevator to Level 3, where all evidence of the experiments has been stripped out. When a gantry collapses, Clark barely manages to rescue Earl and Lex from falling to their deaths. Earl is taken away, but Lex promises that LuthorCorp will take responsibility for getting Earl the best medical treatment possible.

During the course of the episode, Jonathan and Martha celebrate their wedding anniversary in Metropolis, leaving Clark to look after himself. To their great displeasure, he has a wild party in their absence!

Speech Bubbles: Clark: 'I heard there was a third level to the plant, is that true?' Gabe Sullivan: 'Yeah, that's where we do the alien autopsies.'

Lex (on Lionel): 'He doesn't care about anyone in this room. Because if we all die, his PR firm will spin it, his insurance firm will pay out and you, Earl, will go down as the bad guy.'

Small Town Boy: Clark's parents are away, and he takes the opportunity to have a small gathering at his house, which rapidly turns into a sprawling, crockery-breaking teen party. Clark uses superspeed to run around the house to find a suitable item for a drunk boy to vomit into. Earl worked on the Kent farm for six seasons, where he tried to teach Clark how to play guitar. Clark had to give up because he kept breaking the guitar strings.

Earl's jitters affect Clark in the same way the meteors affect him. This leads to him avoiding Earl, including refusing to help Whitney disarm him. However, when Earl and Lex are about to fall to their deaths on Level 3, Clark manages to fight his way through the pain to save them. It's an interesting situation, Earl's condition making him a genuine challenge and threat to Clark and requiring him to demonstrate real heroism and strength of purpose.

Girl Next Door: When she turns up at Clark's house without Whitney, Lana insists that she's capable of having fun on her own. She tells Whitney that when they got back together she needed to have breathing room, hence her going places on her own. She suspects that Whitney doesn't trust her with Clark – and who can blame him? Lana looks at Clark with slight disappointment when he refuses to confront Earl during the hostage crisis, while Whitney bravely steps forward to take Earl on.

Not an Evil Genius: Lex provides the firework display for Clark's party, as well as making sure the police don't interrupt, showing a talent for manipulating law enforcement that is expanded upon in later episodes (see **14**, 'Zero' and **22**, 'Vortex' for two examples).

The situation at the Luthor plant demonstrates the tension between the two Luthors, as Lionel doesn't tell Lex about the existence of Level 3, then allows Lex to be locked in with Earl as the plant fills with gas. When Lionel puts his hand on Lex's arm, trying to stop him from going into the hostage situation, Lex tells him never to touch him again, and when they hug for the cameras Lex looks enviously at the Kents and their genuine affection.

By walking into a hostage situation and offering to take the deeply unstable, gun-wielding Earl to a location he thinks doesn't exist, Lex demonstrates a fearlessness which comes either from bravery or recklessness; there's evidence for either interpretation, but wisely the programme-makers don't lean too far either way.

Torch Bearer: Chloe thinks that Earl is a drug addict and that his jitters are withdrawal symptoms. Her father embarrasses her – there's a fantastic irony that Chloe, who paints herself as the sophisticate from the big city, is the daughter of a man who runs a factory that turns dung into fertiliser. Gabe making bad jokes on the plant tour doesn't help Chloe's embarrassment. However, Chloe is genuinely terrified when Earl takes her father hostage.

The Quarterback: Whitney sustains another beating for his recklessness, trying to disarm Earl and getting injured in the process. According to Lana, Whitney is becoming distant.

Love's Young Dream: Lana turns up to the party without Whitney. They're going through a period of distrust. However, Whitney's attempt to disarm Earl leads to Lana nursing him, while in comparison Clark looks timid for not getting involved.

Down at the Farm: Jonathan and Martha spend their wedding anniversary in Metropolis. When Jonathan asks his wife if she misses the city, she replies that sometimes she does, but that she didn't move to Smallville for action and adventure. Jonathan won't let Clark accompany him to talk to Earl, afraid that Clark collapsing in a hospital will lead to some awkward questions. Jonathan has met Lionel before, but it's uncertain whether Martha has too.

Strange Visitors: Earl, the former farm hand who took a job with LuthorCorp, only to wind up with the severe jitters after being caught in an explosion in Lionel Luthor's secret research project on Level 3. Earl is the meteor mutant closest to the Kents; Clark describes him as having almost been one of the family. Earl, quite brilliantly played by ubiquitous but underrated character actor Tony Todd, has lost everything due to Lionel Luthor's betrayal, left unable even to hold his baby son safely owing to the jitters. Thus, even though his actions endanger all of Clark's friends, Earl is one of the most sympathetic and tragic protagonists in the series.

Man or Superman?: The difference in parental approaches on the part of the Kents and Lionel Luthor couldn't be more pronounced. While the Kents are concerned for the safety of Clark and the other students, Lionel is more concerned with protecting his own secrets. Lionel doesn't give Lex the information he needs to resolve the crisis, and then allows Lex to be sealed in the building as the gas levels rise. He later tells his son that it was Lex's fault for putting himself in danger – another harsh lesson from the Luthor school of fatherhood.

Teenage Kicks: The whole party sequence, obviously, and the wreckage the day after.

Secret Identities: Tony Todd, seen here as the unfortunate Earl, is a legend in the world of fantasy, science fiction and horror. Best known as the eponymous monster in the *Candyman* series of horror films, he's also been in such genre series as *Hercules: The Legendary Journeys*, *Xena: Warrior Princess*, *Angel*, *The X-Files*, *Star Trek*'s *Deep Space Nine* and *The Next Generation*, a *Babylon 5* TV movie and, most recently, *Andromeda*. His film roles also include *Platoon*, *The Rock* and *Final Destination* (as well as its sequel).

This episode sees the debut of Robert Wisden as Chloe's father, Gabe Sullivan. Wisden memorably appeared as the manipulative Robert Modell in *The X-Files*' episodes 'Pusher' and 'Kitsunegari'. His film roles include *Final Destination*, *Look Who's Talking Now* and *Legends of the Fall*, while a vast list of TV credits includes *Millennium*, *Stargate SG-1* and *Highlander*.

Writers Cherie Bennett and Jeff Gottesfeld are known chiefly for their work on books for young adults, which led to them co-writing *Smallville* novels for that readership.

Music: The music at Clark's party is 'Tie Me Up' by Handsome Devil and 'Bad Idea' by Bad Ronald. Other tracks heard are 'Pacific Coast Party' by Smash Mouth, 'The People That We Love' by expatriate British rock group Bush and 'My Bridges Burn' by The Cult.

Trivia: This episode went into production earlier in the season but took a long time to complete. In an interview with Judy Sloane in the *Starburst TV Special*, Annette

O'Toole says: 'That episode was the third one that we shot and it had some problems, so we kept coming back to it. We didn't finish it until a week before it aired.'

Loose Ends: When did Jonathan and Lionel first meet, and under what circumstances? What was the nature of the experiments on Level 3? What criminal charge does Earl face, and can even the best medical care Lex can buy cure him and return him to his family?

The Last Word: 'Just because you spend a lot of time with someone, it doesn't mean you know their darkest secrets.' An all-out, tension-fuelled thriller, 'Jitters' is harder, darker and more aggressive than most episodes. Much of the story's paranoid and cynical feel must be credited to Tony Todd's Earl, a tragic, unbalanced man driven over the edge after losing everything in an incident no one admits ever happened. The fact that when we reach Level 3, the entire place is empty – Lionel Luthor having destroyed all evidence of his experiments – echoes the downbeat endings of many conspiracy thrillers. The senior Luthor is fantastically malevolent here, covering up his experiments from everyone, including Lex, then allowing his own son to be sealed in the plant with a gun-toting madman. Whatever past encounter Lionel had with Jonathan Kent, it can't be good.

Aside from the spectacular gantry sequence on Level 3, one of the most tense, well-executed action scenes to appear in the series so far, there are a couple of stand-out character moments. There's something wonderful about Clark rebelling by having a party, then spending the whole time conscientiously cleaning up after people. Then there's the final scene, which beautifully underscores the difference between Clark's upbringing and Lex's.

9
Rogue

Production #227608
1st US Transmission Date: 15 January 2002
1st UK Transmission Date: 13 February 2002

Writer: Mark Verheiden
Director: David Carson
Guest Starring: Kelly Brook (Victoria Hardwicke),
Cameron Dye (Sam Phelan), Hiro Kanagawa (Principal Kwan)
Co-starring: Mitchell Kosterman (Deputy Ethan Talbot), Danny Wattley,
Costa Spanos, JB Bivens

Synopsis: Clark attends an exhibition in the Luthor Hall of the Metropolis Museum. One of the prize exhibits is a bejewelled breastplate that once belonged to Alexander the Great. When Clark goes out to get some air, he sees an out-of-control bus about to hit a homeless man. Clark runs and stops the bus, not realising that corrupt police detective Sam Phelan has been watching from the bushes.

Phelan, who used to be Lionel Luthor's fixer within the Metropolis PD, proceeds to blackmail Clark into doing his work for him, threatening to expose him to the world. Separately both Clark and Jonathan refuse, but Phelan threatens Clark that he'll hurt his family. Clark travels to Metropolis with Phelan and goes into the home of the Deputy Chief of Internal Affairs to steal his files on Phelan. Clark cheats Phelan, dropping the Deputy Chief's safe on to Phelan's car and leaving him to deal with the mess. Phelan strikes back by dumping a corpse in the Kents' barn and incriminating Jonathan in the killing. Phelan offers to make the murder charge disappear in exchange for Clark helping Phelan steal Lex's breastplate. Lex follows them to the museum and alerts security. Clark escapes, while Phelan is shot dead. Later, the charges against Jonathan are dropped.

While Clark tries to do the right thing with Phelan, Lana tries to help Chloe by taking over the editorship of the *Torch* after Chloe is sacked. Lana just wants to help Chloe keep control over the paper, but Chloe sees this as Lana moving in on her territory. When Lana runs a story about Principal Kwan crushing freedom of speech by sacking Chloe, Lana is sacked and Chloe is reinstated.

Lex strikes up a relationship with an old flame, Victoria Hardwicke.

Speech Bubbles: Clark (on the breastplate): 'I can't exactly see myself going into battle with that on my chest.' Lex: 'Darker times called for darker methods.'

Lex (to Clark): 'Your first visit to Metropolis and you're involved in a police investigation? That has to be some kind of record.'

Phelan (to Clark): 'You might be strong, but you're not bulletproof.'

Small Town Boy: The inevitable happens as one of Clark's superheroic acts is witnessed by someone other than a mutant – in this case the corrupt police detective Sam Phelan, who proceeds to blackmail Clark into doing his dirty work, threatening to expose him. Clark is torn between his desire to do what's right and his need to protect his family from the consequences of his secret being revealed, and he even begins to wonder if the Kents might not be better off without him and his gifts. His attempt to get rid of Phelan is ingenious and indicative of Clark's teenage desire to shock, as he drops a safe on Phelan's car, but can't match the stitch-up Phelan has for them.

When Jonathan is arrested on suspicion of murder Clark flies into a rage, punching through one of the support struts in his kitchen and slamming Phelan against a wall. Phelan goads Clark about wanting to kill him, and it looks like Clark might just be capable. After Phelan has left, Clark gently touches the broken beam, restraining himself after having seen just how far his anger gets him. He tells his father that he was scared by how much he wanted to kill Phelan.

Clark tells Lex that he doesn't consider Whitney his enemy, continuing to reject Lex's strategic approach to romance. He is disgusted that Lex has had dealings with Phelan.

Girl Next Door: Lana's attempts to lobby Principal Kwan on Chloe's behalf after the closure of the *Torch* leads to Lana being appointed the editor. Although Lana does this purely to help, Chloe accuses Lana of trying to notch up CV points for her college applications. Later Lana regrets her actions in trying to help Chloe, feeling that she's just made things worse, but in the end her gamble pays off and Kwan reinstates Chloe. Lana tells Chloe that she has no interest in getting between her and Clark, repeating the oft-heard mantra about them being just friends (a phrase that Chloe echoes about herself and Clark).

Lana instantly presumes Jonathan is innocent when he's arrested. When she was ten she tried to run away to Metropolis but was found at the bus stop by Nell. While Nell drove her home Lana asked her if she regretted adopting her, and Nell replied it was the best thing she ever did.

Not an Evil Genius: Lex isn't a big scholar of history, but he's interested in Alexander the Great because he ruled the world before he was thirty. (He and Lionel have almost constantly referred to Alexander before, and will do so again: see **16**, 'Stray'.) The battle on Lex's mind this week is that between Clark and Whitney over Lana's heart. He doesn't tell Clark that Lana will be at the opening, and then disappears to let them talk in private. He tells Clark to engage with the enemy – Whitney – and stop retreating, paraphrasing the old adage of keeping your friends close and your enemies closer.

This episode introduces Victoria Hardwicke, an old friend (and old flame) of Lex and daughter of Lionel's business rival, Sir Harry Hardwicke. By the end of the episode their affair has been renewed, and they're both trying to seduce each other into betraying their parents.

Another old acquaintance of Lex is corrupt cop Sam Phelan, who was on Lionel Luthor's payroll and pulled Lex out of a few misadventures when he was younger (the most serious of these incidents is seen in flashback in **14**, 'Zero'). Lex visibly despises Phelan, who he sees as both an unpleasant reminder of his past and a tool of his father. When Phelan is looking for Clark, Lex is uncooperative and, after Jonathan is arrested, he offers to help Clark. Lex follows Phelan's car to the museum, and is so confident that the 'bomb' Phelan planted to distract the museum guards is a decoy that he opens it himself.

To add to his obsession with how Clark rescued him from the car crash, and his growing interest in the meteors,

Lex now has his footage of a superspeed blur running through the museum to pore over. The dying Phelan refuses to tell Lex what hold he had over Clark, but Lex guesses that Clark was at the museum. Bit by bit Lex seems to be gathering evidence which can only point in one direction . . .

Torch Bearer: Chloe is relieved of the editorship of the *Torch*, an unbelievable blow considering how much it's a focus of her life. When Lana is made the new editor Chloe freaks out completely, storming out of the office in tears. However, when Lana's anti-Kwan editorial leads to Chloe's reinstatement, she has to admit that Lana may be a love rival, but she's also a decent person. She also has to reassess her journalistic abilities when Kwan insists that she should only print stories she can prove – previous episodes have suggested that Chloe's editorials are well-written tirades, but here she takes a step towards a more professional approach. She tells Lana that one of the reasons the school paper is important to her is that it's one of the few things she and Clark do together.

Down at the Farm: Jonathan and Martha's fears that Clark's heroic behaviour might expose him to unwanted danger come true when Sam Phelan enters their lives. Jonathan does as much as he can to protect Clark, including assaulting Phelan in public, but ends up paying a heavy price when Phelan frames him for murder. He goes quietly, insisting that Clark shouldn't do anything with his powers in front of the police. Jonathan is more scared by Clark losing his temper and nearly killing Phelan than by anything else. Even though they're sure there are more Phelans out there ready to exploit Clark's abilities, Jonathan and Martha insist that he has to go on helping people – it's his gift.

The Quarterback: Although he does appear in this episode in the first museum scene, Whitney gets no dialogue.

Mild-mannered Reporters: The *Torch* gets closed down due to Chloe's scaremongering headline SMALLVILLE: MUTANT CAPITAL OF THE WORLD. Although Chloe considers the article to be a necessary account of the truth about the town, Kwan has had concerned parents calling him since the headline, and has been giving them the official line – that the meteor rocks are harmless. It's hard to argue with Kwan's argument that a school newspaper is for reporting school events, not as a soapbox for its editor!

Lana shows a brief burst of journalistic activity by being appointed editor, although she does so only to try and get Chloe reinstated. Lana finds herself lost as editor, but her inflammatory editorial about Chloe's sacking does the trick, and Chloe is reinstated – but not without a lecture from Kwan on journalistic ethics.

Strange Visitors: No mutants outside of Chloe's editorial this week, with the main villain being Sam Phelan, a bent Metropolis cop manipulating Clark into using his powers to serve his selfish ends. Cameron Dye's performance is not exactly subtle, his eye-rolling menace and fits of rage reminiscent of Gary Oldman's similar detective character in *Leon*, but at least he makes Phelan a suitably obnoxious and evil threat. It's remarkably convenient for everyone else that Phelan gets killed in the shoot-out at the end of the episode, but then with knowledge like that in his possession it's dramatically necessary for him to bow out . . .

Secret Identities: Cameron Dye, who plays corrupt cop Sam Phelan, is the husband of actress Laura San Giacomo. His films include 80s cheese masterpieces like *Body Rock* and *The Last Starfighter*, but on TV he's taken in such well-respected shows as *Frasier*, *Brooklyn South* and *M*A*S*H*. Kelly Brook is an English actress best known in the UK for her modelling work and a disastrous stint as a co-presenter of *The Big Breakfast*.

David Carson was a prominent director on *Star Trek: The Next Generation* and *Star Trek: Deep Space Nine*, which led to him directing the feature film *Star Trek: Generations*. Since then he's directed episodes of *Witchblade*, *Odyssey 5* and the mini-series *The 10th Kingdom*.

Music: Two early 90s British dance acts appear on the soundtrack to this one – Stereo MCs with their unforgettable 'Step It Up' and Massive Attack with 'Angel'. Other tracks are 'Breathing' by Lifehouse (whose 'Everything' was so memorably used at the end of the pilot), 'I Have Seen' by Zero 7, 'She Lives By The Water' by Club 8, 'Not Looking Back' by Driver, 'Numb' by Grant Park and 'Take Your Time' by Radford.

The Last Word: 'I guess that's what you get when you try and be a hero.' The series' first straight crime episode is not just a welcome respite from meteor mutants, but a study in the risks involved in helping others, and the moral boundaries you risk cutting across. The villain of the week, Phelan, can get whatever he wants because he has no moral restraints. Clark has to work within the limits of what is right, while also trying to preserve his own secrets and interests. The presence of Phelan gives some more hints about Lex's past, while his present gets more interesting with the arrival of Victoria. Both characters allow more of Lex's darker side to become visible, while Kelly Brook defies cynical expectations of her acting abilities by effectively bringing Victoria to life.

Best scene of the episode has to go to the moment when Lana and Chloe reassure each other that neither of them is romantically interested in Clark. Kristen Kreuk and Allison Mack invest the scene with a vulnerability and slight edge of desperation that leaves you in no doubt that, whatever those two characters may be saying, they're not even kidding themselves.

10
Shimmer

Production #227609
1st US Transmission Date: 29 January 2002
1st UK Transmission Date: 20 February 2002

Writers: Michael Green and Mark Verheiden
Directors: DJ Caruso
Special Guest Star: John Glover (Lionel Luthor)
Guest Starring: Kelly Brook (Victoria Hardwicke),
Jesse Hutch (Todd Turner), Kett Turton (Jeff Palmer),

Sarah-Jane Redmond (Aunt Nell), Glynis Davies (Mrs Palmer),
Azura Skye (Amy)
Co-starring: Brenda M Crichlow

Synopsis: A completely invisible attacker assaults a jock who mocked young Amy Palmer for her crush on Lex Luthor. Amy's parents work for the Luthors, and the whole family, including Amy's brother Jeff, live in the grounds of Lex's mansion. The invisible attacker strikes again at the Luthor house, vandalising Victoria's room and attacking her in the bath. When Clark finds out that Amy has been stealing from Lex and has a shrine to her parents' employer in her room, Lex and Clark think the case is closed. However, after Amy and her parents leave, Lex is attacked – the invisible attacker isn't Amy, it's Jeff, who's covered himself in meteor-tainted flower sap in order to disappear. Clark fights Jeff, dousing him in paint in order to find and defeat him.

Clark helps Lana with a blood drive, and they become closer. Lana tells Clark that Whitney is being distant. Clark finds out that Whitney's father is suffering from a serious illness and tells Lana to talk to him.

Victoria goes through Lex's computer and finds files on Cadmus Labs. Clark sees Victoria do this and tells Lex. Lionel is also worried about Victoria; he tells Lex he's making a fool of himself.

Speech Bubbles: Lex: 'Relationships aren't always about love, Clark. Sometimes they're about mutual goals.'

Chloe (on Lana): 'Just remember, Clark, once you cross that line you can't hide behind the cloak of friendship any more. Proceed with caution.'

Jeff: 'You're not interested in love.' Lex: 'That kind of love could get me arrested.'

Small Town Boy: With Whitney neglecting Lana, Clark sees a chance to win her over – as he tells his parents, if Whitney doesn't appreciate Lana then he doesn't deserve her. This involves dropping the 'just friends' pretence and taking an aggressive stance. When Chloe describes Clark's meeting with Lana to discuss the blood drive as romantic, he doesn't say anything but avoids her gaze, a definite change from his usual denials. After their near kiss on Nell's porch, Clark seizes the moment with Lana to ask her over to his barn the following night, a definite overture that Lana accepts. Clark tells Pete that his stomach was in knots as he asked Lana over to see the sunset. However, when Clark finds out about Whitney's father's illness, he can't stop himself from advising Whitney to tell Lana even though it'll repair their relationship and squeeze Clark out of the picture. Clark tells Lex he almost wishes he didn't know about Whitney, as now he feels that taking a shot at Lana would be wrong. When Lana comes to visit him as arranged, Clark stumbles over his words, telling Lana that he would never hurt her, and to tell her what he wanted to say would do just that. Lana replies that he should try – she's strong, she can take it. Clark replies that Whitney needs to know that too – he needs her. Clark tells her he's glad that they're friends, and he doesn't want to lose that.

Clark doesn't think Victoria is Lex's type, and is shocked by the anti-romantic nature of their relationship. (However, in fighting for Lana, Clark is, of course, following the advice Lex has been constantly giving him – to be more ruthless in love.) Clark is wonderfully sheepish about telling Lex that he caught Victoria going through his computer files. Ultimately, Clark can't understand an intimate relationship where the partners are constantly plotting to betray each other.

It's uncertain whether this qualifies as a superpower, but Clark demonstrates an incredible memory for detail when recalling where and when Amy gave blood. One of his main challenges in this episode is avoiding the blood drive so that no signs of his alien nature will be revealed. Clark is, of course, worried that telling Lana he's afraid of needles will make him look weak or unhelpful, but she doesn't mind and is grateful for his help with the blood drive anyway.

Girl Next Door: Lana is still trying to find her place in the world, her latest venture being the organisation of a blood drive. She feels let down by Whitney pushing her away, and the fact that Clark is always there for her when she needs him makes her feel closer to him. Although their kiss on the porch is interrupted by Nell, Lana instantly accepts Clark's offer to come over to his barn the following night. When he meets her there, Lana asks him what he was about to say the previous night, encouraging him to reveal his feelings. Clark backs away, telling her he doesn't want to hurt her and encouraging her to talk to Whitney. She's reluctant to take his advice. Lana is clearly very keen on Clark by this stage, but she now feels obligated to stay with Whitney because of his father's illness.

Not an Evil Genius: Lex's watch was given to him by his mother when she knew she was dying. It's made from a Napoleon franc from 1806, in reference to Jacques Louis David's painting *The Coronation of Napoleon I*, an event which Napoleon's mother was unable to attend, but in which she is shown in the painting due to Napoleon's instruction. Lex's mother always hated Lionel's war room with its collection of antique weapons, believing that as war was in their nature they didn't need to display it. The condition that Lex's mother had when she was dying must have been related to her heart as Lex says that she was using the drug Amlodipine Besylate (see **The Quarterback**).

Lionel tells Lex that he's being a fool in having any dealings with Victoria, while Lex claims he knows what he's doing. Lex is still piqued by his exile, telling Lionel that the future of the massive LuthorCorp isn't Lex's concern. Lionel tells Lex that if he betrays his family, he really will be alone.

Contrary to his previous advice, Lex tells Clark that he likes the fact that while he (Lex) would take advantage of Whitney's situation to win Lana, Clark wouldn't. He admires Clark's standards and says that he shouldn't lose them. Lex tells Clark that his relationship with Victoria isn't about love, it's a game they're playing, and their relationship is built on mutual goals. There's an obvious connection in Lex's life between the death of his mother and this later cynicism about love. Lex may fear, or simply be incapable of, engaging with others emotionally. With Lionel as a father, he seems to have learned a lot about relationships being seeded with mistrust.

Lex is quite generous with Amy, treating her infatuation as a crush of no consequence, but remaining kind to her nonetheless. He refuses to get rid of her when Victoria asks him to, and tells Amy that Victoria isn't as bad as she thinks. Even when they find out the truth about Amy's stealing, and later Jeff's invisible activities, Lex doesn't punish the Palmers but offers them support – he either rewards loyalty, or is paying to avoid a public scandal.

Torch Bearer: After their conversation about the bloodied piece of glass found at the scene of the attack on Victoria, Chloe watches Clark walk away with a smile and a brief expression of distracted longing. Later, when Clark runs out of his barn to confront Jeff, Chloe is left to slump on the sofa, alone. Chloe has a wonderful phrase to describe the traditional concept of ghosts, referring to it as 'the Casper paradigm' (in reference to the 'Friendly Ghost' seen in numerous comics, cartoons and a couple of live-action movies).

Just the Funny Guy: When Clark tells him about Lana coming over to see the sunset, Pete suggests he should start scripting what he's going to say now, and goes as far as offering to give Clark some notes. Good to see Pete still thinks of himself as the ladies' man.

The Quarterback: Whitney doesn't have time to help Lana with the blood drive, and has been evasive with her for a week. He insists that he just needs some space and that nothing is wrong. This leads to Lana drifting away from Whitney and towards Clark. However, Whitney has reason for his defensive behaviour – his father has developed a serious illness, and is taking Amlodipine Besylate, a medication used for people with serious heart problems. Whitney's desperately macho solution to this family crisis is to push people away: he rejects the offer of help from a teacher; he's downright aggressive with Clark; and he pushes Lana away from him, telling Clark that he doesn't want to add more loss to her life. It's good to see Eric Johnson getting more to do, as Whitney becomes less shallow and more sympathetic as the season goes on.

Love's Young Dream: Whitney's neglect of Lana while she's working on the blood drive gives Clark an opportunity to

strike, and they do indeed get closer. But Whitney's family
problems and Clark's sense of honour cause Clark to bring
Lana and Whitney back together. This is a pivotal
development in the romance, setting a new course for this
plotline: Lana and Clark's mutual attraction is now
acknowledged, but their sensitivity over Whitney's predicament stops them from acting on these impulses. In the
meantime Chloe is there on the sidelines, visibly aching for
Clark in some scenes. How long before he notices?

Down at the Farm: Jonathan has an unusual lesson for
Clark – as opposed to his usual earthy honesty, he counsels
Clark that he can't always be entirely honest with people,
and needs to keep secrets to protect himself. Martha teases
Clark about his worries concerning the blood drive,
knowing that the only thing he's really worried about is
losing face in front of Lana.

Clark and Lana's conversation confirms that Jonathan
and Nell used to date, that it ended badly and that Nell
doesn't like talking about it now.

Mild-mannered Reporters: Chloe can get blood analysed.
Clark does some investigating of his own when he sees the
pill bottle in Whitney's bag, researching the drug in
question.

Strange Visitors: Jeff Palmer, son of the servants at the
Luthor mansion. Not only does Jeff resent being considered
invisible by the Luthors and their peers due to his low social
status, he also detests Lex for rejecting the affections of Jeff's
sister, Amy. The fact that Lex is always perfectly charming
to Amy, and that she's too young for him (underage, in fact),
doesn't deter Jeff from his hatred. Jeff gets his opportunity
for payback when he discovers a meteor-infected rose, the oil
from which allows him to become invisible. Judging by the
strength with which he attacks people and throws things
around, rubbing the oil into his skin has also given him the
usual meteor-enhanced strength. Like so many meteor
mutants, Jeff's power is strongly related to his personality,
his natural meekness making him nearly invisible already.

Loose Ends: Why do Lana and Clark work on the blood
drive schedule out on the porch when it's visibly freezing

out there? What happens to Jeff? Is he really going to keep the secret of invisibility to himself? Isn't Chloe going to do anything with the sample of invisibility oil she has?

Music: Two tracks by Vigilantes of Love – 'S.O.S.' and 'Galaxy' – are heard in this episode, along with 'When I'm With You' by Simple Plan, 'Evolution Revolution Love' by Bristol-based trip-hop artist Tricky, 'If I Go' by Thrift Store Halo, 'Blend' by Something Else, 'Poor Misguided Fool' by Starsailor and 'Caught in the Sun' by Course of Nature.

Secret Identities: Azura Skye, who plays Lex's stalker Amy, was Jane, sister to Michael Rosenbaum's character Jack, in *Zoe, Duncan, Jack and Jane*. On the big screen she was Cheri in *Bandits* and Spider in *Town & Country*. She plays Karen in the new TV drama *John Doe* and appeared in the *Buffy the Vampire Slayer* episode 'Help'. Kett Turton, who plays Amy's brother Jeff, has done the usual rounds of *The X-Files*, *Millennium*, *Dark Angel* and *First Wave*, as well as the movies *Gypsy 83* and *The Water Game*. Glynis Davies (Amy's mother) played Buffy's Mom in *Scary Movie*, as well as three different roles in *The X-Files* and an appearance in the short-lived *Wolf Lake*. She has also filmed *Bang, Bang, You're Dead* with Eric Johnson. Jesse Hutch played a 'Gill Boy' in *Dark Angel*.

From the Pages of: Pete tells Clark that he's not the flying type. Cadmus Labs, the company Lex is supposedly researching in this episode, has been a regular fixture in the comic books for many years, being involved in such dubious scientific projects as trying to clone Superman during his period of being dead (if you don't know, don't ask). This project resulted in them having a 'Superboy' of their own, although this was a Kryptonian clone rather than a young Clark Kent.

Clark's blue jersey is Superman-esque, the kind of thing George Reeves would wear in the role (it *was* the 1950s).

The Last Word: 'That's the thing about Clark Kent: he's not always there when you want him, but he's always there when you need him.' An episode about people left out in the cold, 'Shimmer' sees Clark getting closer to Lana than

ever then forcing her away from him, while elsewhere the
child of a servant takes his revenge for being made to feel
unnoticed. There's an obvious parallel between Clark,
Lana's reliable friend, and the Palmers, the loyal servants
of the Luthors – both have been overlooked in favour of
more obviously glamorous and ruthless individuals. However, these perceptions prove to be false because Lex treats
the Palmers very well and has sound reasons not to get
involved with the infatuated Amy. In the other plotline,
while Whitney may initially seem to be treating Lana
badly, he is, in fact, trying to protect her.

Both Lex and Whitney, morally ambiguous characters at
the best of times, come out of this episode with a common
nobility and vulnerability. Lex becomes rather a tragic
figure, scarred by the death of his mother and engaged in
an emotionally cold relationship with Victoria. If anything,
Lex seems more romantic when vicariously encouraging
Clark's attachment to Lana; he admires Clark's chivalry
and optimism, qualities he knows are lost to him. To Lex,
Clark seems to represent a kind of innocence and roman-
ticism completely lost to the Luthors.

This, then, is a downbeat episode, full of lovers frozen
out (Clark, Chloe, Amy), family tragedies and unfulfilled
passions. The 'invisible attacker' scenes are well executed
and suitably creepy, with a neat double-bluff concerning the
identity of the assailant. More significantly, the development in the Clark–Lana–Whitney story sets things up nicely
for the second half of the season and demonstrates that the
show is willing to move its long-term plots forward.

11
Hug

Production #227610
1st US Transmission Date: 5 February 2002
1st UK Transmission Date: 27 February 2002

Writer: Doris Egan
Director: Chris Long

Guest Starring: Kelly Brook (Victoria Hardwicke),
Rick Peters (Bob Rickman), Gregory Sporleder (Kyle Tippett)
Co-starring: Ben Cotton, rnelsonbrown, Mark Lukyn, Leanne Adachi

Synopsis: Tycoon Bob Rickman is a very persuasive man. With one handshake, he prompts a representative of the Centre for Environmental Protection to kill himself rather than accuse Rickman of pollution. When Rickman Industries set their sights on Smallville as the site of a new plant, the Kent farm is in Rickman's way. To everyone's surprise, after a handshake from Rickman, Jonathan signs away the farm to him. The victims of Rickman's handshake have no memory of what they did.

Kyle Tippett has the same gift as Rickman (see **Strange Visitors**), but instead of using his power for gain he has become a recluse in the woods near Smallville. After Lana falls off her horse and Kyle is seen nearby, Whitney and a dazed Lana suspect Kyle of having tried to attack her. Rickman, determined to eliminate the only person who shares his ability, uses his handshake to get Whitney to attack Kyle. Clark saves Kyle, but Whitney is left convinced that Kyle attacked him, causing a chasm to open up between Clark and his friends.

Rickman's attacks escalate, and he uses his handshake to send Lex after Kyle and Clark with a machine gun. Clark knocks out Lex, while Kyle and Rickman face off with a handshake and a handgun between them. Kyle wins the battle of wills, with Rickman shooting himself. Lex's lawyers break the contract Jonathan signed, and the farm is free from Rickman Industries.

Speech Bubbles: Lana: 'What do you want to do?' Clark: 'I'm not sure . . . as long as it doesn't involve putting on a suit and doing a lot of flying.'

Kyle: 'Haven't you heard of Crazy Kyle, who lives in the woods by himself? He's somewhere between Bigfoot and the Blair Witch.'

Lex (under Rickman's influence): 'Friendship's a fairytale, Clark. Respect and fear are the best you can hope for.'

Small Town Boy: Clark sees Kyle's isolation as a possible future for himself, and Kyle discloses that some people just aren't meant to have a normal life. Clark reveals that he understands what it's like to be hidden from the world, and persuades Kyle that he can't hide his gift, that he has a responsibility to stop Rickman misusing his. Clark potentially turns the antisocial Kyle into a hero – perhaps the character might even return.

Kyle and Rickman are, of course, a mirror to Clark and Lex, although both lead characters dismiss the parallels in the episode's bitterly ironic final scene. Clark's desire to believe in Lex's better side causes him to dismiss some fairly glaring evidence – the hypnotised Lex says a lot of truths he wouldn't usually reveal, expressing his suspicions about Clark and his lack of faith in friendship.

Clark can't imagine being a farmer, although he doesn't know what career he does want. It's good to see that Clark is willing to alienate Lana for what he believes in, standing up for Kyle in the face of Whitney and Lana's accusations. In his feud with Lana, Clark can doubtless see the seeds of isolation that might lead him to become a recluse.

Clark finally takes a bullet in this episode, when Lex unleashes a hail of gunfire in his direction. Although they don't break the skin, each bullet does leave a nasty bruise. Needless to say, Rickman's ability has no effect on Clark.

Girl Next Door: After the restatement of Clark and Lana's 'just friends' status at the end of the previous episode, it looks as though Clark might lose even that when he refuses to corroborate Whitney's side of the story after his fight with Kyle. Lana can't remember what happened in her first encounter with Kyle in the woods, but after Whitney and Kyle's fight she can't believe that Whitney would attack Kyle, saying that he isn't capable of harming anyone. She thinks Clark is looking for an excuse to attack Whitney out of bitterness over the 'scarecrowing' incident so, after their confrontation in the barn, Lana tells Clark she wanted to clear the air and maintain their friendship, but now she doesn't know why she bothered. However, in the end it is Lana who repairs their friendship – even though she never gets any explanation as to Clark's stance, she decides their friendship is too important to throw away.

Not an Evil Genius: Lex is less than impressed with Bob
Rickman, with whom he has had previous dealings. That
Rickman knows Lionel Luthor doesn't help. Lex is –
rightly – suspicious of the way that Rickman seems capable
of getting whatever he wants. When Lex falls under
Rickman's spell, after spending most of the episode
refusing to shake hands or in any way let himself be
touched by the man, he unleashes a number of his
resentments about the way the Kents, and the people of
Smallville in general, look at him with contempt. It's a rare
thing to see Lex cutting loose without his usual poker face,
and Michael Rosenbaum takes the opportunity to play this
uninhibited, murderous Lex to the max. After seeing Clark
use his powers, the hypnotised Luthor tells Clark that he
knew he had secrets, but that he didn't know they were
that good. When Clark approaches Lex, and tells him he's
his friend, Lex replies that friendship is an illusion.

Lex compares Clark to Atticus Finch, the hero of
Harper Lee's *To Kill A Mockingbird*, who takes a stand
against the rest of his small town to do the right thing.
When Clark asks how the book ends, Lex tells him it's not
about the ending – it's about the journey. (One of the
characters dies at the hands of another in the book's
ending, in spite of Atticus's best efforts.) Lex sees leader-
ship as being about not only knowing you're right, but
being able to convince others of it.

After Kyle is injured, Lex calls on the services of Toby,
a shady doctor-for-hire who patches up rich people. Toby
refers to getting blood all over his Mustang after an
incident at Club Zero (see **14**, 'Zero').

Torch Bearer: Chloe is not a good horse rider. She finally
gets to kiss Clark this week, but as she's under the power
of Kyle at the time she doesn't even get to remember it
afterwards, and can't believe what has happened. In
another case of Chloe exaggerating her own sophistication,
she tells Kyle that she's used to 'living dangerously'.

Chloe tells Clark about dozens of incidents in the last
decade of people wandering out of the woods with no
memory of how they got out. While Chloe knows about

recent lurid incidents, it's Clark who puts it into historical context – those stories go back to the Civil War. Yet again, Chloe knows a lot of weird, sensationalist stuff but doesn't get her facts *quite* right.

The Quarterback: According to Lana, Whitney is working extra shifts at the family store while his dad is ill, though Whitney doesn't want to inherit the store when he leaves college. From the start, Whitney thinks Kyle is a psycho and takes a gung-ho approach, and it only takes one magic handshake from Rickman and Whitney is trying to kill Kyle, though Whitney says Kyle is a maniac who attacked Lana, then him.

Down at the Farm: Jonathan tells Rickman that if he was interested in money, he wouldn't be a farmer. Martha describes the Kent farm as being their legacy, which is Jonathan's word for it. This makes Jonathan's sale of the farm to Rickman even more baffling. When Clark describes Lex as his best friend, Jonathan and Martha exchange glances. When Clark tells them that Lex can help get them out of the contract Jonathan signed, Jonathan says he doesn't want to owe Lex Luthor any favours, but Martha replies that he doesn't have many options.

According to Lex, the contract Jonathan signs is quite generous, paying three times the market value of the farm. The bad news is that the contract is sound, and would take a dozen lawyers to break. Luckily, Lex has that many lawyers.

Strange Visitors: Bob Rickman and Kyle Tippett were salesmen of farm equipment in the mid-80s. They were trapped in a car in Smallville during the meteor shower and in 1989 and the two subsequent years they were salesmen of the year. Thanks to their encounter with the meteors, Rickman and Kyle have the ability to convince people to do anything with one handshake. When the task is complete the victim reverts to normal, with no memory of what they've done. If they can't fulfil their task the victims will keep trying unless they're forcibly snapped out of the trance.

After two years of successful sales, Kyle retreated into the woods and Rickman set up business on his own. Kyle has been hiding because he was afraid he couldn't control the power, staying in the woods and making sculptures which he sells in town. He says he doesn't believe in friends – they always betray you in the end.

Rickman, on the other hand, used his abilities in business. According to Lex, Rickman's gift for persuasion has allowed him to destroy communities and cause appalling pollution damage. Rickman finally returns to Smallville to build a plant, breaking the agreement with Kyle never to come there. Rickman says the rules of engagement between him and Kyle were made a long time ago, and things have changed.

In the end Clark manages to persuade Kyle that he needs to use his gifts and take responsibility for his former friend. In their final confrontation, Kyle's abilities prove greater than Rickman's, the latter shooting himself. Afterwards, Kyle tells Clark he saw him get shot, but that he won't reveal Clark's secret. Kyle also advises Clark not to hide in the woods all his life – he has a gift and should use it. Kyle goes out in the world to use his.

While Gregory Sporleder brings an abrasive weight to the part of Kyle, making him believable and sympathetic without losing his edge, Rick Peters is a little too broad in his portrayal of Rickman. Nevertheless, they make for a suitable contrast of characters.

Secret Identities: Rick Peters' film career includes *Leprechaun 4: In Space* and a number of TV movies including *Elvis Meets Nixon*. He has also appeared in *CSI: Crime Scene Investigation* and *Providence*. Gregory Sporleder played Galentine in *Black Hawk Down*, a drunk in *Being John Malkovich* and Frye in *The Rock*. His TV roles include an episode of *Friends* and David Lynch's extremely weird *On The Air*.

The Last Word: 'Trust me Clark, our friendship is going to be the stuff of legend.' Another excellent episode from the writer of **6**, 'Hourglass', 'Hug' is a bittersweet story about friendship and betrayal, given a tragic edge by the knowledge that, like Kyle and Rickman ten years before, Clark and Lex are going to end up enemies, one a hero and the other a manipulative villain. In Kyle, Clark also gets to see a possible future for himself as a recluse, afraid of his own power. By encouraging Kyle to go back into the world and use his gifts, Clark gets a little restatement of the import- ance of his friends and family. The producers get to play with the reset possibilities of the memory loss caused by the handshakers' gift. So we get to see Lex and Clark go head to head, and Chloe kissing Clark . . . neither with any long- term consequences.

Though Clark and Lana's falling out is only a blip, Lana's dutiful feelings towards Whitney seem set to keep her and Clark just friends for a while yet. Simultaneously, Clark's kiss with Chloe should surely leave him appreciat- ing the options open to him . . .

12
Leech

Production #227611
1st US Transmission Date: 12 February 2002
1st UK Transmission Date: 6 March 2002

Writer: Tim Schlattmann
Director: Greg Beeman
Guest Starring: Kelly Brook (Victoria Hardwicke),
Kevin McNulty (Eric's father), Sarah-Jane Redmond (Aunt Nell),
P Lynn Johnson (Eric's mother),
William Samples (Sir Harry Hardwicke), Tom O'Brien (Roger Nixon),
Shawn Ashmore (Eric)
Co-starring: Will Sanderson (Brent), Ashley Presidente,
Julian Christopher, Mitchell Kosterman (Deputy Ethan Talbot)

Synopsis: When nerdy teacher's son Eric Summers nearly falls off a dam, Clark is there to catch him. But Eric has a meteor rock in his bag and, when lightning strikes them both, it flows through the rock, causing Clark's powers to transfer to Eric.

Clark has to come to terms with being powerless. After initially being alarmed by his weaknesses, Clark sees the advantages: he can play sports without having to hold back for fear of hurting anyone, and he can approach Lana without her necklace making him sick.

Eric goes public with his powers as soon as the opportunity arises, using them to stop a thief who snatches Chloe's bag. Chloe writes a story on Eric, and he soon becomes a local hero. But when the full extent of Eric's powers become clear, and he uses them in rage, the crowds turn on him. Eric's parents want him to be studied by scientists, and are afraid of him. Clark realises that Eric can't be trusted with these powers and, even with his own vulnerability, it's Clark's responsibility to stop him. Clark borrows Lana's necklace and goes to confront Eric. They fight, and electricity flowing from a junction box, through both them and the necklace, restores Clark's powers.

Roger Nixon reports back to Lex about the car crash with a computer model showing how the car must have hit Clark straight on. Lex confronts Clark with this theory but, as he catches Clark while he's vulnerable, Lex is left with hard evidence that Clark is a normal kid. Lex tells Nixon there'll be trouble if any information on the Kents leaks out.

While he's pursuing the truth about Clark, Lex is also pursuing opportunities elsewhere. Victoria thinks she has persuaded Lex to join her in a coup against LuthorCorp. Having gained the information from Lex's computer (see **10**, 'Shimmer'), Victoria has advised her father, Sir Harry Hardwicke, to purchase Cadmus Labs, hoping to take LuthorCorp without needing Lex. After they invest they soon find out that Cadmus Labs is worthless – Lionel and Lex having scammed the Hardwickes – and now it's they who will be selling up. The Luthors have won, and will be taking over Sir Harry's company. Nixon has one more piece of information for Lex – Lionel has been sleeping with Victoria.

Lana finds that the deserted cinema attached to Nell's florist's shop, the Talon, is up for sale. Lana is distressed that Nell is selling up to move to a smaller store as the Talon was where Lana's parents first met.

Speech Bubbles: Chloe: 'You know what Clark, the second you start throwing people thirty feet I'll write nice things about you too.'

Lex (to Victoria): 'You call sleeping with me business? I hate to think what that makes you.' And then, one slap later, the classic . . . Victoria: 'We could have been great together.' Lex: 'I plan on being great all by myself.'

Small Town Boy: Clark goes through a cycle of feelings in relation to his loss of powers. First he's scared by his lack of strength, worried that he's vulnerable and not knowing what has happened to him. Then he becomes exhausted by his daily routine – chores that previously took him five minutes now take two hours. When Eric reveals his powers, and Clark realises the change may be permanent, he becomes depressed and bitter, especially with the attention Eric is getting for stopping Chloe's mugger. Clark wonders whether the years of hiding his abilities were worth it, considering Eric seems so popular going public.

Clark does begin to accept his loss of powers when he realises that the self-control he has needed to use all his life doesn't apply any more. Clark no longer feels responsible for everyone as he used to, and can get closer to Lana now her necklace doesn't poison him. However, he comes to see how Eric misuses his powers, at which point Clark realises that his powers are a part of him, as is the feeling that they need to be used responsibly. Clark gets in Eric's way and, subsequently, gets injured because, although he's lost his abilities, he still feels responsible for them.

Welling plays the scene where he talks to Lana about Eric's powers brilliantly, half-distracted and disturbed as he casually talks about something he's lost. At this point Clark knows there's a definite possibility he might die trying to take Eric down. However, his inherent heroism leads him to take that risk. After he gets his abilities back, Clark tells Jonathan that his powers complicate all their lives, but that Eric didn't get Clark's two greatest gifts – his parents.

Lex finally challenges Clark about his powers, trying to get to the bottom of how Clark saved him from his Porsche. This conveniently comes in an episode where Clark doesn't have those powers. Clark shows little patience for Lex's theories and tells him that he's just a guy who tried to do the right thing – isn't that enough? It's who he is, whether he has his powers or not. Clark asks if Lex wants to take him outside and hit him with a car, just to make sure he's telling the truth. However, Clark, being Clark, forgives Lex quickly after he apologises.

Clark doesn't think much of Chloe's 'Super Boy' name for Eric. Before losing his powers, Clark uses his X-ray vision to find rocks and his strength to punch them out of the ground – field trips made easy!

Not an Evil Genius: Nixon's investigation into the car crash reveals startling – and completely accurate – information. It says a lot about Lex that he doesn't actually want to use this information against Clark, and it says even more that he refuses Clark's invitation to hit him with a hammer. Lex tells Clark that he's the closest to a real friend Lex has ever had, and that Clark doesn't have to hide anything from him. When he sees Clark injured, Lex is convinced that he was wrong. He apologises for questioning Clark's honesty, and pleads insanity for his recent investigation. Lex warns Nixon that if any of these findings become public, there will be trouble.

In the other plot thread, another of Lex's enterprises comes to a head, with Victoria and her father using the information they stole from Lex to try to oust Lionel from LuthorCorp. Not a good move – the information they obtained from Lex's study was part of a set-up, and the business they invest in is worthless. Even though Lex doesn't like Lionel, he knows he can trust him more than Victoria. There's a nasty twist in it for Lex, though – his father turns out to have slept with Victoria too.

Girl Next Door: Lana's parents met in the Talon, the old cinema that Nell is about to sell. Her father was working at the cinema, and his mother went to see *Close Encounters of the Third Kind*, got bored, and spent the night talking to him in the lobby. Lana tells Clark she feels that with the cinema about to be sold, the evidence of her parents existence is being chipped away.

Lana tells the powerless Clark that he doesn't seem to be carrying the weight of the world on his shoulders as he usually does, but by the end of that episode she realises he's carrying that responsibility again. Lana admits to always wanting to be able to fly.

Love's Young Dream: Clark bids Lana an emotional farewell when he borrows her necklace to confront Eric. She's scared by the fact that he doesn't seem to know whether he'll be coming back, and Clark kisses Lana on the cheek. However, by the end of the episode it's still Whitney that Lana has to take her home.

Torch Bearer: Chloe is pivotal to this episode, being present when Eric performs his big act of heroism, and naming him 'Super Boy'. Getting her by-line in the *Ledger* is a big step towards her becoming a proper journalist. When Chloe is mugged, the bag stolen contains her laptop. She later admits to Eric that the computer is her life, which she acknowledges sounds pathetic. Chloe is clearly flattered by all the attention.

Yet again Chloe shows herself unsuited to the outdoor life, complaining that the geology field trip is pointless as she could just order the rocks over the Internet and have them delivered to her house.

The Quarterback: In between running the shop and looking after his sick father, Whitney is pretty busy. So busy, in fact, that he's barely in this episode.

Just the Funny Guy: Pete thinks Clark is jealous of Eric's new heroic status – and he's right.

Down at the Farm: Clark asks if his parents were ever scared of him. Jonathan replies that although young Clark had some temper tantrums and put the odd hole in the wall, he was generally good and no one to be afraid of. Clark asks his parents if they feel differently about him now he doesn't have powers, and they reassure him he's still their son. Jonathan admits to Martha at being slightly relieved when Clark loses his powers – Clark can now lead a normal life. Jonathan tells Clark that seeing how Eric reacted when given that power just made him realise how special Clark is.

Strange Visitors: Eric Summers is the classic comic-book wish-fulfilment character, the unloved, bespectacled nerd who gets picked on until fate gives him superpowers. Except that Eric isn't the hero of this story, he's the villain.

As Jonathan says at the end of the episode, Eric had problems before he got superpowers. His father, a teacher, is harsh on him, clearly considering him a disappointment. When Eric becomes a local hero, his father's response is to arrange medical examinations and an appointment with a scientist in Metropolis. Eric realises he's just a scientific curiosity for his father and, even worse, he later finds his father is scared of him, calling the police when he comes home. No wonder, then, that Eric redirects his abilities into rage, trying to beat up the jock who bullied him, throwing around police cars and using his powers to gain attention. For a child denied any form of power or respect, the chance to wield such abilities proves intoxicating.

Man or Superman?: The three male leads in this episode are deeply affected by their different fathers. Clark's father is warm and respectful of his son, teaching him to use his powers properly. Eric's father denies him love and any appreciation, causing Eric to go off the rails. And Lex's father repays his son's loyalty by sleeping with his girlfriend. Yuck.

Secret Identities: Shawn Ashmore, who plays Eric, was on the other side of the superheroic fence as Bobby 'Iceman' Drake in *X-Men*, a role he reprises in the sequel *X2*. Kevin McNulty played another dad in *The Neverending Story III*, and has appeared in the movies *Timecop* and *Bird on a Wire*, as well as playing the recurring role of Dr Arnett in *Millennium*. William Samples, who plays Victoria's ambiguously accented father, has appeared in the TV version of *Highlander* and *MacGyver*. Writer Tim Schlattmann started his career as a writer on *Roseanne*, and has since gone on to write for *Roughnecks* (the animated spin-off from *Starship Troopers*) and *Get Real*.

From the Pages of: Lex refers to Nixon's sources as a 'Rogues Gallery' – an expression used in comic-books to describe a superhero's cast of villainous opponents. The local paper refers to Eric as a 'Super Boy', Superboy being the old comic-book alias used by a young Clark Kent when he lived in Smallville.

The Last Word: 'Sometimes letting go is the only way to move forward.' Clark's powers being accidentally transferred to another person is the oldest Superman story in the book, but 'Leech' manages to breathe fresh life into this hackneyed material. It's the fact that Clark isn't yet a superhero that makes his predicament so interesting – it isn't entirely a loss, and there are some wonderful scenes as he adjusts to having a normal life. Being able to play basketball without fear of hurting anyone, being able to approach Lana without her necklace making him sick – all great fun as Clark finds himself free of his old responsibilities. It's hard to see any angles to the situation that the episode doesn't deal with, including Clark's inevitable decision to risk his – now far more vulnerable – life to stop Eric. Eric is confirmation that Clark is one of the few people qualified to wield the power he has, and Shawn Ashmore is wonderfully bitter, yet strangely sympathetic, in the role.

That this should be the moment that Lex decides to accuse Clark of being more than human is, of course, convenient, but there was a limit to how far Luthor's investigation could continue without him discovering the truth. The resolution is a bit too neat, but allows the characters to move forwards. Yet again, it's a Superman cliché get out, but one which works with this strength of writing and performances. 'Leech' is helped by some stunning set pieces and great sight gags: Eric throwing cars around; some clever direction used to make Clark seem almost smaller once he's lost his powers; the headline of the *Smallville Ledger*; the image of Eric and Clark consumed by lightning; and, best of all, the shot of a police car embedded in the roof of Eric's house. It's this flair of execution that lifts 'Leech' above its rather predictable premise, making it one of the best episodes of the season.

13
Kinetic

Production #227612
1st US Transmission Date: 26 February 2002
1st UK Transmission Date: 13 March 2002

Writer: Philip Levens
Director: Robert Singer
Guest Starring: David Lovgren (Scott), Kavan Smith, David Coles,
Sarah-Jane Redmond (Aunt Nell)
Co-starring: Kwesi Ameyaw

Synopsis: A gang of thieves who can walk through walls rob Lex Luthor's hidden safe. During the course of the theft, Chloe is thrown off a balcony and seriously injured. Clark is determined to catch the assailants, feeling guilty over Chloe's injury. Meanwhile Lex is more interested in getting back a computer disk the thieves took. The disk contains evidence of Lex's appropriation of his father's funds for his own researches, and the gang uses it to blackmail Lex.

The thieves are Wade, Scott and Derek, three former jocks who fell on bad times and resorted to crime. Their powers come through tattoos using meteor-rock-based green ink, but the effects are short-lived. The gang needs new blood, so they draw Whitney – since he lost his scholarship, he is now also a failed potential sports star – into their group. When he realises what he's involved in, Whitney turns to Lana for help, and she in turn talks to Clark. Clark and Lex manage to retrieve Lex's disk and save Whitney from the gang, though Lex has to rescue Clark when he is weakened by one of the gang's meteor tattoos. Scott and Derek are arrested, while a falling car crushes Wade when his powers fail him.

Lana finds that Lex is buying the Talon and tries to persuade him to keep it as a café-bar and venue rather than turning it into office space. Lex isn't persuaded by Lana's sentimental stories, but when she comes to him with a sound business case, he's convinced.

Speech Bubbles: Chloe: ' "Clark Kent, investigative reporter." It has a nice ring to it.'

Lex: 'Clark, you can't save the world. All you'll end up with is a messiah complex and a lot of enemies.' Clark: 'I saved you, didn't I? That turned out all right.'

Chloe: 'These so-called "healthcare professionals" just want me to stay in bed and eat Jell-O.' Clark: 'Those fascists!'

Small Town Boy: When Chloe gets injured while he is incapacitated by the gang's meteor-type effect on him, Clark berates himself for not getting to her in time. He can't shake this feeling of responsibility, even though his parents, Lex and Chloe herself tell him it isn't his fault.

Clark says that he sometimes wishes he could leave town and get away from the meteor rocks; like Whitney he has plans for himself beyond Smallville, although like Whitney he doesn't have a definite plan as yet. Clark is determined to help Whitney – partially because of Lana, but mainly as a form of atonement for his perceived failure to save Chloe.

While everyone else gets Chloe bouquets from Nell's shop, Clark brings her hand-picked wild flowers. Clark kisses Chloe on the forehead while she's in hospital. He clearly has very strong feelings for Chloe which come more to the surface due to her injury, but these feelings aren't quite moving in a romantic direction yet.

Clark relieves his tension at one point by angrily breaking up logs with his fists, but is stopped by Jonathan – they need firewood, not splinters! A degree of tension develops between Clark and Lex because of the dubious nature of the information the gang has obtained. However, Lex's rescue of Clark goes some way to proving that Lex puts his friends before his masterplans.

Not an Evil Genius: When Chloe is injured during the robbery of the Luthor mansion, Lex is determined to deal with it his way. Matters are complicated because a disk the gang stole from the vault reveals that Lex is tapping into his father's money to fund his own project. Lex claims it's a methane processing plant, but apparently it involves a particle accelerator. Because of this information, Lex can't tell the police anything has been stolen, leaving Clark dubious about Lex's intentions. Lex is extremely ruthless in dealing with his enemies. He tells Clark that the gang is going to learn the consequences of stealing from the Luthors – and Whitney is going to have to take his share. When the surviving gang members have been arrested, Lex tells them that if they keep his secret, he'll keep theirs, and makes it clear that if they don't, he's perfectly capable of getting to them in prison.

Lex is the first to realise that Clark's determination to help Whitney is motivated by Chloe's injury, and he tells Clark that he can't save everyone. Lex manages to convince Clark that he came to the gang's lair to help him, not to retrieve his disk. At all times, Lex reveals as little of his more dubious activities as possible to Clark.

Lex quotes Benjamin Franklin: 'Our critics are our friends – they show us our faults.' Lex seems to like Chloe's interview technique, describing it as 'verbal judo'.

Girl Next Door: Nell and Lana discuss how much the Talon means to Lana, but Lana accepts that a single-screen cinema can't compete with a multiplex. Nell wants to be able to afford to send Lana to any college she wants, and so she can't keep holding on to the Talon. When Lana finds out that Lex is the new owner, she concentrates her attempts to preserve the Talon on him. She initially appeals to him by telling him what a wonderful place it is, and what memories it has. When he rejects this approach, Lana approaches Lex for a second time with a better business plan for the Talon including a café, screenings of art-house movies and letting local bands play. As an historic building the Talon will have certain tax benefits, which is part of the plan she pitches to Lex.

The Quarterback: This is probably the strongest episode Whitney gets. Having lost his scholarship, Whitney doesn't think he'll ever get out of Smallville, and that he'll inherit the shop and spend the rest of his life there. His depression has led him to become distant from Lana, walking past her in the street without noticing and forgetting when they're supposed to meet.

Whitney doesn't have a plan of what he wants to do now his football career has collapsed, he just knows he wants to get away from the store. When he meets several former jocks who seem to have turned similar circumstances to their advantage, Whitney readily gets drawn into their circle, even letting them give him a tattoo. He finds his new powers – the ability to move through solid objects –

exhilarating, but when he gets drawn into the plot to blackmail Lex, Whitney has second thoughts and turns to Lana for help. To the character's credit, Whitney helps Clark retrieve Lex's disk at the end of the episode, risking his life in the process.

Lana tells Clark that she thinks there's more to Whitney than football, but that Whitney sees it as his only way out and she can't convince him otherwise. Whitney still lacks direction at the end of the episode – but at least he avoids death or jail.

Torch Bearer: Chloe's interviewing technique with Lex is hardcore – she demands to know if there are any more secret levels at the LuthorCorp plant (see **8**, 'Jitters'). Clark is put out by Chloe's aggressive interviewing style, but Lex isn't offended. Chloe flatters herself, wondering if Lex is pretending to take a phone call from Lionel just to avoid her. While Lex is out of the way she snoops around the mansion.

The main thing to happen to Chloe is her fall from a high window in the Luthor mansion. Immediately after the fall, Lex's doctors aren't sure of Chloe's condition; the fall was bad, and she broke her left arm and has concussion. The doctors want to check there's no brain swelling. Lex's huge bouquet of flowers makes her feel like she's won the Kentucky Derby. When Chloe finds out that Clark and Pete are investigating the gang, she insists that they let her be involved as she's bored having to rest in hospital. When she gets out, Chloe acts as though her stay was a few years in prison, and immediately starts investigating a possible conspiracy around the disappearance of the gang's ink.

Just the Funny Guy: Pete somehow manages to get Chloe's computer connected to the Internet from inside the hospital. Clark gives Pete a funny look – and he has the decency to look sheepish – when this unorthodox behaviour is exposed. Pete thinks that the explanation for how the gang moves through walls is insane.

Down at the Farm: Jonathan tells Clark that an important lesson when you become an adult is that you can't save everybody.

Strange Visitors: A gang of former local sporting heroes regain the adrenaline rush of their youth – and go out for the rewards they failed to get legitimately – using tattoos drawn with meteor-rock-based ink. Chloe theorises that the tattoos speed up their metabolisms, allowing their molecules to vibrate so that they can move through solid objects. She also believes that their bodies won't be able to handle the stress, leading eventually to death. They need new blood on board, someone they can trust, and recruit Whitney, another sports hero fallen on hard times.

The main gang are Wade (the leader), Scott (the muscle) and Derek (the clever one with one arm). As Lana tells Clark, in 1996 Wade and Scott *were* Whitney – successful school athletes – but after Wade had a knee injury and Scott was involved in drugs they lost it all. Like many of the villains in *Smallville*, the gang use their incredible powers for the mundane task of just taking what they want. If anything, though, this group are even sadder than the rest, artificially boosting their performance to constantly relive their glory days of booze and sports.

Love's Young Dream: When Clark and Lana discuss Whitney in the barn, the emotional connection between them is clear, something they both seem embarrassed by. Ironically they seem closer now that Whitney's family problems bind Lana to him.

Teenage Kicks: Whitney's booze and tattoos night of shame represents a high point for adolescent vice in the show.

Secret Identities: David Lovgren played Danny Solskjaer in *AntiTrust* and appeared in the comedy *Cool Runnings*, as well as *The X-Files* episode 'Memento Mori'. Kavan Smith plays Flynn in the pilot for the new version of *The Time Tunnel*, and has a role in *Mission to Mars*. David Coles has appeared in *Dark Angel*.

Director Robert Singer was an executive producer and director on *Lois & Clark: The New Adventures of Superman*, and has played similar dual roles on the TV series *Timecop*, *Turks* and *Falcone*. Writer Philip Levens worked on *Wolf Lake* and *Night Visions*.

Trivia: Lex's address is 2116 Beresford Lane.

From the Pages of: The gang's ability to vibrate through solid objects is a trick practised by DC Comics' superhero the Flash, 'The fastest man alive'. However, even though they're all ex-athletes, the gang don't gain any superspeed powers from their tattoos.

The Last Word: 'You take the ultimate rush, you pay the ultimate price.' A strong episode for Whitney, 'Kinetic' also strengthens the bond between Clark and Chloe. Most of the episode is a lesson in the exercise of power: Lex uses his power vengefully, Clark uses his to protect people, while the gang use their superpowers to take what they want and extend their youth. The gang members are one-dimensional, but good examples of the 'remember him' guys Whitney said he didn't want to become back in **1**, 'Pilot' (it's satisfying for those paying attention to have another detail from the very start of the series being paid off). If that isn't enough character development, Lana's deal with Lex shows how quickly the characters are growing up and taking on responsibilities.

The tattoos are a muddled metaphor – do they represent hormones, or drugs, or the adrenaline that groups of young males get when they feel they can do what they want? However, a muddled message is better than another treatise on the relationship between fathers and sons. Although 'Kinetic' isn't brilliant, it's a fair change of pace.

14
Zero

Production #227613
1st US Transmission Date: 12 March 2002
1st UK Transmission Date: 20 March 2002

Writer: Mark Verheiden
Story: Alfred Gough and Miles Millar
Director: Michael Katleman
Guest Starring: Corin Nemec (Jude Royce),
Cameron Dye (Sam Phelan), Eric Breker

Co-starring: Jud Tylor (Amanda), Michasha Armstrong, Darryl Quon, Mark Gibbon, Mitchell Kosterman (Deputy Ethan Talbot), Glenn Ennis

Synopsis: Three years ago: Lex gets into a fight with Jude Royce at the Zero Consequences nightclub in Metropolis, during which Jude is shot dead by a bouncer called Max.

Now: Lex hangs upside down, kidnapped and beaten. Lex's kidnapper reveals himself as the supposedly dead Jude.

One week ago: Jude applies for a job at the soon-to-reopen Talon, while Max comes to Lex claiming that he's seen Jude, which Lex knows is impossible. Lex is plagued by a series of threatening pranks, including Max's severed hand being sent to the Talon in a box. Lex can't locate Max, but gets his people to try and find Amanda, Jude's old girlfriend. Lex remembers how, three years ago, Phelan (the corrupt cop from 9, 'Rogue') helped cover up Lex's involvement in Jude's death, with Max being paid off for his trouble. Jude arriving and pulling a gun on him interrupts Lex's reminiscing. Jude finds it interesting that, with Lex's apparent involvement, Phelan is now also dead. Clark arrives, but Jude flees and Lex denies there was anyone there. Jude poisons the Kents cattle with Luthor-Corp chemicals, setting Lex up to take the fall.

Lex is then kidnapped, and hung upside down in the deserted Club Zero. 'Jude' is shot dead by Lex's real tormentor, Amanda's brother, who has been seeking vengeance because his sister killed herself shortly after Jude's death. The Jude lookalike was just a double he found.

Lex tells the brother that he took the blame for the shooting to protect Amanda, who really fired the shot. Clark rescues Lex and knocks out Amanda's brother, but Lex tells Clark he has no idea what has been going on.

Clark is plagued by questions from Chloe, who has been set the task of writing his biography as a school assignment. Chloe digs into irregularities concerning Clark's adoption, the only adoption ever to be handled by Metropolis United Charities, but is encouraged to drop it by Clark. However, Chloe keeps her files on his mysterious adoption.

In spite of the delivery of a severed hand and the abduction of its owner, the Talon reopens for business.

Speech Bubbles: Pete: 'In a world full of designer water, Clark came straight from the tap.'

Clark (to Chloe): 'I'm not some mystery for you to solve.'

Amanda's brother: 'You can't escape your past, Lex.'

Small Town Boy: Clark is understandably worried by Chloe snooping around in his past, and compares her to *60 Minutes'* presenter Mike Wallace. He keeps avoiding her attempts to get an interview out of him, and when she starts digging into the minutiae of his adoption he gets angry. Clark tells Chloe that his biological parents are either dead or didn't want him, and that he's not interested in finding them, but later admits to her that he wonders about them every day of his life. If Clark isn't too hot on Chloe's assignment, he's rather more excited by his own – the prospect of investigating Lana, although in practice this turns out to mean an (off-screen) interview. Clark is also helping Lana with the reopening of the Talon, but it's never clear exactly *how* because his involvement seems to be asking Lana about her feelings concerning the reopening.

Not an Evil Genius: This is Lex's story first and foremost, adding background to his relationship with Phelan as well as his misspent youth in Metropolis. Lex's taking Amanda to Club Zero, where he knows she'll find Jude cheating on her, can be read either as a desire to let her know the truth or a fairly low way to break the couple up – as Lex is a fairly conflicted character, probably a bit of both.

Although Lex turns out not to be a killer, he *is* an unashamed liar, covering up his involvement in Jude's death and spending the entire present-day section of the episode lying to Clark and Lana about his past.

Girl Next Door: Lana is now developing well beyond her cheerleader roots, taking responsibility for the reopening of the Talon. She feels like she's escaping from her past as the girl from the *Time* magazine cover. She seems far more willing to doubt Lex's sincerity than Clark is, especially when the results of his past threaten to taint the Talon's reputation.

Torch Bearer: Chloe jokes that she's going to apply her journalistic skills to her assignment writing Clark's biography – however, she goes too far in the process, falling out with Clark. The final shot of the episode is of Chloe uncertain whether or not to delete her file on Clark's adoption, torn between loyalty to her friend and loyalty to her journalistic instincts. Chloe knows Clark well enough to guess his assignment is Lana by the look on his face when she asks, and describes him as Lana's surrogate boyfriend. Chloe's interrogation of Jonathan and Martha goes into incredible detail about Clark's adoption, and she records her interviews on ordinary C90 audiotapes. Chloe has a brilliant extra question for Jonathan and Martha: 'I don't want you guys to take this the wrong way, but has your son always been this strange?'

She demonstrates an ability common to teenagers in this kind of TV show – a knack for hacking into government computers whenever plot information is needed in a hurry. Here she manages to hack the DMV (Department of Motor Vehicles) website to get information on Jude.

Just the Funny Guy: While Chloe gets to write about Clark, and Clark gets to write about Lana, Pete doesn't get to interview any of the eligible ladies in his class, instead being assigned to write about Stan Gibson, manager of the student store. Understandably, he suspects that the assignment process has been rigged. At last we get some more depth to Pete's character as his antipathy to Lex is revealed. The Luthors did something very bad to the Ross family (see **15**, 'Nicodemus'), and Pete still bears a grudge.

Down at the Farm: Clark's adoption is a subject Jonathan and Martha don't want to get into too deeply, as the process seems to have been rather unorthodox. Jonathan is devastated when his cows are poisoned with toxic waste, and when the finger points to LuthorCorp it only confirms his prejudices. The clean-up operation involves the CEP – presumably the Cumulative Exposure Project, a part of the Environmental Protection Agency that measures exposure to toxic contamination. Martha talks about growing up in Metropolis – she knows the Luthors and their world. Martha asks Clark to back away from his friendship with Lex rather than getting pulled into the Luthors' problems.

Love's Young Dream: Not a very romantic episode. Clark and Chloe are at loggerheads over her paper, Lana is involved in the reopening of the Talon, and even Clark is too preoccupied with Lex's problems to chase after Miss Lang. The viewer doesn't even get to see Clark interview Lana for his school assignment, although there are some decent scenes with the two of them discussing the Talon. Whitney is sidelined even more; he appears in one scene, and doesn't even have any dialogue. Not exactly a key episode for followers of the love triangle.

Secret Identities: Corin Nemec is in the regular cast of *Stargate SG-1* and has also appeared in the mini-series of Stephen King's novel *The Stand* and the film *Operation Dumbo Drop*. Jud Tylor was in the first episode of Kristin Kreuk's other TV series, *Edgemont*, as well as guesting in the Kevin Sorbo vehicle *Andromeda*. Director Michael Katleman directed the pilot for *Lost In Oz*, as well as episodes of *Dark Angel*, *The X-Files* and *ER*. He worked in lesser capacities on films such as *Jumping Jack Flash*, *Predator* and *La Bamba*.

From the Pages of: Amanda's brother lived in Central City, home of the original incarnation of the DC Comics' hero the Flash. In the current *Justice League* cartoon, the Flash is voiced by Michael Rosenbaum. Amanda's brother met his convenient Royce double in a café in Bludhaven, another city from the DC Comics' universe. Bludhaven is home to former Robin, Dick Grayson, who in current comics continuity works there as a policeman while serving double duty as the superhero Nightwing.

The Last Word: 'No more games, Lex. It's time for the truth.' A story about dark secrets and loyalty, 'Zero' constantly plays with what we know, never quite giving up its own secrets. By the end we're left with uncertainty: uncertainty over Lex's intentions, over what Chloe will do next, and over what on *Earth* Jonathan and Martha did to secure Clark's adoption. All the flashbacks and ambiguities lead to confusion in places – the Royce double seems to appear from nowhere to assault Lex in the gym – and the idea of the identical double is hokey, and looks like a rather desperate plot fudge. But in thematic and character terms this is a very strong episode, adding layers to Lex's character while building up a strong set of mysteries and tensions between the other characters. With the early part of the season mostly concerned with one-off, meteor-powered villains of the week, this seems to be the point where the serious ongoing storylines kick in.

15
Nicodemus

Production #227614
1st US Transmission Date: 19 March 2002
1st UK Transmission Date: 27 March 2002

Teleplay: Michael Green
Story: Greg Walker
Director: James Marshall
Guest Starring: Hiro Kanagawa (Principal Kwan),
Joe Morton (Dr Hamilton)
Co-starring: Bill Mondy (James Beales), Julian Christopher, Nicki Clyne

Synopsis: James Beales, a LuthorCorp employee, is driving like a maniac when he is involved in a car crash with Jonathan Kent. Beales is in possession of a Nicodemus flower, stolen from the lab of Dr Hamilton. The Nicodemus sprays its pollen on Jonathan, causing his behaviour to become more and more irrational as time goes on. Lex finds out from Hamilton that the Nicodemus is an extinct flower that caused an outbreak of irrational behaviour and death many years before. Hamilton has revived the flower using the meteor rocks.

When the bank rejects his latest loan application, Jonathan heads over there with a shotgun. Clark stops him and Jonathan passes out, sinking into a coma. While investigating the crash site, Lana is also sprayed by the

Nicodemus. Lana becomes uninhibited, making sexual advances towards Whitney, Clark and then Lex. Lana steals Lex's car and tries to climb a windmill she's always wanted to get to the top of. Lana passes out halfway up the ladder, but Clark is there to catch her. The Nicodemus infection has killed Beales, and it looks like Jonathan and Lana don't have long to go. Pete is infected while searching Hamilton's lab. Hamilton manages to find a cure in an old book, but as Lex is about to send it to his team in Metropolis, Pete bursts in with a gun. Lex manages to help Hamilton escape with the book, but Pete is unleashing his buried resentment towards Lex, and it takes Clark to stop Pete from killing Lex. Lex convinces Clark that Pete's rambling about Hamilton being involved with Lex was a hallucination.

Thanks to Lex's work in finding and implementing a cure, all the infected people recover. Lex banishes Hamilton to Cadmus Labs to continue his work in controlled conditions.

Speech Bubbles: Jonathan (to Lex): 'If all of you Luthors were to dry up and die I wouldn't shed a tear.'

Chloe (to Clark): 'The choice is yours. You can either sit in your loft and play with your telescope, or move on.'

Lana: 'For once I'm not scared of life and no one can handle it because you all prefer the insecure little girl. Well I'm sick of her and all her talk about her dead parents.'

Small Town Boy: Initially, Clark is worried that the pressures of the farm are causing Jonathan to have a nervous breakdown. Clark tells Chloe that in spite of the 'no-fly zone' over Lana since Whitney's father became ill, he can't stop his feelings for her.

When Lana seductively tells Clark to trust her, he stammers as he replies that he does. Where he tells Lana what they're doing is crazy, Tom Welling delivers the line in a very strange and over-the-top way. Clark is torn between his suspicion that Lana isn't herself and his desire to go along with her delirium. Being Clark, he of course tries to act honourably, although his father's illness leaves him vulnerable. Although he does kiss Lana by the pool, he refuses to go any further, getting dunked for his trouble. Later, Clark tells Lana it's good to have her back to normal, but admits that he liked what she was wearing. He has the decency to spare her feelings when she asked if she did anything embarrassing with him.

Clark becomes distressed as his father and friends become ill, and finds it hard to accept Lex's lies, going as far as to grab Lex's arm and shout at him. In the end, when a delirious Pete tells Clark that Lex is in league with Hamilton, Clark believes Lex, although he does throw him against a wall to knock him out. Clark clearly has great control over his strength – he knocks Pete unconscious with a finger-flick to the forehead.

Girl Next Door: When asked for her deepest desire as part of Chloe's poll, Lana says hers is to climb the windmill in Chandler's Field. You can, allegedly, see the Metropolis skyline from there, but Lana has never had the nerve to see for herself. When Chloe and Clark seem doubtful about this, she offers to make something up instead. In fact Lana has a greater range of deep desires than her answer suggests, as seen after she loses her inhibitions owing to the influence of the Nicodemus flower.

First, Lana vamps into school and tries to get Whitney to skip class. When he refuses she tells him how dull he's become and dumps him. Lana tells Clark that though things are rough, Clark needs to let his friends distract him – in this case, by going down to the pool so that Lana can do a striptease for him. When that doesn't work out, she moves on to Lex, smearing whipped cream on his lips and asking what his ulterior motive in buying the Talon was. Lana tells Lex she's nervous and needs guidance from someone more experienced. When Lex proves as reluctant as Whitney and Clark, Lana steals his car and heads for the windmill to fulfil her desire. At the windmill, Lana tells Clark she has self-confidence, she's free. She demands to know whether he's in love with her then, when he won't reply, calls him a coward. Kristin Kreuk excels as the uninhibited Lana, showing some real acting range as a ruthless, sexually predatory and manipulative young woman. Is this how Lana would act if she felt she could get away with it? If so, it's bad news for Whitney, but great news for Clark and/or Lex ...

Not an Evil Genius: Lex lies constantly in this episode to cover himself. When Clark confronts him about reading *The Nicodemus Diary*, Lex claims that he read the book out of casual interest because the events took place on land he owns. Lex claims that when Jonathan became ill, he checked out the story, but didn't want to share it with Clark because it was so irrational. Clark asks if Lex knows Hamilton; Lex claims to not even recognise the name. When Clark tells Lex that the Nicodemus outbreak isn't Lex's fault, Lex looks guilty (a clever inversion of Clark's visible guilt whenever someone mentions the meteor shower). To his credit, Lex is incredibly determined to find a cure for the Nicodemus at any cost. Lex manages to preserve his secret and save lives, getting Hamilton's cure to the doctors while convincing Clark that Pete's accusations are the Nicodemus talking.

When Lex hears that Beales was rescued from his crashed car, he automatically asks if the rescuer was Clark, which shows the extent to which he thinks of his friend as a hero. Lex isn't impressed with Hamilton messing about with extinct flowers, telling him that he's supposed to be studying the meteors' effects on humans, not plants. Hamilton is understandably irked by this lack of respect for the scientific process. Would Lex be happier if Hamilton moved straight to working on human subjects? Lex's approach would seem to suggest that.

When Lana goes out of control, Lex tells her that no one is impressed by her attitude, and he should know because he wrote the book on adolescent rebellion.

Torch Bearer: Principal Kwan, presumably in his ongoing campaign to improve Chloe's journalism, gets her to do a survey revealing the feelings of her fellow students. When Clark watches Lana walk away, and Chloe is asking him to answer the 'Deepest Desire' survey, she reminds him that it's a PG-13-rated survey. Chloe gets exasperated at Clark's Lana obsession, catching her breath in frustration as he stares at her. She tells him there are other girls out there – a heavy hint which Clark fails to pick up on. When Clark tells Chloe about the incident in the pool, she tells him that at least he'll have something to daydream about in detention. Chloe actually persists with one of her stories this time, going back to Hamilton's lab at the end of the episode to find it empty.

Just the Funny Guy: Pete, a leading member of the cast who has had woefully little to do so far this season, finally gets some character development as his contempt for the Luthors is finally explained. It's in this episode that he proves that he's not just 'the funny guy', displaying bitterness at the label. Pete tells Clark that he isn't keen on Lex because Lionel cheated the Ross family out of the creamed corn factory. Pete claims that he hasn't mentioned it before because he thought Clark would come around. Pete believes Lionel Luthor betrayed Pete's family, and now Lex is souring things between Clark and Pete – Chloe tells Clark that Pete feels he and Clark haven't been as close since Lex came on the scene.

Once under the influence of the Nicodemus, Pete's dislike of Lex turns into murderous rage. He tells Chloe how beautiful she is, then becomes bitter that he's always ignored and that Chloe doesn't worry about his feelings because she's only interested in Clark.

Before being infected, when asked what he'd do without any restraints, Pete says he'd make out with a pretty girl nearby. When Chloe says that all the answers to her survey so far have been either sex- or violence-related, Pete replies that this is just human nature, before rushing off to pursue his target. When told about Jonathan, Pete thinks Clark's father has become a teenager.

Down at the Farm: Presumably in a conscious attempt to differentiate between Jonathan before and after being infected by the Nicodemus flower, John Schneider plays him as being unconcerned when Beales tries to drive him off the road, which seems a little odd.

There is a more romantic side to Clark's parents – by the looks of it more romantic than Clark is entirely comfortable with – when Jonathan loses his inhibitions after being infected by the Nicodemus flower. He gleefully tells Lex that suing him over the accident would solve all of his financial problems, and goes on to tell Lex exactly what he thinks of him. This less responsible Jonathan, who is more keen to sit around watching TV and drinking beer than working on the farm, is a lot of fun, although things go badly wrong when Jonathan gets his loan rejected by the bank and decides to go down there with a shotgun to settle the matter. When Clark stops him, Jonathan becomes dizzy and passes out, lapsing into a coma for most of the episode.

When Jonathan is dying, Martha tells Clark about their first meeting. Jonathan came to Metropolis University to take a finance course and was sitting by a fountain eating an apple. Martha asked to borrow his notes – Jonathan not knowing that Martha was the notetaker for the class. Jonathan handed his notes over without question, and when Martha asked how sure he was that she would give them back, Jonathan replied that he preferred to believe in people. (Clark directly echoes this sentiment to Ryan in **16**, 'Stray', showing the level of his father's influence.) Martha, who just thought he was 'cute' up until then, found herself hoping he would marry her. She still thinks that to this day.

The Quarterback: Visiting his father in hospital and looking after the Fordmans' store has left Whitney behind on his school work, so he refuses to skip class to go play with Lana. This results in him getting dumped by a pollen-fuelled Lana, which leaves him (unsurprisingly) upset.

Mad Scientist: Hamilton resurrected the Nicodemus flower to try and find out if its toxins could have useful applications. When Lex criticises his methods, Hamilton tells him that science is a long process, and if he doesn't understand that he can get someone else to do the work. Hamilton claims the Nicodemus story is folklore but still doesn't want to open the case containing one of the specimens and sniff it. Hamilton tells Chloe that he's an antisocial man. Hamilton wrote a paper while at Metropolis University saying that the meteor rocks could be used to irradiate dormant plant cells. Lex relocates Hamilton to

Cadmus Labs at the end of the episode, determined to keep him on a shorter leash. To what extent is this motivated by the results of the Nicodemus outbreak, and to what extent is Lex worried about Lionel closing in on Hamilton's work (as evidenced by Beales' theft)?

Strange Visitors: Not a person this time, but a flower. The Nicodemus sprays a pollen that causes people to become uninhibited, reckless and violent, eventually slipping into a coma then dying. Surprisingly, the Nicodemus' properties are not caused by the meteor rock, although it is exposure to meteor radiation that allows Hamilton to revive the long-dead species from dormant seed pods. The Nicodemus flower caused the deaths of all 200 people in the Morley settlement in 1871, as told by the priest who wrote *The Nicodemus Diary*. According to the book the Nicodemus caused the settlers to act out of character and behave violently. It caused them to unleash their repressed feelings, then go into a rage, then fever, and finally death. After the massacre the cavalry torched the settlement to destroy all of the flowers, and it's been extinct ever since. Fortunately for those poisoned by the flower in the present day, the Native Americans had a cure for the Nicodemus' effects, a cure which Hamilton finds and which Lex's medical team manage to re-create.

Loose Ends: In **5**, 'Cool', Lex's mansion had a security system, so how did Pete just walk in late at night? Does Cadmus Labs still have all the Nicodemus flowers to work on, or did Lex have them destroyed? Are the plants still alive around the crash site?

Music: When Jonathan is driving at the start of the episode 'Good Ol' Boys', performed by Waylon Jennings, is heard – it was the theme tune to John Schneider's most famous TV series, *The Dukes of Hazzard*. Other tracks are 'I Will Make You Cry' by Nelly Furtado, 'Destiny' by Zero 7, 'Supernatural' by Divine Right, 'Sadie Hawkins Dance' by Relient K, 'Big Day' by Puracene, 'Love Sweet Love' by Josh Clayton-Felt and 'Saturday Night's Alright' by Hal Lovejoy. The music in the final scene is, of course, 'Beautiful Day' by pretentious billionaire rock group U2.

Secret Identities: Bill Mondy plays Stuart Lightman in *The Burial Society* and his TV appearances include episodes of *Wolf Lake*, *Star Trek: Deep Space Nine*, *LA Law* and the *Babylon 5* spin-off series *Crusade*. Julian Christopher played Calvin Simms in *The Commish* and also guest-starred on *Star Trek: Deep Space Nine* as well as *The Outer Limits* and *Murder, She Wrote*.

James Marshall started out as second assistant editor on Peter Greenaway's *Drowning By Numbers*, and has worked his way up through Second Unit Director or Assistant Director gigs on projects such as *Highlander: The Series* and the film *Stanley & Iris*, to directing episodes of *The Sentinel* and *Viper*.

From the Pages of: Lana asks Clark if he is 'made of steel', an obvious reference to Superman being 'the Man of Steel'.

Trivia: The responses to Chloe's 'Deepest Desire' survey include 'To catch the big one (named Cathy)', someone wanting to sail around the world with a man, and a couple about falling in love. The sign at the Talon reads 'NOW OPEN – POETRY READING THURSDAYS'.

The Last Word: 'I think the operative word is "gulp".' With so many suppressed feelings and buried tensions in the show to date, it was probably inevitable that an episode about unleashing these desires and freeing oneself from social constraints would come along sooner or later. Well, this is it, and it has too many good moments to list. John Schneider and Sam Jones III both shine as Jonathan and Pete lose their inhibitions, but the absolute standout star of the show is Kristin Kreuk. Kreuk plays her role to the vampish hilt as Lana sequentially attempts to seduce Whitney, Clark and Lex, all of whom prove lacking, far too restrained for her newly unrestrained desires. Each of these Lana scenes is a gem, very funny and slightly disturbing. The Lana plot also provides one of the season's most memorable scenes, as Lana does her poolside strip-tease to a partially excited, partially reticent Clark.

How very convenient that, like the victims of hypnotism in **11**, 'Hug', everyone infected by the Nicodemus flower loses their memory, so Pete no longer knows about the connection between Lex and Hamilton, or the unearthly speed with which Clark snatched the gun off him. Far too convenient. That's one of only two flaws in a funny and exciting episode, though, which isn't too bad a score.

The other fault is the very silly matte shot at the end of the episode which makes Metropolis look as though it's about a mile away.

16
Stray

Production #227615
1st US Transmission Date: 16 April 2002
1st UK Transmission Date: 17 April 2002

Writer: Philip Levens
Director: Paul Shapiro
Special Guest Star: John Glover (Lionel Luthor)
Guest Starring: Ryan Kelley (Ryan), Jim Shield (Stepdad),
Brandy Ledford (Stepmom)
Co-starring: Rekha Sharma, Bill Finck, Joe Maffei,
Courtney Kramer (Skye), Jayme Knox, Shelley Adam

Synopsis: Young Ryan has the ability to read minds, but his step-parents get him to misuse this gift, helping them to commit crimes. When his stepfather shoots a pawnbroker during a robbery, Ryan runs away, only to be knocked over by Martha Kent's car. The hospital discharges Ryan to the Kents' care, where he forms a strong bond with Clark, using his gift to discover Clark's secret. Ryan, pretending not to know where he came from, spends some time with Clark. He tells Clark a lot about his friends, and tips off Lana that one of the Talon's waitresses is stealing from the till. Ryan's step-parents eventually take him back (see **Down at the Farm**), threatening to kill the Kents if Ryan squeals. They use Ryan to try and rob Lex, but Ryan gives them a false code for Lex's account. After an argument in which his stepfather kills his stepmother, Ryan tries to escape again, but his father chases after him. Clark arrives and knocks out Ryan's stepfather. Chloe locates an aunt of Ryan's, and Ryan leaves the Kents to live with his newfound relative.

Lionel Luthor, pleased with his son's work in Smallville, tells Lex that his exile is over and he can return to Metropolis. Lex refuses.

Speech Bubbles: Lionel: 'You know, Philip of Macedonia raised his son among lions to instil fearlessness in him.' Lex: 'Didn't he also try to impale the kid with a spear?'

Lex (to Lionel): 'You know what those emperors you're so fond of talking about were really afraid of? That their sons would become successful and return to Rome at the head of their own army.'

Small Town Boy: The main thrust of the episode is 'what if Clark had a little brother?', with the relationship between Clark and Ryan at its heart. Making Ryan a fan of superhero comics is a masterstroke – the way that he idolises Clark provides a flash forward to what it will be like for Clark to be looked up to as Superman. Clark tells Lana that he always wanted a little brother, someone he could trust and rely on. (Lana says that's how she sees Clark – which doesn't exactly please him, although he thanks her nonetheless.) There's far less desperation in Clark's approach to Lana, and he twice stops Ryan from letting on how she feels (although the way in which Ryan offers to tell him is a dead giveaway anyway). When Ryan says he's in love with Lana, Clark tells him to join the club.

Clark is surprised that Lex was a comic-book fan, doubtless seeing him as too cynical to have ever had such an innocent and optimistic hobby. When Ryan tells Clark about Lex's dark side, Clark replies that he prefers to believe the best of people – in other words, he's not unaware of Lex's dark side, but thinks that the good side will outweigh the bad if given the chance.

Ryan tells Clark that Chloe is interested in him, and would like to be invited to the Prom by him. Although Clark denies this as a likely scenario, Chloe almost confirms it later. However, Clark somehow manages to dismiss all this and normalise his relationship with Chloe, not addressing her feelings for him until **19**, 'Crush'.

Clark's perpetual lateness is referred to again; he jokes that Ryan is making him look bad by getting up early to prepare a family breakfast. Clark has another special ability, in that he can prevent Ryan reading his thoughts (It's Martha's thoughts that reveal Clark's powers). However, psychic contact is possible between Clark and a human, as it happened in **6**, 'Hourglass', when Clark shared Cassandra's visions.

Girl Next Door: There's a not-exceptionally-shocking revelation in this episode, as Ryan's mind-reading antics pretty much give away that Lana has feelings for Clark. Well, duh! Lana tells Clark that she always wanted a sibling, and has a classic only child's idealised idea about what this imaginary brother or sister would be like: 'someone to talk to, help fill the silence'. Lana has to deal with the responsibilities of management, as she finds out that the Talon has a thief on its staff – fortunately Ryan tips her off. She kisses Ryan on the cheek to thank him, winning her another fan.

Not an Evil Genius: Lionel offers Lex the chance he thinks Lex has been waiting for – to return with him to Metropolis, to take a position as Lionel's Special Adviser at LuthorCorp. When Lex refuses Lionel's offer, he tells his father that he thinks he wants Lex back because he's doing well for himself, not going clubbing or getting arrested. Lex thinks that Lionel is scared by this resurgent Lex, and wants him back where he can keep an eye on him. Though Lionel tells Lex that he's making a mistake, Lex says he'll return to Metropolis when he's ready – possibly with an army. Lex tells Lionel that the games they play between them are all that they have left, an achingly sad statement on the coldness of their relationship.

Another bit of Luthor family history is revealed, as Lex talks about his brother, Julian. Lillian Luthor became pregnant when Lex was eleven. Lionel was never happier, and the day of Julian's birth was the one time in Lex's life when he felt like he was part of a family. But on the day of Julian's christening he was found in his cot, having stopped breathing. Lillian was never the same, and Lionel became more and more distant, having lost his second chance to have a son and heir that he could truly love. Lex claims that if Julian had lived, Lionel would have made sure he and Lex hated each other.

Lex claims to be a fan of the *Warrior Angel* comics, owning an original, first-edition panel from the comic as well as a full run of the issues. He says the Angel was his idol, at least partially because he was bald. Like Ryan, Lex seems to have changed his allegiances from his original comic-book hero to Clark as a personal hero – his parting gift when he thinks he may be leaving Smallville is to give Clark a foil, saying that every hero should have one.

Bad Dad: As part of his justification for inviting Lex to return to Metropolis, Lionel gives his son a rare compliment, telling him that his performance at the plant has been more than adequate. Lionel admits to pushing Lex, but says it's necessary if Lex is to attain greatness. Lionel talks about Alexander the Great, leading Lex to ask if Lionel has come all that way just to lecture him on Greek history *again*. Lionel tells Lex that his offer is what Lex has been waiting to hear, and Lex replies that there are things he's been waiting for Lionel to say for a lot longer.

Lionel quotes General Carl Von Clausewitz's *On War*, originally published in German in 1832: 'The backbone of surprise is fusing speed with secrecy.'

Torch Bearer: According to Ryan, Chloe wants Clark to invite her to the Prom, and has already picked out a pink dress. When Clark mentions this to her jokingly, Chloe says she hadn't bought the dress, but was just looking at it. (The dress she wears to the Spring Formal in **21**, 'Tempest' is more red than pink.)

Chloe has a source in the Sheriff's department that turns out to be an attractive traffic cop who called Chloe plucky after she talked her way out of a speeding ticket. Chloe pointedly suggests she may take said officer to the Prom.

Chloe compares Ryan to Kaspar Hauser, a boy in the nineteenth century who turned up in a German town without any memory of who he was, and became a cause célèbre across Europe. Chloe avoids saying that Hauser was murdered. (The story of Hauser has been filmed twice, in 1974 [*The Enigma & Kaspar Hauser*] and 1993 [*Kaspar Hauser*], so is not as obscure as Clark suggests.) Chloe is curious how Ryan knew about Hauser but, as Clark says, she doesn't exactly have a poker face. When she realises Ryan has some kind of intuitive ability, Chloe suggests that he may be an alien, or have called Miss Cleo (a telephone astrologer, presumably).

Chloe tells Clark that although Lex may be leaving, she's not going anywhere. This turns out to be not strictly true a few weeks later (in **21**, 'Tempest'). It's Chloe's researches that locate Ryan's aunt in Edge City.

Down at the Farm: When Martha is watching Clark and Ryan playing hoops, she asks Jonathan if they made the wrong decision not adopting another child. Would having a younger brother to share his secret with have helped Clark as he grew up? Jonathan notes that both Clark and Martha are getting very fond of Ryan, and later he himself is visibly depressed when Ryan leaves with Child Services (in fact it's Ryan's stepmother who takes him). By the end of the episode Ryan has become a part of all the Kents' lives, and they're sad to see him go.

In one scene Martha agrees with Ryan that Clark is the best thing that ever happened to her and, hesitantly, that Clark makes up for them not being able to have children themselves. When Ryan asks if Clark has always been strong enough to do things like rip open the back of the garbage truck, Martha claims that Clark couldn't have done that. Ryan asks what Martha's greatest fear is and, from the fact that Ryan uses what he reads in her mind to go straight to the storm cellar, it's clear that fear is of Clark's alien origins being exposed. Both Clark's parents eat huge breakfasts – one presumes they work it off on the farm!

Strange Visitors: Not all people with special abilities get them from meteors – young Ryan has the ability to read minds, yet has no meteor connection. Ryan has an unpleasant background, his mother dying and leaving him with his evil stepfather, who then remarried giving Ryan an evil stepmother as well. These wicked step-parents have been using Ryan's abilities to commit crimes, until Ryan runs away. Ryan settles into the Kent family well, and asks if they could adopt him as they did Clark. Ryan even lets himself be taken away by his stepmother to protect the Kents. By the end of the episode, he has found an aunt to live with – as she approaches he tells Clark he can tell she is a nice person, and that she is as nervous as he is.

Ryan's abilities allow him to read people's surface thoughts, and he uses questions to bring the thoughts he wants to the surface: witness his interrogation of Martha or Lana. Ryan can't turn off his power to block out people's thoughts, though; he can't read Clark's mind at all, so he likes his company because it's peaceful. When he finds out Clark's secret, Ryan promises not to reveal it and to use his ability to tell when someone is getting close to finding out. Ryan tells Clark he feels like a freak, and this makes him resistant to Chloe, worried she'll put his picture on the 'Wall of Weird'. He's sick of hiding his abilities, something Clark can relate to.

Ryan is a big fan of the *Warrior Angel* comics, which he likes because the title character protects the weak. By the end of the episode he has a new hero, Clark, and so gives his comics away.

Ryan seems unimpressed with Lex and his first-edition panel from Ryan's favourite comic. He claims to know Lex has one because buying something like that is just what rich people do – a brilliant put-down.

Man or Superman?: Both Lex and Ryan are rebelling against their fathers, choosing the Kents and Smallville over more aggressive and ruthless lives elsewhere. They seem to benefit from the heroic influence of Clark, who acts as a surrogate brother to them both. Lex is, of course, deeply envious of the Kents' family life, and Ryan gets the chance to live it for a while.

Loose Ends: Why is the bowling alley left with its doors open and its outer lights on, when it's clearly closed? Did the real Child Services arrive to pick up Ryan the night his stepmother came for him? If not, what happened to them?

Why doesn't Ryan's stepfather come back for him again after he goes to live with his aunt? Or is he in jail?

Lex and Ryan give each other significant looks when Ryan raids Lex's mind for the password. Considering the password Ryan gives his stepfather is false, does this mean Lex manages to trick Ryan, or that he lets Ryan read a plan in his mind to get them out of there? Certainly, setting Ryan's step-parents at each other's throats seems like a very Lex thing to do.

Music: The songs heard in this episode are 'Free to Change Your Mind' by Regency Buck, 'Lonely Day' by Phantom Planet, 'Is It Love?' and 'Dragging Me Down' by Todd Thibaud, 'Hollywood' by Micah Green and the memorable 'Superman' by Five For Fighting over the last scene.

Secret Identities: Young Ryan Kelley's brief CV takes in the movies *Stolen Summer*, *Stray Dogs* and *Roommates*. Jim Shield played a gambler in the Gough and Millar-scripted *Shanghai Noon*, and was a stunt man on *Dudley Do-Right*. Brandy Ledford played Vicky in *Rat Race*, made an appearance in *Demolition Man* and was in *Baywatch* for a year as Dawn Masterton. Rekha Sharma had a recurring role as Dr Beverley Shankhar in *Dark Angel*, and also appeared in *The Lone Gunmen*.

Director Paul Shapiro has helmed episodes of *The X-Files*, *Millennium* and *24*. He was also behind the camera for a few episodes of *Roswell*, including the classic 'Michael, the Guys and The Great Snapple Caper'.

From the Pages of: Lex's description of the Warrior Angel as a 'strange visitor from another planet who protects the weak' is a catchphrase associated with Superman, and comparisons are made between the Angel and Clark throughout. Chloe compares Clark to Zorro, the swash-buckling character created by Johnston McCully in his 1918 novel *The Curse of Capistrano*, who went on to appear in numerous comic strips. Chloe also refers to Lex as a millionaire playboy, a description usually applied to Bruce Wayne, a.k.a. Batman. 'Edge City' is the name of a syndicated newspaper comic strip created by Terry and Patty LaBan.

Trivia: Neither Pete nor Whitney appear in this episode. The headlines on the *Smallville Ledger* read LUTHORCORP PLANT POSTS PROFIT and CITY COUNCIL REJECTS PLAN. The first line of the Talon's sign reads OPEN MIKE NIGHT, but the angle is never clear enough to read the rest. The name James Gibson is clearly visible underneath the picture of Ryan's father, but it's not clear whether this is his name or that of the arresting officer, or even Chloe's contact.

The Last Word: 'Greatness is a rarefied air one has to be taught to breathe.' The importance of parenting in the development of a person's character has been a consistent theme throughout the season so far, and this provides an overt example, with an outsider being integrated into the Kent family and Lex being offered the chance to return to his father's side. Although it's refreshing to have Clark acting the big brother, there's little original in the Ryan plot; depending on your viewpoint the nameless wicked step-parents are either a clever bit of fairytale storytelling, or an exercise in tiresome cliché. The production may have been attempting the former, but it winds up with the latter, a situation not helped by the flavourless acting from the two evil parents. Fortunately Ryan Kelley is a much better actor in spite of his tender years, and it's a credit to the show that Ryan isn't always entirely sympathetic; he's a tough kid who had a hard upbringing, and it shows.

The Lex and Lionel plot is much more fun, and the Julian story provides more insight into how dysfunctional the Luthors are. Although there are some fun moments – Chloe and Clark searching for evidence by the roadside and Clark's stunt with the bowling ball – 'Stray' doesn't really add up to much.

17
Reaper

Production #227616
1st US Transmission Date: 23 April 2002
1st UK Transmission Date: 24 April 2002

Writer: Cameron Litvack
Director: Terrence O'Hara
Special Guest Star: John Glover (Lionel Luthor)
Guest Starring: Reynaldo Rosales (Tyler), Jason Connery (Dominic),
Sheila Moore
Co-starring: Tiffany Knight, Brian Drummond, Patrick Keating,
Rheta With An H, Ralph Alderman, Dale Wilson

Synopsis: Tyler Randall tries to help his dying mother to find peace by suffocating her with a pillow, but hospital security tries to stop him, and Tyler falls to his death in the struggle. A piece of meteor rock in Tyler's bracelet lodges in his flesh and, when the pathologist removes it, a green taint spreads through Tyler's system. Tyler returns from the dead with the ability to turn people to dust with a single touch.

Tyler goes to Smallville, where he volunteers with the same Mobile Meals scheme as Martha, taking food to the housebound elderly. Tyler uses his power to kill Mrs Sykes, an old woman complaining of the pain of her illness. Clark and Chloe investigate, and Clark only narrowly manages to save his mother from Tyler. Tyler is about to euthanise Whitney's dying father when Clark tells him that his entire crusade has been based on a false premise – Tyler's mother didn't die at the hospital, she is still alive in Smallville. Tyler goes to see his mother, then turns his power on himself in remorse, dissolving into ash.

Whitney is avoiding visiting his ailing father. Clark eventually persuades him to go, but Whitney gets knocked out when Tyler arrives to kill his father. Lex arranges a treat for Whitney and his father: the Metropolis Sharks come to the school to practise with Whitney.

Clark has a disagreement with his own father when Clark suggests they use Lex's tickets to go to the big ball game rather than take their annual fishing trip. Relations remain frosty between father and son, but after Martha tells Clark about how when Jonathan's father died there was still tension between them, Clark makes an effort to reconcile himself with his dad.

Lex has father problems of his own when Lionel sends Dominic to investigate Lex's expenses. Dominic starts looking into Lex's investigation of the Porsche crash, causing Jonathan to find out about Lex's investigation for the first time. Lex eventually delivers Dominic back to Lionel in Metropolis – drugged and stuffed into a car boot.

Speech Bubbles: Lex (to Jonathan): 'I just want you to understand that if I'm guilty of anything regarding your family, it's envy.'

Lex (to Clark): 'You have no idea how lucky you are. When my father dies, kings will come to his funeral. But when yours does, his friends will come.'

Dominic (after listening to another rant about Lionel): 'There are some things best left between patient and therapist, Lex.'

Small Town Boy: This week Clark comes to terms with mortality (following on from this theme in **6**, 'Hourglass'). Clark doesn't like helping his mother with the Mobile Meals, as there's nothing he can do for the old and the sick. Martha tells him he can save them from loneliness. This doesn't convince him but, in fighting Tyler, Clark comes to realise that where there's life, there's still hope, and that spending time with those who haven't got long left is a worthwhile cause.

Because of this, Clark learns to appreciate the time he has with his father, and the opportunities that fishing trips have for quality time. Although early in the episode Clark doesn't want to go on the trip, and admits to his father he doesn't even like them, after seeing the relationship Lex has with his father, the loss Whitney is facing and being told by Martha about Jonathan's lack of closure with his own dad, Clark sees the fishing trip as a positive thing he should treasure while he can.

Clark is resistant to Tyler's lethal touch, although his face is briefly bruised where Tyler touches him, and he says it felt like the life was being drained from him.

Girl Next Door: This is a Lana-light episode, with her acting mainly as a link between Clark and Whitney. Lana persuades Clark to try and talk to Whitney about visiting his father in hospital, something Lana has already failed at.

Not an Evil Genius: Lex talks about his childhood after his mother's death. Lex tells Jonathan that the only photo of

Lionel and Lex together is in the LuthorCorp prospectus. He admits to being envious of the Kents.

In trying to help Clark and his father spend some time together, Lex offers them football tickets for the box at the Metropolis Sharks. However, after being accused by Jonathan of using the Kents as pawns, Lex withdraws his offer and tells Clark to go fishing – Jonathan just wants to spend time with him, and Clark doesn't know how lucky he is. Lex also has to patch up his worsening relationship with Jonathan after Kent senior finds out about Lex's investigation into the crash. At the end of the episode Jonathan is mollified slightly by what Lex does for the Fordmans, and they're capable of talking civilly about Lex's investigation and why he did it. Lex reassures Jonathan that he doesn't want to stop Clark from being good.

The main Lex thread of the episode is Dominic's investigation into Lex's accounts on Lionel's behalf, searching out financial discrepancies. Lionel would have been happy with Lex spending his money on excesses, but he knows Lex isn't the party fiend he once was, so he wants to know where the money went. Lex warns Dominic that, in spite of himself, he's still his father's son, and that Dominic should tread carefully. Lex tells Dominic that the reason he's been sent to Smallville is that Lex is doing well and Lionel presumed Lex would fail; but now Lex is turning into competition – and the only way Lionel knows how to deal with competition is to destroy it.

Bad Dad: For Lex's tenth birthday Lionel gave him a copy of Friedrich Nietzsche's *The Will to Power*, from which Lex quotes – 'Behold the superman, man is something to be overcome.' Other highlights of the juvenile Luthor reading list include Sun Tzu and Machiavelli. Lionel and Lex were once lowered into the sea in a cage to get close to Great White Sharks – Lex only went because Lionel didn't think he would. It was their last father–son trip.

Torch Bearer: Chloe takes a ghoulish and not terribly sensitive interest in Mrs Sykes' death and cites a case of a spontaneously combusting disco dancer from 1978. When

Chloe asks if she's transparent in terms of her determination to investigate, Clark and Pete chorus an affirmative. Unlike Clark, Chloe is unconcerned by disturbing a crime scene at the Sykes' house. Chloe alludes to Michael Jackson's zombie-filled video for *Thriller* when talking about Tyler.

Chloe tells Lana that Clark is always running off and that she has no idea why. However, considering her sometimes huge leaps, she doesn't seem to have any opinion about this unusual behaviour, or any curiosity as to why Clark does it.

Just the Funny Guy: Pete finds the autopsy reports Chloe keeps waving around particularly distasteful. Pete and Clark perform as more of a double act this week, responding almost identically to Chloe's theories.

The Quarterback: Whitney's father is dying and, after he has another heart attack, Whitney finds it hard to visit him in hospital – it doesn't seem like his father, whom he remembers as the strongest person he's ever known. Whitney's father will never get to see all the things Whitney will do in later life. He doesn't want his memories to be of a sick man in hospital, but is given something to consider when Clark says that he should take the man over the memory.

Whitney has never visited the grave of Lana's parents before this episode, which he thinks is unacceptable, even though Lana says it's all right. He didn't want to think of his parents dying because the prospect was so awful. Lana tells Whitney that's why he needs to see his father and make the best of what time he has, and Whitney does. Whitney takes a bruising while trying to stop Tyler from killing his father. Thanks to Lex, Whitney's father gets to see him play with the Metropolis Sharks – albeit just at a practice on the school field.

Down at the Farm: Jonathan and Clark have been going fishing once a year since Clark was young. Jonathan is seen lovingly working on his reels and rods. He isn't happy that Clark wants them to use football tickets from Lex, and is even less happy when he finds out Clark knew about Lex's investigation into the car crash and didn't tell him. When

Lex accuses Jonathan of only ever viewing him as a Luthor, Jonathan replies that Lex hasn't given him reason to see anything else.

Martha tells Clark that when Jonathan's father, Hiram Kent, died, there were a lot of things Jonathan didn't get to say to him, which he now regrets. Later, Jonathan tells Clark that the fishing itself doesn't matter, it's spending time with him. Jonathan saw his father every day, and they never really talked. By the end of the episode, the fishing trip is back on and Jonathan has resolved a couple of issues with Lex.

Even after the events of **14**, 'Zero', the produce from the Kent farm is still being described as organic. Martha volunteers for a Mobile Meals service.

Strange Visitors: After trying to help his mother to die, Tyler himself gets killed but rises again with the ability to kill with a touch. Tyler's resurrection seems to have been due to a fatal dose of painkillers he had taken combining with the meteor rock lodged in his flesh at the point of death. For some reason helping in euthanising his mother, and then rising from the dead, seems to convince Tyler he's been given a sacred duty to wander around bumping off the sick and the old with his hand-of-death. When he finds out his mother is still alive, Tyler changes his mind and kills himself by touching his palms together.

Man or Superman: Jonathan and Clark's storyline isn't very good and doesn't lead anywhere, but it's nicely paralleled by Lex's story about his one fishing trip with Lionel, where they were lowered into the water in a cage to get close to some Great White Sharks. Lex thinks that Jonathan is giving Clark something he never got from Lionel – limitations. All Lex's father taught him was not to get caught and not to cause a scandal. As Lex says, that's public relations rather than love.

Music: This episode's music includes an encore for Rubyhorse (who had a track used in **11**, 'Hug'), this time with the track 'Sparkle'. The other songs used are 'Friends and Family' by Trik Turner, 'The Weight of My Words' by Kings of Convenience and 'Falcor' by Firengine Red.

Secret Identities: Reynaldo Rosales, who plays meteor-fuelled Tyler, has appeared in episodes of *Charmed* and *CSI: Crime Scene Investigation* as well as the mini-series *Fidel*. He's often credited as Reynaldo Christian. Other cast members with multiple names are Rheta With An H (a.k.a. Rheta Hutton), who has played numerous old women and grandmothers, and Ralph Alderman (otherwise known as Ralph J Alderman) who played a locksmith in *Freddy Got Fingered* and Rusty in *Wolf Lake*. Sheila Moore played Liesel Jurgensen in *Snow Falling On Cedars*, Ruth in *The Reflecting Skin* and guest roles in *The X-Files* and *Millennium*.

Director Terrence O'Hara has shot episodes of *The Huntress*, starring Annette O'Toole, as well as episodes of *The X-Files*, *Angel*, *Star Trek:Voyager* and *Brimstone* (which featured John Glover as the Devil).

Loose Ends: Lana is never seen to meet Tyler – how does she know him?

The Last Word: 'I don't want to hurt anyone Lana, I just want to bring them peace.' There's some excellent direction, especially in the mortuary scene, but otherwise this is little more than a competent space-filler. Although the intermingling of the various characters coming to terms with mortality is well done, it isn't the most sensitive or complex handling of the euthanasia issue. Tyler's motivations aren't particularly well thought through or interesting, and to be honest the character is a bore. Reynaldo Rosales portrays him well enough, but really doesn't have much to work with.

The fishing trip subplot is unspeakably hackneyed, a series of rank clichés that should never have been allowed to shamble across the screen; Clark wants to do something else, Jonathan wants to preserve the tradition. It's all about spending time together, blah blah *blah* – but at least it allows another set of contrasts between the two pivotal father–son relationships in the show. Lex's treatment of the odious Dominic is simultaneously a hint of his villainous future, and a heroic rejection of his father. Staggeringly average, 'Reaper' really isn't a matter of life or death.

18
Drone

Production #227617
1st US Transmission Date: 30 April 2002
1st UK Transmission Date: 1 May 2002

Writers: Michael Green and Philip Levens
Director: Michael Katleman
Special Guest Star: Marguerite Moreau (Cassandra Castle)
Guest Starring: Shonda Farr (Sasha), Chelan Simmons,
Hiro Kanagawa (Principal Kwan)
Co-starring: Simon Wong

Synopsis: At Smallville High it's time for the elections for school president. When Chloe's pick for the top job, Paul, is injured in a mysterious bee attack, Pete puts Clark forward as an alternative candidate. As Clark learns to cope with his new high profile, it becomes clear that a rival candidate for the presidency, Sasha, is controlling the bees and using their attacks to advance her campaign, targeting rival candidate Felice as well as putting Paul out of the race. When Clark intervenes, Sasha uses the bees to attack his family.

Meanwhile, Clark and Chloe have a falling out when she backs the hospital-ridden Paul for the presidency over Clark. Clark manages to defeat Sasha as the swarm turns against her, but loses the election to Paul, in spite of Pete's vigorous campaigning techniques. Clark realises that Chloe needed to do the right thing in backing the candidate she believed in, and they make up.

A persistent female journalist, Cassandra Castle of the *Metropolis Journal*, is determined to get an interview from Lex at all costs. After faking a car failure and replacing his masseuse, Castle manages to persuade Lex that an exclusive interview would help him in his publicity battle with his father. The interview turns out to be a hatchet job, but Lex gets to read it before it goes to press. Lex thinks Lionel persuaded Cassandra to write such a hostile piece, and is frustrated when Cassandra won't be threatened or bought off. Lex finally wins Cassandra over by arranging for her to get a promotion if she drops the hostile story. Cassandra confesses that Lionel was involved.

The Talon is running low on customers as the Beanery is competing aggressively with them. Lex advises Lana to get her hands dirty, and she does, finding out about the Beanery's health violations and then tipping off the *Smallville Ledger* through Chloe. Lana isn't exactly proud of herself, but it works – the Talon is busy again.

Speech Bubbles: Pete (to Clark): 'All you've got to do is show up, shake a couple of hands, give an election speech – it's easy!' Chloe: 'And we wonder why our politicians aren't great leaders.'

Lex coins Clark's campaign slogan: 'The man of tomorrow is forged by his battles today.'

Small Town Boy: Being thrust into the political spotlight for much of the episode constantly bewilders Clark. His frown at his parents' encouragement, as they pretty much bully him into staying in the race, is a wonder to behold. He's flattered, however, when Lana tells him that he has all the qualities for a great class president, which encourages him to stay in the race. He offers to have his campaign rally at the Talon to bring people in, which Lana likes, but which raises Chloe's suspicions that Clark doesn't really have a point to his campaign other than impressing Lana. Clark is offended when Chloe doesn't back him, even though he knows full well that he doesn't have a platform. Clark never really gets time to work out what he stands for, being too busy meeting new people. Clark becomes quite delirious at the power of popularity, telling Chloe that he's even been invited to parties over the weekend.

When Lana tells him that the owner of the Beanery described his attempts to put the Talon out of business as just business, Clark asks why everyone over forty insists on constantly quoting *The Godfather*.

Girl Next Door: The Talon is deserted thanks to the aggressive campaign by the Beanery to keep the local coffee drinkers there. Lana is furiously determined to get the Talon busy again – she's tried coupons, offers and adverts, but so far nothing has worked. If business doesn't improve, the Talon will close within a month. Lana says that if the two-for-one deal doesn't work out, she'll have to institute topless waitresses. Lana agrees with Clark that people quoting *The Godfather* is annoying, and when Lex then quotes it she says the movie should be banned. With a fight on her hands, Lana is becoming more aggressive, leading to her ruthless elimination of the competition. While Lana isn't proud of herself for what she had done, she admits it felt good to be underhanded for once.

Lana supports Clark's campaign and helps him write his election speech (a speech, in the end, only she hears), but she also insists he should have more faith in his friends and support Chloe for standing up for her convictions. (As in **9**, 'Rogue', Lana is one of Chloe's most ardent supporters.)

Not an Evil Genius: Lex's offer to get his mechanic, Hans, to help with Cassandra's car is wonderfully described by her as post-modern chivalry. Lex knows that Cassandra is from Metropolis because of her witty dialogue and the fact she is wearing Dolce & Gabbana. Cassandra wants to do an article on Lex, which will help to raise his profile and get him out of his father's shadow – her employer, the *Journal*, is more respectable than the *Inquisitor*, Lex's main source of good press. Lex turns her down, but gives her points for style. Lex tells Cassandra he's impressed that she fooled him for so long – few people have ever caught him with his guard down. Eventually Lex gives in to her demands for an interview, but when she turns the piece into a hatchet job, Lex has to follow his own advice and 'get creative' to deal with her.

Lex ran for student office at school, which surprises Clark. He didn't have the most noble of aspirations, and refuses to give Clark any tips on the methods he used to get elected – Clark will win on his own terms. Lex admits that he might want to run for President one day (see the other Cassandra's vision in **6**, 'Hourglass'). Lex tells Lana that most new ventures fail, and you have to be prepared for that going in. Although he doesn't like to lose, it isn't his fight and, as an investor, he needs to be prepared to cut his losses. If the Beanery is fighting hard, then Lana needs to get creative and be willing to get her hands dirty, although Lex insists he isn't suggesting anything illegal. He's impressed when Lana pulls out all the stops.

Torch Bearer: Chloe isn't impressed with any of the candidates, including Clark, and insists that Paul could still win the election from hospital, which he eventually does. Chloe's main objection to another candidate, Felice, is that her name rhymes with the French word for suitcase. As Pete says, it's good to see Chloe isn't reaching for reasons to hate Felice. Chloe bombards Clark with important student issues, and he doesn't have a stance on any of them, leading to her refusal to back his campaign. Chloe is as sardonic as ever about the value of being popular at school, saying that she'll be head cheerleader before Clark is president. To Chloe, Clark even pursuing mainstream popularity is a betrayal, and she seems to fear his descent into a shallow set of priorities. Chloe doesn't gloat when Clark loses, admitting that her preferred candidate may have won, but her friend lost. She congratulates Clark on displaying dignity in defeat.

Just the Funny Guy: Pete comes into his own in this episode, nominating Clark for class president then managing his campaign.

Pete sees a great future for Clark in politics, and recommends the perks of power. He sees himself more as the power behind the throne, leading Chloe to describe him as a kingmaker. Pete's campaign is a combination of saturation with leaflets and a series of meets and greets. He books Clark in at a girls' volleyball game to get the 'jock vote', and gets him to attend a concert by the school band to show that he's a friend of the arts, even though the band are no good. Pete isn't interested in the issues or Clark's speech – he thinks if enough people like Clark, he'll win. According to Clark, Pete is also obsessed with his poster campaign, thinking the election will be won primarily on wall space. Clark himself describes Pete as overzealous.

Pete is very allergic to bees, so for him the attacks are a nightmare scenario.

Characteristically, Pete is looking forward to topless waitresses at the Talon.

Down at the Farm: To his surprise, Clark finds that his parents actively encourage him taking the political spotlight – it's a school activity where he can shine without using his gifts and risking exposure. Jonathan tells Clark that he can quit if he wants, but quitting is a habit that's hard to break. Martha is still trying to stop Clark drinking milk straight from the bottle (**1**, 'Pilot'). Clark tells Chloe that Martha is addicted to the Discovery Channel – which is why he knows about bees. After attacking Clark with bees at the Talon, Sasha tries to assassinate Martha with a swarm, leading to a tense chase across the fields as the bees zoom towards her.

The Quarterback: Whitney appears in this episode, drinking with his friends in the Talon to support Lana. However, he doesn't have any dialogue.

Strange Visitors: Sasha, the nerdy student politician with the power to control bees, wants to make Smallville High her own personal hive by becoming class president. Sasha has no sense of humour, and certainly doesn't consider the lighthearted approach to campaigning taken by her opponents to be funny. Sasha says Felice is trying to buy the election, while she doesn't rate Clark's chances at all. According to Chloe, swarms of bees haven't migrated from any of the usual places – beekeepers across the state are finding their hives empty, which explains the unnatural number of bees in one place that Sasha controls. Sasha's powers come from an accident in which she was stung by over a thousand bees; bad at the best of times, but these were the bees living in the largest meteor crater in Smallville.

According to Sasha, she suffers from parental pressure, feeling that she needs to become president to get into a good college and make her parents proud. (Her family are never seen, so it's hard to tell how true this may be.) Certainly, Shonda Farr plays Sasha as someone who is bitter to the point of derangement, rather than a seriously wronged party. Sasha's dress sense slightly gives the game away – all those horizontal stripes make her look like a big bee! The hexagonal, hive-like windows on the barn where Sasha has her campaign headquarters are great.

Music: One of the most musically heavy episodes, there are a lot of different tracks heard in **18**, 'Drone'. They are 'Stick Em Up' by Quarashi, 'If There's Love' by Citizen Cope, 'Not What I Wanted' by Evan Olson, 'Drink to Get Drunk' by Sia, 'The Middle' by Jimmy Eat World, 'Wogs Will Walk' by British guitar band Cornershop, 'Opaline' by Dishwalla, 'Big Day' by Puracane, 'Wake Up Elvis' by Alan Charing, 'Fever For The Flava' by Hot Action Cop and 'Here Is Gone' by Goo Goo Dolls.

Secret Identities: Marguerite Moreau has a recurring role in the *Mighty Ducks* franchise of hockey movies, and also has roles in *Queen of the Damned* and *Mighty Joe Young*. Shonda Farr appeared in Britney Spears' road movie *Crossroads*, as well as the 2001 'reimagining' of *Planet of the Apes*, and her TV roles including *Buffy the Vampire Slayer*, *CSI: Crime Scene Investigation* and *Beverly Hills, 90210*. Chelan Simmons appeared in the mini-series adaptation of Stephen King's novel *It*, as well as *Special Unit 2*.

From the Pages of: Pete's political ambitions come straight from the comics, where he eventually becomes Lex's Vice President, and in the course of the episode Lex admits that he wants to hold that office. Shuster's Gorge, where Sasha had the accident that gave her the power to control bees, is named after Superman co-creator Joe Shuster.

Paul's campaign flyer features him in Superman costume (the costume of the Crows' mascot) with his fists raised and the slogan I'LL FIGHT FOR YOU. A number of the slogans abbreviate President to 'Prez'. *The Prez* is a largely forgotten DC Comics' character, the world's first teenage president of the United States.

Sasha's powers make her not unlike an old DC Comics' villain, The Queen Bee. Is this a Queen Bee prequel story?

Trivia: The headlines on the *Torch* are STUDENT STUNG BY SWARM and STUDENT WALK-A-THON EXCEEDS FUND RECORD, so Chloe's editorial style has calmed down of late. Cassandra stages her breakdown on Route 90 – the same road on which Martha hit the runaway Ryan in **16**, 'Stray'. The sign at the Talon indicates the desperate situation – HALF PRICE LATTES ALL WEEK. Chloe's election editorial is headed

PAUL FOR PREZ. The headline of Cassandra's article on Lex reads PAPER TIGER. Clark's speech, in its references to making a difference, is reminiscent of the speech made by Lana's mother heard at the end of **4**, 'X-Ray'.

The Last Word: 'I stand for truth, justice, and ... other stuff.' Witty and sharp, 'Drone' is the closest the series has come so far to the best teen movies of recent years. The opening sequence is an impressive technical achievement, following a solitary bee around the election campaign and then segueing into a *10 Things I Hate About You*-style deconstruction of school cliques. A funny running joke about *The Godfather* is another tip-off that this is a more pop-culture savvy version of the show than we've previously seen. Cassandra is a good potential recurring ally for Lex, while Sasha has equal possibility as a returning nemesis, certainly if she's a *Smallville*-ised version of a certain character (see **From the Pages of**).

Above all, the episode has a point to make – that the love of the crowd can't be relied upon, and that the public always turns against people – that is delivered as a highly entertaining action show. It's light and fluffy, but considering the contents of the next three episodes that's probably not too bad a thing . . .

19
Crush

Production #227618
1st US Transmission Date: 7 May 2002
1st UK Transmission Date: 8 May 2002

Writers: Philip Levens, Alfred Gough and Miles Millar
Director: James Marshall
Special Guest Star: John Glover (Lionel Luthor)
Guest Starring: Adam Brody (Justin Gaines),
Hiro Kanagawa (Principal Kwan), Donna Bullock (Pamela)
Co-starring: James Purcell, Kevan Ohtsji (Danny Kwan), Anaya Farrell,
Catherine Barroll, Serge Houde (Mr Frankle)

Synopsis: Justin Gaines, former cartoonist for the *Torch*, has spent five months in a Metropolis hospital recovering from a hit-and-run accident that left him with crushed hands. Justin has a new ability: telekinesis, allowing him to draw without the use of his hands, and to take bloody revenge on anyone he feels is responsible for his current condition. Justin causes an elevator accident that cuts off the hands of the surgeon Justin felt didn't do enough for him. Justin returns to Smallville, where he rekindles his friendship with Chloe, a friendship that soon becomes a romance. Chloe finds out about Justin's power, but doesn't realise he has murderous intentions. Justin discovers it was Principal Kwan's car that ran over him, and he takes his revenge by smashing Kwan's car into him, killing the Principal. Justin doesn't realise that Kwan wasn't driving the car that night; it was his son Danny behind the wheel. When Chloe sees Justin's drawings of his revenge fantasies, she tries to get away from him to tell Clark, but Justin tries to kill her. Clark gets there just in time to stop Justin from chainsawing Chloe to pieces, and defeats Justin.

Lex's old nanny, Pamela, tracks him down in Smallville after having deserted him shortly after his mother's death. Pamela wants to reconcile, but Lex doesn't trust her, suspecting that she's after his money. Pamela claims that Lionel paid her off to leave, while Lionel claims that Pamela is nothing but a gold-digger. Lex rejects Pamela, but after he finds out that she is dying, and that Lionel approves of him rejecting her, he goes to visit Pamela at her hospital bed.

Whitney's father dies.

Speech Bubbles: Clark (on discovering Chloe likes him): 'I just can't believe I never saw it before.' Lana: 'Sometimes the right person can be right in front of your eyes and you never even know it.'

Clark: 'I've got these two amazing friends who both happen to be girls.' Lex: 'For argument's sake lets call them "Lana" and "Chloe".'

Small Town Boy: Clark alienates Chloe when he fails to book tickets to attend the Student Journalism Conference in Metropolis. Clark can't see why Chloe is so upset, especially over the fact that he was with Lana instead of arranging the tickets, until Pete finally reveals Chloe's feelings for Clark. As Justin and Chloe begin a romance, Clark's feelings for Chloe become increasingly confused.

Clark becomes resentful of Justin, which Chloe notices, causing her to dismiss his suspicion of her new boyfriend as jealousy. After Chloe berates him about his insensitivity, Clark reads *Men Are From Mars, Women Are From Venus*, the 1992 self-help bestseller by John Gray, and goes through a phase of self-examination. It's Lex who encourages him to make a decision – if he tries to protect his friendship with both girls, then he'll never be able to have either. Lex tells Clark that love is about risk.

Clark tells Lana that he regrets that they just stayed friends, and that he's not going to make the same mistake with Chloe. After saving Chloe from Justin, Clark says he admires her for being open with her emotions, and wishes he could be more like that. By the end of the episode Clark has got tickets to the Student Journalism Conference for himself and Chloe, and they hold hands over the table, seemingly settling where Clark's romantic ambitions now lie. While his friends look for summer jobs, Clark has to help out on the farm all summer.

Girl Next Door: Lana tells Clark that her relationship with Whitney is fine, but she isn't very convincing. With his father recovering, Whitney lavishes attention on Lana, but she tells Clark that their relationship can't just go back to what it was – it needs redefining. Lana becomes upset when she sees Clark and Chloe holding hands, and seems intent on telling Whitney something – until he announces that his father is dead.

According to Whitney, Lana has been reading Thornton Wilder's 1938 Pulitzer Prize-winning play *Our Town*, and he invites her to see it performed in Metropolis.

Not an Evil Genius: Lex's mother, Lillian Luthor, died in 1993, and he visits her tomb to place flowers. She seems to have passed a love of Walt Whitman on to Lex – the book that's constantly passed around during these scenes must be Whitman, as the lines Lionel reads and Lex quotes are from Whitman's *Song of Myself*, although Lionel slightly misquotes the first line. Pamela, Lex's former nanny, is the first person in the show to call Lex 'Alexander'. Lex tells Clark that he's only ever loved two women in his life – one died, and the other betrayed him. He tells Clark that some people – presumably including himself – are supposed to be alone. Tellingly, it's after Lionel feels reassured that Lex won't have any dealings with Pamela that Lex decides to visit his former nanny – rebellion against his father is still the main thing that drives him.

Bad Dad: After Lex's mother died, Lionel allegedly paid Lex's nanny, Pamela, to leave and never come back. Pamela claims that this was to make sure that Lex became Lionel's son, and had no civilising influence to tame him. Lionel retorts by claiming that Pamela was a hanger-on who conned Lex's mother out of valuable shares then ran off with the money before the body was cold.

Having bankrupted Sir Harry, Lionel thinks it's time to sell Cadmus Labs.

Torch Bearer: This is a very strong Chloe episode. Chloe has her heart set on working for the *Daily Planet* as an intern, rejecting Lex's standing offer of a gig at the *Metropolis Inquisitor*. The *Planet* takes four high-school interns from the whole state, and as there have been over five hundred applications Chloe is a bit concerned. She wanted to go with Clark to the Student Journalism Conference in Metropolis, and trusted Clark to book them in. When Clark forgets to do this because he was so busy with Lana, Chloe is understandably annoyed – especially as a day alone with Clark was the opportunity she needed to ask him to the Spring Formal. She lays into Clark for neglecting everyone else in favour of Lana and Lex.

Chloe's romance with Justin seems a natural one, as they're both passionate about their work: he loves his art, and she lives for journalism. When Justin shows her his telekinetic powers, Chloe takes it in her stride, accepting him for who he is. Chloe wants to think the best of Justin and rejects Clark's theory that Justin is involved in Kwan's death, blaming it on sour grapes on Clark's part. In spite of her attempts to break away from her infatuation, she's back to worshipping Clark by the end of the episode, although that handholding scene suggests she's closer to her goal than before . . .

Just the Funny Guy: Pete's mother is a judge, but rather than work for her over the summer Pete opts to go into politics (see **18**, 'Drone'), working at the Mayor's office.

The Quarterback: Early in the episode Clark mentions that he's heard Whitney's father is feeling better. This is clearly the pain fading before the end, as Fordman senior is soon dead. However, before then, Whitney is at his happiest, with his father at home and feeling better. Whitney, seeming nicer than ever before, is determined to repair his relationship with Lana, inviting her to the theatre.

Love's Young Dream: With Clark beginning to feel more for Chloe, and Lana still obligated to Whitney, they have a difficult and subtext-heavy discussion at Clark's house, where the unexpressed feelings between them are clear. Lana seems to be close to manoeuvring out of her relationship with Whitney – until his father dies, and he needs her once more.

Strange Visitors: Justin, artist of the 'Flaming Crow's Feet' comic strip in the *Torch*, who returns to school after five months recovering from a hit-and-run accident that left his hands broken. In spite of being able to create art using the power of telekinesis, Justin is still bitter at losing the use of his hands, taking revenge on the doctor who failed to do more for him, and the man he thinks ran him down. Justin goes full-blown psychotic when he feels even Chloe has betrayed him, using his powers to try and chainsaw her in half. Justin is knocked out at the end of the episode, and according to Chloe he's safely locked up in a psychiatric ward although, ominously, the police don't seem to know what they can charge him with. How long can they hold him, either legally or, considering his powers, physically? Justin is played with aggrieved passion by Adam Brody, and any return for the character would be welcome.

Music: The songs used in this episode are 'You and I' by Micah Green, '40 to 5' by Leave The World, 'Nothing To

Do' by Bottlefly, 'Light in Your Eyes' by Louise Goffin and '2001 Spliff Odyssey' by Thievery Corporation. The song heard at the funeral for Whitney's father as our characters exchange glances in the rain is 'Time After Time' as performed by posthumous chart sensation Eva Cassidy.

Secret Identities: Adam Brody was in *American Pie 2* and MTV's *Undressed*, and played Coop in *Once and Again*. Donna Bullock appeared in farcical Presidential thriller *Air Force One*, played Adair Peck in the two-part *Frasier* story 'Three Dates and a Breakup' and was Connie in three episodes of *Dallas*. James Purcell appeared in the *Robocop: Prime Directives* mini-series and *Death Wish 4: The Crackdown*. Kevan Ohtsji is sometimes credited as Kevin Ohtsji or Kevan Ohsji – he appeared opposite his screen father here, Hiro Kanagawa, in the *Lone Gunmen* episode 'Bond, Jimmy Bond', and played Takeshi in manga adaptation *Crying Freeman*. Serge Houde has a long career in film, including *The Score*, *Grey Owl*, *The Jackal* and *Look Who's Talking Now*, as well as episodes of the tawdry horror anthology *The Hunger*.

From the Pages of: Mayor Siegel is named after Jerry Siegel, co-creator of Superman. There's another joke about Clark flying while wearing a costume in the future, as he's courted by the Air Force.

Trivia: At the careers fair there are booths for the Air Force, the Navy, Kansas State University, the *Daily Planet*, the *Metropolis Inquisitor*, Polaroid, the Metropolis Police, Mayor Siegel's office, the local Fire Department and LuthorCorp.

The tombstone for Lex's mother reads 'Lillian Luthor, Loving Wife and Mother, 1951–1993'. The headline on the *Metropolis Inquisitor's* front page concerning Dr Wallace's accident reads GOING DOWN! DOCTOR LOSES HANDS IN FREAK ACCIDENT.

There's a wonderfully silly message on the Talon's sign this week: SONNET SATURDAYS – FREE PICK UP LINE WITH PURCHASE.

The Last Word: 'You know, most men are from Mars, Clark, but you're from some distant galaxy I've never even heard of.' The series starts punching some serious emotional buttons as tensions and romantic rivalries break out for real. Clark and Lana clearly still have a great mutual attraction, but an equally great awareness that they can't be together, leading to the wonderfully painful scenes where they discuss Chloe and Whitney at the farm and later at the Talon. The final funeral scene is beautiful, lacking any dialogue but telling a story simply with exchanged glances. Lingering images like Clark standing in the rain at the funeral, or Justin and Chloe kissing as items lift into the air around them, mark James Marshall out as one of the show's finest directors, one who can handle both action and subtler character moments. Possibly the best episode of the season, and certainly the most emotional, this is the moment when *Smallville* graduated from being entertaining and dramatic to really moving the audience with the fate of its characters. Wonderful and melancholy.

20
Obscura

Production #227619
1st US Transmission Date: 14 May 2002
1st UK Transmission Date: 15 May 2002

Story: Greg Walker
Teleplay: Michael Green and Mark Verheiden
Director: Terrence O'Hara
Guest Starring: Tom O'Brien (Roger Nixon),
Darrin Klimek (Deputy Gary Watts), Aaron Douglas (Deputy Birdego),
Robert Wisden (Gabe Sullivan), Joe Morton (Dr Hamilton)
Co-starring: Frank C Turner (Eddie Cole), John Dadey,
Mitchell Kosterman (Deputy Ethan Talbot)

Synopsis: Lana is caught in a gas explosion in which she is blasted with meteor fragments. The first people to reach her after the blast are Whitney and Deputies Watts and Birdego. In hospital, Lana finds that she has visions, seeing through someone else's eyes – and that person has kidnapped Chloe.

Initially everyone believes Chloe is in Metropolis with her cousin, as planned, but when she is confirmed missing a search begins. When Lana has a vision of Chloe being buried alive in a field with a windmill, Clark realises that she's in Chandler's Field. Clark rescues Chloe by pulling the coffin she's in out of the ground, but doesn't catch her kidnapper. Clark connects Lana's visions to the explosion, and presumes that one of the first people on the scene must be the kidnapper since the psychic bond was probably formed between people together at a traumatic event.

At the Talon, Birdego is interviewing Lana when Watts creeps up and knocks him out. Watts takes Lana to his fairground lair, the same fluffy-toy-filled space that Chloe was kept in. Watts tells Lana that he kidnapped Chloe so he could rescue her and take the credit. Now he'll become a hero by solving Lana's murder. Clark runs in and fights Watts, who is then gunned down by the police.

Roger Nixon has a story for Lex, concerning a crop-duster called Eddie Cole who claims to have seen a spaceship land on the night of the meteor shower. Lex pays Cole for his story, but tells Nixon it's just a tall tale. Lex gets Hamilton to check out the crash site, and they find an octagonal fragment made from an alien alloy – a piece which is exactly the same shape as an opening on the top of Clark's spaceship . . .

When his information is dismissed by Lex, Nixon follows up another lead, stalking Clark as he uses his powers.

Lex pays Jonathan compensation for the events of **14**, 'Zero'. Jonathan almost accepts the cheque, but refuses it when he finds out that Lex is investigating the crash site.

Clark invites Chloe to be his date for the Spring Formal.
Speech Bubbles: Lex: 'You look at the stars, Clark. Some of them have been extinguished for thousands of years, but their light is only reaching us now. The past is always influencing the present.'

Lex: 'I don't like riddles, Doctor.' Hamilton (on the fragment): 'Then this object will make you profoundly unhappy.'

Small Town Boy: Clark finally has to make a choice between Lana and Chloe as the Spring Formal approaches. When he says he doesn't want to close the door on the possibility of a relationship with Lana, his mother points out bluntly that the door is already closed. Chloe's kidnapping further reminds Clark of how much she means to him. Clark was assigned to show Chloe around school when she transferred from Metropolis, and his first kiss was with her. They have been friends ever since. Clark promises to visit Chloe in Metropolis over the summer while she's doing her internship. When he finally asks her to the Spring Formal, he apologises for not doing so earlier.

Clark tries to persuade Lex not to become obsessed with the meteor landings, but to no avail.

Girl Next Door: Lana develops psychic powers after being thrown about by a gas explosion, leading her not to trust whether she's having visions or becoming deluded. Kreuk plays Lana's disturbance well – when Lana arrives at the *Torch* looking for Chloe she's wonderfully jumpy, eyes darting back and forth. When Chloe is rescued, Lana is uncomfortable watching her being close to Clark. Lana then gets the eerie experience of seeing through Watts' eyes while he stalks *her*, and manages to get kidnapped. Again (see **2**, 'Metamorphosis' and **4**, 'X-Ray').

Not an Evil Genius: Lex reiterates to Nixon that the Kents are not just off limits, they are under his personal protection. However, when the meteor story comes into his hands, Lex can't stop delving into it, although he does get rid of Nixon before investigating. Lex lies about his purpose investigating the crash site, claiming that he's considering buying the land and needs to check what environmental effect the meteors had. Lex wants to pay Jonathan fair compensation for the toxic spill in **14**, 'Zero', but Jonathan returns the cheque. Lex's obsession with the meteor strike, and the crashed ship, is heightened by his possession of a genuine alien artefact.

Torch Bearer: Chloe is kidnapped early in the episode, but as she was supposed to be driving to Metropolis to take an

interview for the *Daily Planet* internship programme, no
one initially realises she is missing. Her disappearance leads
to some reminiscing from Clark: Chloe moved to Smallville from Metropolis in the 8th grade, and the first thing
she wanted to know from Clark was where she could get a
copy of the *Daily Planet* and keep in touch with civilisation. The young Chloe was fascinated by the fact that
Clark lived on a farm, and demanded to be invited over to
see for herself. She apparently confused being a farmer
with being Amish. When they first went up to the loft,
Chloe kissed Clark, telling him that she knew he'd been
thinking about it, and she wanted to get it out of the way
so they could be friends.

Chloe gets her internship, in spite of missing the
interview, meaning she will be in Metropolis through the
summer. Her kidnapping is big news, but Chloe doesn't
want to be in the *Planet* as a story, she wants to get there
as a journalist. Chloe has a cousin in Metropolis who she's
supposed to be staying with. This cousin is probably of
university age, as Chloe refers to staying in her dorm room.

Perhaps wary of Whitney's record at writing off trucks,
Chloe insists that she should drive her car when they go to
warn Lana.

Just the Funny Guy: Pete is taking Erica Fox, the hottest
girl in his class, to the Spring Formal, and asks Clark if he
wants to know his secret. The secret is that he asked her –
a technique he advises Clark to try.

The Quarterback: Whitney asks Lana to be his date to the
Spring Formal, saying that he isn't taking anything for
granted any more. While going through his late father's
property, Whitney finds medals for Fordman senior's
service in the Vietnam War, something he never talked
about. One is for exceptional valour, after Whitney's father
rescued three men in his unit during a firefight. Whitney
thinks this is a message from his father, that there's more
ways to do something with your life than throwing a
football. He talks about how good it feels to win games
and be called a hero, but that there's something more he
could be doing.

Down at the Farm: There's some traditional mother and father banter over Clark at the start of the episode, as Martha nags Clark about his love life while Jonathan wants to leave him to sort it out himself.

The generous compensation cheque the Kents receive for the chemical spill is, according to Lex, an exact reflection of the herd and grazing land lost. Jonathan tells Clark that he may be stubborn, but he's not blind, and that he's going to pay in the money. It seems that Jonathan is coming to an accommodation with Lex at last, Clark having persuaded him that pushing Lex out is just going to guarantee he'll become their worst fears.

Everything seems cosy, until Jonathan finds out that Lex is digging over the crash site, at which point he hands the cheque back.

Mad Scientist: Lex has Hamilton working on the field where Clark's ship crashed. Hamilton smiles for pretty much the first time, getting overexcited when he finds evidence of something alien landing in the field. Hamilton's cursory knock on Lex's study door as he barges in demonstrates again his wonderful lack of social skills.

Love's Young Dream: The stress of losing Chloe removes the sexual tension between Clark and Lana, to the extent that when she puts a comforting hand on his arm he barely registers it – something previously unthinkable. Chloe asks Clark to stay with her in the hospital after she's been rescued, and they hold hands. Clark asking Chloe to the Spring Formal is a romantic high point of the season.

Strange Visitors: Deputy Gary Watts, who plans to make a name for himself by kidnapping Chloe then rescuing her himself. He buries Chloe alive so he can find her, but Clark gets there first. Watts then decides that kidnapping Lana, killing her and solving the murder will be just the thing for his career. (There is no explanation as to who he will pin the murder on.) Watts is a loser – he moonlights as a security guard at the fairground.

The psychic connection between Watts and Lana after the gas explosion is, according to Clark, a case of De

Kretser Syndrome, which apparently causes these links to develop in times of stress or anger.

Another Planet: The first new alien artefact since **1**, 'Pilot' appears: an octagonal piece of alien alloy that fits into the front of the ship that brought Clark to Earth.

Mild-mannered Reporters: Clark is left holding the fort at the *Torch* while Chloe is in Metropolis. On his first morning the printer jams, the scanner breaks and the schedule for the Spring Formal is late. As Lana says, there doesn't seem to be any danger of Clark being claimed by the journalistic life at this stage . . .

Music: The songs heard in this episode are 'No Such Thing' by John Mayer, 'Just Another' by Pete Yorn, 'Two Stone in My Pocket' by Neil Halstead, 'Piano Fire' by Sparklehorse and 'Silent to the Dark' by indie youngsters Electric Soft Parade.

Secret Identities: Since appearing as a taxi driver in *Muriel's Wedding*, Darrin Klimek has done the usual rounds of *First Wave* and *Andromeda* as well as making an uncredited appearance in *The Thin Red Line*. Aaron Douglas plays another Deputy in *Final Destination 2*, and has had roles in *Stargate SG-1* and *Dark Angel*. Frank C Turner is a recognisable face from many films and TV shows, including the epic *Air Bud* trilogy, *Unforgiven*, *The X-Files*, *We're No Angels*, *Cats & Dogs* and *Insomnia*.

From the Pages of: The symbols on the bottom of the alien fragment are the same shape as the Superman symbol.

Loose Ends: Why doesn't Lana recognise the windmill in Chandler's Field in her vision, when in **15**, 'Nicodemus' she was obsessed with climbing it? Is this because the writers want Clark to work things out, or because they decided to reuse an old location and barely altered the script? When Clark rescues Chloe, why isn't she suspicious that he found her buried in the middle of a field then pulled a coffin out of the ground without any visible assistance? Watts is a bowling friend of Gabe Sullivan's, but it's never shown how Gabe reacts to his friend kidnapping his daughter. However, the biggest question of all is how Nixon traces Clark and manages to shadow him so effectively.

Trivia: The flyer for Cole's crop-dusting business has the slogan GREAT RATES FOR ALL JOBS, NOTHING TO LARGE, NOTHING TO SMALL (sic). The sign at the Talon reads JUMPIN JAVA – BEBOP FRIDAYS.

The Last Word: 'Clark Kent leaps tall theories in a single bound!' An exciting but very silly episode, 'Obscura' is tense but nonsensical. Lana's visions are very similar to the sequences in Joss Whedon's TV series *Angel*, right down to Lana's spasms of pain as they set in (although the visual language of these kind of scenes has been fixed for quite a while in television and film, so they're not an invention of the *Angel* production team). Watts' plan is exceedingly stupid, and as such the kidnapping plot fails to hang together. However, Lana's visions are suitably scary, and all the plot development with Lex and Nixon leave the audience breathlessly awaiting the season finale. All this, and Chloe and Clark possibly getting it together? One can forgive plot problems when the overall arc is moving in such an interesting direction.

21
Tempest

Production #227620
1st US Transmission Date: 21 May 2002
1st UK Transmission Date: 22 May 2002

Story: Philip Levens
Teleplay: Alfred Gough and Miles Millar
Director: Greg Beeman
Special Guest Star: John Glover (Lionel Luthor)
Guest Starring: Robert Wisden (Gabe Sullivan),
Tom O'Brien (Roger Nixon)
Co-starring: Don Thompson, Scott Bellis, Angelika Baran
Musical Guest: Remy Zero

Synopsis: Lionel Luthor visits the LuthorCorp plant to make an announcement – the plant is closing immediately. Lex is disgusted, but Lionel tells him he doesn't belong in Smallville – it's time to come home to Metropolis.

The closure of the town's biggest employer makes Lex a pariah in Smallville, although Clark still wants to believe in him, and casts a shadow over preparations for the Spring Formal, as Chloe and her father may be going back to Metropolis for good now the plant is closing.

Whitney is also leaving – he is following in his father's footsteps and joining the US Marine Corps. He ships out for training on the night of the Spring Formal.

While Clark and Lana try to come to terms with Chloe and Whitney's imminent departures, Lex battles to save the plant through a management buyout. One of his former associates has something to sell – a story on Clark Kent – but Lex isn't interested. Nixon steals the alien fragment from Lex's desk, and causes the Kents' truck to explode, taping Clark's survival as evidence of his superhuman powers. Nixon later confronts Clark, saying he wants to write a story about him. Lionel blocks Lex's attempt at a management buyout by buying up the Smallville Savings & Loan. If the workers take out loans to buy shares, Lionel will foreclose on their loans and ruin them all.

As the Spring Formal begins, a storm is brewing. Clark and Chloe arrive at school just as Lana and Whitney are leaving to take him to the bus station. Whitney asks Clark to look after Lana for him while he's away. Lana drives Whitney to the bus station, but on her way back finds herself blown off the road by a storm.

In the Kents' storm cellar, Nixon's alien fragment jumps out of his hand. The Kents confront Nixon, and Jonathan chases him out into the storm, while in the cellar the spaceship begins to come to life and rise up.

At the dance, Clark and Chloe are about to kiss when an announcement is made about tornadoes in the area. Clark realises Lana is in danger and runs out, leaving Chloe.

Lionel confronts Lex in his office, the confrontation becoming increasingly violent. The storm shatters the windows of the mansion, and masonry crumbles. Lionel is trapped under rubble, leaving Lex hesitant as to whether he should help his father and enemy.

Lana hides from a number of twisters as they approach, sheltering in her truck. As a tornado sucks up Lana in her truck, Clark arrives. As Lana is swept away, Clark runs into the maelstrom after her.

To be continued . . .

Speech Bubbles: Chloe: 'Just promise me Saturday night's going to be great.' Clark: 'It'll be a night you won't forget.'

Lana: 'I guess we get left behind, Clark.'

Lionel: 'You're not my enemy, you're my son.' Lex: 'I never saw the distinction.'

Small Town Boy: Everything is coming together for Clark with the Spring Formal approaching, until Lionel Luthor announces the closure of the LuthorCorp plant, raising the possibility that Chloe will be returning to Metropolis forever. Clark then has to deal with Nixon finding out about his powers, proving Clark's abilities by blowing up the truck that he's sitting in. Clark tells Whitney that he'll look after Lana while he's gone. Clark reassures Chloe that he's going to the Formal with her because he wants to, not as a default. Clark promises to Chloe that her night will be perfect, and that he won't desert her. But when the tornadoes approach, and Clark knows that Lana is out there, he leaves Chloe to help Lana.

With the announcement of the plant's closure, Clark retains his faith in Lex, defending him and blaming the decision on Lionel. Clark knows that Lex had big plans for Smallville.

The development of Clark's strength and invulnerability continues. When Nixon blows up the truck, Clark emerges without a scratch, having barely felt the heat. After he finds out that Chloe may be leaving, Clark works out his aggression by throwing fence posts into the ground on the farm. The greatest potential test of Clark's powers comes in the cliffhanger, when he runs straight into a tornado to try and help Lana.

Girl Next Door: When Whitney takes her on a romantic picnic, and says he's got something he wants to ask her, Lana seems to panic as if he's about to propose. Her reaction to his announcement that he's shipping out to join the marines is one of shock. As she tells Clark later, she just stood there in silence. Lana can't believe that Chloe and Whitney could be out of their lives for good. Lana doesn't answer when Whitney asks her to wait for him, but as they say goodbye she rushes to kiss him, giving him her necklace for good luck.

When Lana sees Chloe being kissed on the cheek by Clark, she visibly glowers with jealousy. Her comments about Chloe and Whitney leaving seem ambivalent, as if she partially wants them out of the way.

Not an Evil Genius: In a packed episode, Lex still manages to get some stand-out moments. When Lionel wants to force Lex to return to Metropolis (after his persuasion failed in **16**, 'Stray'), Lex decides to fight back. Putting aside his meteor obsession, Lex concentrates on trying to get together a management buyout to save the jobs of his employees. This is Lex at his most heroic, fighting for his workforce against his father's machinations. Lex's plan relies on the management providing 10 per cent of the capital, but Lionel's takeover of the local Savings & Loan, allowing him to foreclose and evict any management who take out mortgages to fund the bid, cripples Lex's plan.

On the night of the storm Lionel and Lex come into conflict when Lionel finds out that Lex is using his mother's stock to fund the buyout. Lex says he's forging a new future, one free of Lionel. Lionel is aghast – he isn't Lex's enemy. Lex can't see the difference. As the storm tears into the building, and Lionel is trapped beneath masonry that threatens to crush him, Lex is sorely, visibly tempted to let him die. That's the beauty of the episode; Lex goes from his most heroic to potentially his most evil in the space of a scene, from defying his father to letting him die. It's a dazzling, dramatic character arc. No wonder Lex describes his relationship with Lionel as complicated.

Lex's relationship with Clark survives Lex's reputation as the town pariah after Lionel blames the closure of the plant on Lex's failings. Lex warns Clark about Nixon and the *Inquisitor*, advising him to stay away from them. On the night of the Formal and the storm, Lex warns Clark that his attempt to save the plant is going to get worse before it gets better. Lex tells Clark that he wants him to know that whatever happens, he's still his friend and Clark should look after himself. In a lovely moment, Lex helps Clark to tie his bow tie.

Lex loses his alien fragment, which is stolen by Nixon. Lex tries to warn Nixon to stay away from the Kents, but Nixon threatens to go to Lionel with what he has found.

Bad Dad: Lionel believes that he is training Lex to be strong, not making his son into his own enemy. His determination to bring Lex back to his side leads to epic acts of ruthlessness – Lionel gathers the entire staff of the plant to tell them that they're fired due to Lex's incompetent management, effectively ruining 2,500 lives and destroying Lex's reputation. His gambit in buying the Smallville Savings & Loan is even more ruthless – not only is he willing to sack these people, he will evict them as well if Lex doesn't step back into line. Still, Lionel believes he is making Lex into a worthy heir, telling Lex about Alexander the Great leaving his legacy to whoever was the strongest. Lionel tells Lex he'll bury him and anyone who supports him. When Lex describes him as an enemy, Lionel is actually shocked, only then realising how far things have gone between father and son.

Torch Bearer: With the threat of her father taking the family back to Metropolis, Chloe is determined not to cancel her date with Clark; she wants to enjoy it while she can, and gets Clark to promise the night will be perfect. Chloe talks to Clark about how Lana will essentially be a free agent. Chloe says that, even if Lana says she'll wait for Whitney, long-distance relationships never work – just like her and Clark who, she says, will forget her within a fortnight of her leaving for Metropolis. Chloe is afraid that as soon as Whitney is on the bus, Clark will run to Lana and confess his undying love, leaving Chloe alone at the dance. Chloe warns Clark that if he does that, she'll never speak to him again.

In a neat moment, Chloe affectionately flicks a bit of fluff from Clark's collar. Her dress for the Formal is a lovely red affair with a pattern down one seam. At the dance, Chloe and Clark have their picture taken several

times, and dance to Chloe's favourite song. They are about
to kiss when the announcement is made that the tornadoes
are approaching, causing Clark to cut and run, leaving
Chloe alone.

Just the Funny Guy: Pete changes the colour of the tie and
cummerbund he has booked for the Spring Formal so it
doesn't match with Clark – he claims this is so people don't
mistake them for twins!

The Quarterback: Finding his father's medals in **20**,
'Obscura' has had a profound effect on Whitney, who
takes it as a sign that he should enlist with the United
States Marine Corps. (As he had to work at the family
store when his father was ill, who is going to run the place
with Whitney gone and his father dead? Never mind, eh?)
Whitney tells Lana he's loved her since he first saw her,
and will still love her when he comes back. She's the only
thing he will miss in Smallville. On their last day together,
Whitney and Lana look at the Smallville High trophy case,
where all Whitney's achievements are kept. He says these
achievements feel trivial. Whitney has a delightful farewell
prepared for Lana, with them in the gym – set up for the
Spring Formal – dancing alone before the event.

There's a wonderful scene where Whitney talks to Clark
about the weird year they've had, and apologises to Clark
for the bad things he's done to him. He goes on to say that
Lana isn't sure about their relationship, but Whitney is.
Whitney asks Clark to look after Lana until he gets back.

Down at the Farm: The plant was Smallville's biggest
employer, and its closure is going to have a domino effect
on everyone, including the Kent farm. Jonathan believes
Lex has run the plant into the ground in just a year.

When Clark tells his parents about Nixon, and how he
thinks Nixon caused the truck to explode, he berates
himself for not being careful enough about using his
powers in public. Jonathan tells Clark to go on living his
life – if Nixon has something he'll come to Clark's parents,
and they'll deal with him. Having seen the fragment on
Lex's desk, Clark tells his parents that he thinks Lex has
part of the spaceship, and that it is the missing piece.

Jonathan and Martha insist that Lex can't trace the fragment to them. They agree that Clark shouldn't use his abilities and should stay away from the storm cellar. Unfortunately, Nixon has them bugged and is listening in, leading to Jonathan's violent confrontation with Nixon and the activation of the spaceship.

Another Planet: Nixon takes the alien fragment from Lex's desk and to the Kent's storm cellar, where it jumps out of his hand and into its slot on the front of the ship. The ship levitates, glows and begins to open up.

Strange Visitors: No mutants, just the conniving Nixon and a bit of bad weather.

Music: Remy Zero, who perform 'Save Me', the theme tune to the series, appear within the show as the band at the Spring Formal, in a wonderfully cheesy sequence where they lip-sync and Clark shows his appreciation. Apart from 'Save Me' they also perform a song called 'Perfect Memory', which is one of Chloe's favourite songs but mainly accompanies Lana driving after leaving Whitney at the bus stop. The song 'Everything' by Lifehouse, so effectively used at the end of the pilot episode, reappears here during Whitney and Lana's last dance. Other tracks in this episode are 'What Do I Have To Do?' by Stabbing Westward, 'Where This Love Goes' by Sherri Youngward, 'Breathe' by Greenwheel, 'Let Go' by Gigolo Aunts and 'What We've Been Through' by Paul Trudeau.

Secret Identities: Scott Bellis played Max Fenig in three episodes of *The X-Files*, including the eponymous 'Max'. He also played Randy in *Anti-Trust* and Ricky in *Timecop*.

From the Pages of: Lana tells Clark that red is his colour. Her description of Whitney's role in the marines – wearing a uniform and saving the world – makes him sound like a superhero.

Trivia: The headline of the *Ledger*'s special edition reads LUTHORCORP PLANT TO CLOSE – 'MANAGEMENT PROBLEMS' SITED (sic). According to Martha the last time the *Smallville Ledger* rushed out a special edition was for the meteor shower. This week's initial Talon sign caption is SMALLVILLE'S BEST CAPPUCCINO, but later it changes to CONGRATS

GRADS – NOW WHAT. (Presumably Lana doesn't have a question mark.)

The Last Word: 'Storms are a way of life around here, Lex. Trick is not to get caught out in the open.' Now *that* is how you leave an audience on the edge of their seats for the summer. 'Tempest' is relentless, shaking up every status quo and piling on a ton of cliffhangers in its last ten minutes. From the activation of the spaceship to Clark's headlong run into a tornado, the action just doesn't stop in the final act of this show. Most of the characters are left in a state of uncertainty, suspended in peril until next season. There's Lex, blood dripping down his face, caught between good and evil as he struggles with whether he should save his father or let him die. Chloe, deserted at her moment of possible happiness. Jonathan and Nixon running out into the storm, Clark's father possibly intent on murdering to keep his family's secret. Martha and the activated spaceship. And finally there's Lana and Clark, caught up in those fantastic computer-generated twisters.

Will LuthorCorp tear the town to pieces? Can Chloe and Clark be together after he deserted her? Will Lex or Jonathan kill to get what they want? How exactly can Clark save Lana? All questions left tantalisingly open at the end of this brilliant episode. The series seemed to hit a status quo very early in the season, but with 'Tempest' *Smallville* finally proves that it's about more than meteor mutants, and that it can step beyond formula and shake up everything the audience took for granted.

Season Two

Superman created by Jerry Siegel and Joe Shuster
Developed for television by Alfred Gough & Miles Millar
Executive Producers: Alfred Gough, Miles Millar, Mike Tollin,
Brian Robbins and Joe Daviola
Music by Mark Snow

Regular Cast:
Tom Welling (Clark Kent)
Kristin Kreuk (Lana Lang)
Michael Rosenbaum (Lex Luthor)
Sam Jones III (Pete Ross)
Allison Mack (Chloe Sullivan)
John Glover (Lionel Luthor)
Annette O'Toole (Martha Kent)
John Schneider (Jonathan Kent)

The Episodes

22
Vortex

Production #175051
1st US Transmission Date: 24 September 2002

Writers: Alfred Gough and Miles Millar
Teleplay by Philip Levens
Director: Greg Beeman
Guest Starring: Tom O'Brien (Roger Nixon)
Co-starring: Rekha Sharma, Julian Christopher, Jerry Wasserman,
Mitchell Kosterman (Deputy Ethan Talbot)

Synopsis: Clark grabs on to Lana's truck in the eye of the tornado, pulling himself into the truck and protecting her from the storm. The alien ship flies into the tornado after Clark, but when the artefact flips out of its place the ship falls to Earth. Lex tries to help his father, but the building collapses on them. Jonathan chases Nixon through the storm, and they find themselves trapped in an old crypt, their escape route buried beneath a falling motor home. When the storm dies down Clark is left in the devastated landscape with an unconscious Lana.

Lana recovers quickly in hospital, but is haunted by an inexplicable memory of Clark rescuing her. Lex gets Lionel to the hospital, then joins Clark's search for his father. Trapped in the crypt, Jonathan and Nixon argue over Clark's future. The lead-lined crypt stops Clark from using his X-ray vision, and when Lex calls Nixon on his mobile phone Jonathan smashes it, preferring to die than see Nixon tell Lex about Clark. When they hear Clark and the search party outside, Jonathan and Nixon scramble towards the air supply, trying to be heard, but cause a collapse. The air is cut off, and Nixon and Jonathan are left lying in a pile of meteor rocks.

A map provided by Lex leads Clark to the crypt. He bursts in but collapses under the influence of the meteor rocks. Nixon stuffs Clark's pockets with rocks, intending to take him away and show him to the world. Jonathan and Nixon fight, and Nixon is on the verge of killing

Jonathan when Lex arrives, shooting Nixon dead. Jonathan throws the rocks away from Clark.

Clark and Chloe agree to go back to being just good friends.

Under Lex's instructions, surgeons proceed to operate as soon as possible on Lionel. They succeed in saving him from paralysis, but leave him blind.

Speech Bubbles: Jonathan: 'Clark is not a story, he's my son.' Nixon: 'He's not your son, you deluded hick! He's not even human!'

Nixon: 'Dying in a tomb. That's ironic.'

Lana (to Clark in his barn): 'Just remember, you can't hide out here forever.'

Small Town Boy: Clark manages to save Lana, then leaves her at the hospital while he runs off to check on his parents. Much of the episode sees him driven by the need to locate his father and unwilling to tolerate any distractions from that task. He even shouts down Lex when he thinks his friend is still working with Nixon, and says that Jonathan could have been right all along. Clark believes that he brought Jonathan's disappearance upon himself.

Clark takes Chloe's decision that they should just be friends with calm bemusement, perhaps because he has bigger things on his mind. At the end of the episode Clark tells his father one of these distractions – when he was in the tornado, Clark felt as if he were flying.

Clark is still consistently lying to everyone around him, which leads him into trouble with Lana . . .

Girl Next Door: Lana has a memory of Clark flying towards her in the storm. While she isn't sure she can believe that memory, she knows Clark isn't telling her the truth about her rescue. As opposed to many of the characters in the show (Lionel, Lex, Chloe, Hamilton et al), Lana has no great use to which to put the information about Clark's true nature. It doesn't matter to Lana what Clark's secret is – it matters to her that he's a liar and that he doesn't trust her enough to share his secrets with her. With Whitney gone, this sets up a new barrier to keep the series' key romantic couple apart.

It also represents a change for Lana – she tells Martha that she always thought she would die young, so when she saw the twisters she thought her ticket was up. As with Lex in **1**, 'Pilot', Lana feels that Clark has somehow subverted the order of things and given her a second chance.

Lana is not comfortable with being on news reports again, after becoming a *Time* cover star after the meteor shower (see **1**, 'Pilot').

Not an Evil Genius: As in **21**, 'Tempest', Lex's actions signify both his struggles to be heroic and his darker impulses. Lex helps Clark find his father and is far more open with his friend than before, but his motivations are not entirely clear. Most telling of all is the shooting of Nixon. The Kents read this as a brave act, as Lex saving Jonathan's life. This is the first time the audience sees Lex kill someone and the expression as he looks down on Nixon's corpse shows that Lex himself is shocked by what he has done. When he shakes hands with Jonathan at the end of the episode, they commit to a fresh start, and Lex seems set on a new course. He's more open, and no longer involved with the likes of Nixon any more. He's concerned with looking after his ailing father.

But questions remain over Lex's motivations. Did he shoot Nixon just to save Jonathan, or at least partially to make sure Nixon took Lex's secrets to the grave? When Lionel's operation leaves him blind, does this teach Lex that good deeds lead to bad results? Either way, when Lex stands over Nixon with a smoking gun in his hand, a clear picture begins to emerge of exactly how far the young Luthor is capable of going.

Bad Dad: Lionel joins the regular cast of the series with this episode, which sees a period of détente begin between Lex and his father. Lex's decision that Lionel should be operated on immediately is one that Lionel admits he would have made himself, but they both would have been wrong – the operation leaves Lionel blind. Lionel will, however, walk again, and seems conciliatory towards Lex. Lionel tells Lex that he saw him hesitate and thanks him for saving his life in spite of the urge to let him die.

Torch Bearer: Clark's desertion of Chloe at the dance, and his subsequent rescue of Lana, leave Chloe in a catch-22 situation. Her suspicion that Clark will always think of Lana first has been confirmed, but it would be ignoble of her to punish Clark for saving someone's life. Instead Chloe takes the easy way out, telling a baffled Clark that she wants to go back to being just friends. Allison Mack does a brilliant tortured-Chloe routine when she is reduced to tears after she breaks up with Clark. She then feels guilty because she's upset about Clark while those around her are trying to cope with a real tragedy.

It's impossible not to feel sorry for Chloe, especially as she tries to delete the romantic photos of her and Clark at the dance from her computer's memory. In the end she can't bring herself to trash them – like Clark with his infatuation with Lana, Chloe can't move beyond the feelings that are holding her back.

Down at the Farm: Jonathan spends most of the episode trapped in the crypt with Nixon and conducts a long argument with the journalist about who Clark is and what his future should be. Nixon argues that Clark belongs to the world, and that the world deserves to know about him. He thinks Jonathan is deluded to pretend that he's good enough for Clark, since Clark's existence represents a step forward in human knowledge. Jonathan argues that Clark is his son, first and foremost, and that he needs to be protected – from influences such as Nixon and people who would encourage him to use his abilities to gain power.

Another Planet: The spaceship, once activated by the artefact jumping into its slot, lifts out of the storm cellar and seems to head straight for Clark, flying into the maelstrom. However, the artefact gets knocked out of place, deactivating the ship. The ship is left lying in a field at the end of the episode.

Music: This is one of the more score-driven episodes, dominated by Mark Snow's music, but a couple of pop tracks are present. 'Time and Time Again' by Stretch Princess and 'In My Place' by Coldplay can be heard, the latter playing wistfully over the final scene.

Trivia: The new season brought a new title sequence, with new clips and character shots, as well as the departure of Eric Johnson and the inclusion of John Glover in the regular cast.

Chloe alludes to L Frank Baum's *The Wizard of Oz*, calling Lana 'Dorothy'. In that story, of course, a girl was whisked away by a tornado in Kansas, and it also featured a building falling from the sky in a very similar way to the motor home falling on Jonathan and Nixon.

The sign at the Talon reads TORNADO RELIEF CENTER.

The Last Word: 'These events change you, wipe out your illusions. You discover things about yourself.' A fine balance between character and plot momentum, 'Vortex' resolves all the cliffhangers from **21**, 'Tempest', but thankfully stops short of reinstating the status quo, instead leaving questions to be answered and new plotlines on the boil. The arguments between Jonathan and Nixon over Clark's future get to the heart of Clark's character and the importance of his upbringing in making him into the hero he will become. These scenes give a potentially scrappy episode a spine of serious content and underline many of the show's recurring themes.

In production terms, this is a step up from even the heights of the Season One cliffhanger. The pre-title sequence in particular is spectacular as Clark flies towards Lana in the eye of the storm and debris rains down on Jonathan and Nixon. The fight between Nixon and Jonathan at the episode's end is impressively brutal, while all the post-tornado scenes of recovery are suitably crowded. After a highly successful first year, it seems *Smallville* has been given an even bigger budget to play with in its second season.

And this is, most of all, the start of a new season, with the character dynamics subtly – and sometimes radically – changed. Lex's conflict with his father is largely resolved, and he's patched up his relationship with Jonathan. Lana, her life changed by being saved by Clark, knows something is not right with her friend. A wedge has been driven between Clark and Chloe. It's all change, and there's more to come. Excellent.

23
Heat

Production #175052
1st US Transmission Date: 1 October 2002

Writer: Mark Verheiden
Director: James Marshall
Guest Starring: Krista Allen (Desiree Atkins)
Co-starring: Shawn Reis, Mitchell Kosterman (Sheriff Ethan Talbot)

Synopsis: The new school year begins bringing a heatwave, a new biology teacher in the sexy form of Desiree Atkins, and a new problem for Clark – his eyes start sending out rays of heat in class and start a fire as the students watch a sex education film. Clark is attracted to Desiree, but finds out that she is Lex's fiancée and that Lex wants Clark to be his best man at the wedding that night.

Lex and Desiree are married only a fortnight after they met, Desiree controlling Lex with a pink mist that passes from her to him when they kiss. After the wedding Clark talks to Lana, and she begins to mention acting on their passion. Clark accidentally sets the coffee machine at the Talon on fire with his heat vision, so Jonathan gets Clark to practice his heat vision to get it under control by thinking of what was in his mind when it switched on. Clark blows a few things up, but eventually masters his new ability.

Desiree visits Clark in his barn, tries to seduce him, fails and tells Lex that Clark tried to seduce her. Lex is suspicious when he finds out that Desiree changed her name from Alison Sanders, but she hits him with the pink mist and he drops the matter. Lex tries to evict Lana from the Talon, using the fire as a pretext, but Clark realises Desiree is behind the decision and confronts her; Desiree tells Clark that if he gets in her way she'll turn Lex against the town, all his friends and family. Desiree sets her own car on fire, and Clark is arrested on suspicion of causing all the recent fires. Jonathan goes to visit Desiree, but she also uses the pink mist on him. Lana and Chloe visit Clark in jail and tell him Desiree's background (see **Strange**

Visitors) so Clark realises his father went to see Desiree. He starts a fire using his heat vision, and escapes in the confusion.

At the Luthor mansion Lex confronts Desiree, realising he's not himself, but Desiree has Jonathan come at Lex with a shotgun. Clark runs in and blasts a bullet out of the air with his heat vision before it can hit Lex. Clark knocks out his father, and Desiree sets Lex on fire with liquor. Clark puts Lex out and superheats the doorknob with his vision so that Desiree burns herself, collapsing with a scream. The arson charges are dropped thanks to Lex's statement and Clark gets off with a warning. Desiree is gone. Lex apologises to Clark.

Lana makes a video letter to Whitney, but finds her own contribution hard to compose. She eventually decides to tell the difficult truth.

Speech Bubbles: Miss Atkins: 'It looks like we're going to have to suffer through this together.' Pete: 'Bring on the pain!'

Clark: 'Next time I have a date, I'll be able to take her out without setting her on fire!'

Chloe: 'Lucky for us, Clark Kent seems immune to some members of the opposite sex.'

Small Town Boy: New season, new power – Clark develops heat vision, which is turned on when Clark is ... well, turned on. The main source of Clark's excitement is Desiree, but the second time the heat vision is activated it's at the Talon with Lana. Clark is suitably freaked out, and avoids school for fear of starting another fire and hurting someone. After some practice deliberately activating the heat, Clark gets it under control and can use it with enough precision to pop corn and light candles. The slow motion melting of the bullet is exceptionally impressive.

Clark stutters his way through his video message to Whitney, but refers to the agreement they made in **21**, 'Tempest'. He tells Lex that he's willing to wait for Lana to sort out her feelings for Whitney before making his move.

Clark hardly got in touch with Chloe over the summer, and claims this was because of work on the farm. Clark does talk to her at Lex's wedding and she agrees to be friends, but Clark still suffers her waspish and pointed comments throughout the episode.

Girl Next Door: Lana composes a video letter to Whitney, who is abroad with the Marines. She gets quotes from all his friends, but cannot compose her own contribution because she has so much to say. She tells Clark that she misses Whitney, but that it's difficult putting her life on hold, and she doesn't think it was the wisest decision. She decides to be honest with her feelings, and to tell him the truth in her message, even though it will be hard. She tells Clark that a relationship can't be built on secrets and lies.

Lana thinks Lex's whirlwind relationship is romantic, albeit weird. She admires Chloe for taking a risk on her feelings for Clark. They decide to become friends and not to let Clark get in the way of that. Lana is suspicious that Clark was the one person immune to Desiree's charms. She's also suspicious of his presence at all the fires and his jailhouse escape.

Lana has a wonderful involuntary laugh as she watches the boys drool over Desiree in biology class.

Not an Evil Genius: Lex isn't himself, falling under the spell of Desiree and her pheromones. He isn't surprised to find that Clark helped when there was a fire in the classroom but, when he thinks that Clark tried to seduce Desiree, Lex feels betrayed by the one person he could trust. Lex eventually breaks his conditioning as he realises that he's not acting like himself, and gets an annulment to the marriage. He tells Clark that he has learned not to let his passion get the better of him, and he admires the way Clark restrains himself with Lana.

Lex buys the Talon a giant new coffee machine as an apology for trying to evict Lana, and also gives her roses and rewrites the contract to remove his buyout clause.

Torch Bearer: Chloe returns from her summer in Metropolis, and is less than happy to see Clark again after their break-up in **22**, 'Vortex'. Her discomfort is visible when he hugs her, and she confides in him that, while working at the *Daily Planet*, she met a hot young intern who made her forget about Smallville altogether for three months (this is a lie, she still has feelings for Clark). At the wedding, she tells Clark about pheromones, and that some people have chemistry between them and others don't. She admits to letting her feelings get the better of her. This new-model Chloe is deeply cynical, and doesn't believe Clark when he says Desiree tried to seduce him.

Chloe's message to Whitney demands an exclusive interview from him when he gets home. Chloe tells Lana that going to the Spring Formal with Clark was a mistake, and she got hurt. She knows that Clark cares for her, but not as much as he cares for Lana.

Just the Funny Guy: Pete, with his natural showmanship, is perfect on camera when asked for a quote for the video letter to Whitney.

Down at the Farm: The Kents are suffering in the heat as they don't have air conditioning because it would lead to a prohibitively expensive electricity bill. When she finds out about the sex education film Clark was watching when his heat vision kicked in, Martha is the one who diagnoses that it could be hormonal. Jonathan persuades Clark to consider what he was thinking when the heat vision started, and gives Clark a scarecrow to stare at. When Clark is arrested, Jonathan tells him to co-operate. Martha tries to get through to Lex, telling him that she defended him to Jonathan and now thinks her husband was right. When Desiree seduces Jonathan, she uses his resentment of Lex to turn him into a potential killer.

Strange Visitors: Desiree Atkins – briefly Luthor – has a pheromonal power that allows her to control human men, but not Clark. All it takes for her to take command is to get close. Desiree used to be Alison Sanders, and originally came from Smallville. She was in a parked truck with her boyfriend when the meteors hit, gifting her with pheromonal powers to turn men into her slaves. First she got her boyfriend to murder her parents and inherited everything; then she married a shipping executive and one of her students killed her husband. When she invested money in dotcoms and lost it all, she decided to pursue Lex.

From the Pages of: No other version of the Superman story has ever used heat vision as a metaphor for out-of-control teenage hormones!

Secret Identities: Krista Allen played the title role of Emmanuelle in the 90s films, as well as Kristy Hopkins in *CSI: Crime Scene Investigation* and the Oracle in *Charmed*. Shawn Reis has appeared in *Dark Angel* and *Monk*.

Music: The opening song is 'My Friends Over You' by New Found Glory; 'Hot in Herre' by Nelly plays in the classroom scene. While Clark tests his powers, the JXL remix of the Elvis Presley track 'A Little Less Conversation' can be heard. Also in the episode are 'Tomorrow' by punky youngster Avril Lavigne and 'Truth or Dare' by rock/rap outfit N*E*R*D.

Loose Ends: What happens to Desiree at the end of the episode? Lex mentions that she's gone, but is she in jail or has she just been encouraged to leave town?

Trivia: If Desiree is from Smallville, how come no one recognises her at her very public wedding to Lex?

The Last Word: 'Quit staring, Clark. You'll burn your eyes out.' By far the funniest episode of the series so far, 'Heat' isn't quite a full-blown comedy, but gets damn close at times. Whereas the first series seemed perpetually in fear of highlighting the silliness of superpowers, the production team demonstrate a new confidence that allows the development of Clark's heat vision to be played mostly for laughs. The idea of Clark's heat vision being tied to his sexual awakening is fantastic and very funny, and the cast grab this opportunity and run with it. Tom Welling, in particular, demonstrates some sublime comic acting and his reaction to the symbolic popcorn-popping is priceless.

On a more serious note the heat-vision effect is excellent and a radical departure from the laser beams used to denote the power in most other versions of *Superman*.

24
Duplicity

Production #175053
1st US Transmission Date: 8 October 2002

Writers: Todd Slavkin and Darren Swimmer
Director: Steve Miner
Guest Starring: Sarah Jane Redmond (Aunt Nell),
Joe Morton (Dr Hamilton)
Co-starring: Andrew Jackson (Ray Wallace), Michael Kopsa (Dean),
Cameron Cronin (Dr Glenn)

Synopsis: Lex fires an increasingly unstable and unreliable Dr Hamilton. An agitated, pill-popping Hamilton then causes Ray Wallace to drive into a field and flip his truck. Hamilton drives off just as Pete approaches and Pete finds Clark's spaceship in the field near Wallace's truck . . .

Pete thinks that the spaceship is the key to his fortune, and the next day he takes his best and trusted friend, Clark, to the field to retrieve it. Clark reluctantly helps Pete to hide the ship in Pete's shed. That night Clark and Jonathan go to steal the ship back, and find it has already gone but Pete sees them leave and presumes they stole the ship. When Pete confronts Clark, Clark is forced to reveal his secret. Pete freaks out, betrayed by the fact that Clark has lied to him all these years.

After hearing rumours about the ship, Dr Hamilton confronts Ray Wallace and then kills him to cover his tracks before stealing the ship. He wants the octagonal artefact he found for Lex to unlock the ship, but Lex no longer has it. Hamilton interests Lionel in the spaceship, taking Lionel back to his barn to feel it. If Hamilton can unlock the ship, Lionel would be interested in funding him.

Increasingly deranged, Hamilton kidnaps Pete. Prolonged exposure to the meteors is killing Hamilton and he needs Pete to tell him who owns the ship. Clark rescues Pete, while Hamilton dies of a meteor overdose, jittering himself to death. When Lionel takes Lex to Dr Hamilton's barn, the ship is gone. Having seen the dangers of knowing, Pete accepts Clark never told him his secret to protect him. Pete is welcomed into the Kent family circle.

Speech Bubbles: Pete: 'I can see the headlines: "The real Clark Kent exposed".'

Clark: 'Pete, I would never hurt you.' Pete: 'Too late.'

Lionel (touching the spaceship): 'Forgive my scepticism, doctor, but, for all I can tell, this could be a post-modern coffee table.'

Small Town Boy: Clark, the honest boy who lies to all his friends, finally confesses all his secrets when Pete gets too close to the truth. Clark's conflict between his friendship with Pete and the need to protect his secret builds up through the early part of the episode, until Pete's suspicion that Clark stole the spaceship leads Clark to reveal his secrets. Before then, Clark's lies become desperate as he tries to stop Pete going public with the spacecraft, or even telling Chloe that he has it.

Until Pete comes around (after being rescued from Hamilton), it seems that the lesson Clark is going to learn from his experience is that telling the truth can lead to as much trouble as keeping a secret. Not only does Pete freak out when he finds out Clark has been lying to him, but Lex makes it clear that he doesn't forgive friends who deceive him. Bringing Pete into the family gives Clark a confidant, and eases the loneliness that his powers bring him. As the episode opens, Clark shoots hoops from a great distance, using superspeed to run under the net and catch the ball himself; in an expertly used bit of symbolism, in the final scene he's got Pete to play with.

Clark is incapacitated by getting splashed with Hamilton's concentrated meteor essence, which seems to slip into his system by contact with his skin.

Just the Funny Guy: At last – just over a season into the show, Pete gets to take centre stage. His response to finding the spaceship brings out his entrepreneurial instincts and his desire to play the showman. Pete wants to get rich and famous, to make a splash, and sees the ship as a perfect way of doing that. However, all thoughts of fame and fortune fall away when Pete realises that his best friend has been lying to him since they were little – Pete may be shallow, but he's not *that* shallow. It's only when Pete has his run-in with Hamilton that he realises that being kept out of the loop was the safest place to be. Notably, even under threat of death, Pete is fiercely determined to keep Clark's secret, proving that he has the right stuff despite the Kents' initial fears.

Pete becomes a brief, minor celebrity as the hero who took Ray Wallace to hospital after the crash. This mainly leads to Chloe wanting an exclusive interview with him.

Girl Next Door: Lana broke up with Whitney in the video message she was recording at the end of **23**, 'Heat'. After telling Clark her feelings about Whitney, she has another terse conversation with him, disappointed that she shares all her personal thoughts with him, yet he shares nothing with her. She makes it very clear that Clark's secretive behaviour is keeping them apart.

Lana's Aunt Nell has a new boyfriend, Dean. Lana dislikes Dean enough to tell Nell that she's staying with Chloe and then sleep at the Talon. Lana is apologetic when Chloe is put on the spot by Nell because she didn't know about the lie in advance. Lana finds Dean's presence intrusive – perhaps after so long with a single parent, and still feeling the loss of her real parents, she finds this surrogate father figure an imposition? Certainly, when Nell wants Lana and Dean to get to know each other better and for them to spend more time together as a family, Lana finds the prospect unwelcome. In Clark's barn, Lana uses Clark's telescope to spy on her own house – checking if Dean is there.

Torch Bearer: Chloe is flattered that Lana thought of her first as a friend to spend a sleepover with, and suggests that next time Lana wants to get out of the house she should stay over for real. Chloe improvises wildly when interrogated about the sleepover by Nell, saying that Lana and Chloe didn't study, opting for Keanu Reeves DVDs instead. Both Kreuk and Mack show great comic timing as they blabber desperately at Dean and Nell.

Clark shamelessly manipulates Chloe into ignoring the story about the crashed spaceship by suggesting it's a yarn

fit for the *Inquisitor*, a tabloid that Chloe, a devotee of the
Daily Planet, has little time for.

Not an Evil Genius: Since the management buyout of the
LuthorCorp plant, Lex has been the head of his own
company. As such, he no longer has time for conspiracy
theories and other outlandish matters. He has no regrets
about cutting Hamilton loose when he becomes a liability
and, when Hamilton is searching for the artefact, Lex
makes far less effort to find it than he would have done in
his more obsessive Season One phase. Lex's curiosity is
triggered more by his father's interest in the spaceship than
by the spaceship story itself.

Lex isn't comfortable when Lionel comes to stay with
him and, under the mask of medical concern, he encourages Lionel to either return to his doctors in Metropolis or
relax somewhere more exotic than Smallville. Lex doesn't
trust Lionel's claims that he wants to work on their
relationship and, when Lionel decides to stay in Smallville
longer, Lex is instantly suspicious . . .

Bad Dad: Lionel comes to Smallville claiming he wants to
spend some time with his son, but later reveals that he's
trying to escape the doctors and therapists who are leading
him through a slow and humiliating process of recovery.
While tapping his way around the corridors of the mansion
with his cane, Lionel meets Hamilton, who persuades him
to come and examine the spaceship. While Lionel believes
in the usefulness of people like Hamilton – advising Lex
that he should not underestimate the value of eccentrics
and lunatics – he tells Hamilton that he will only get his
funding if he can find the artefact to open the ship. Lionel
uses a handheld electronic reader to scan text and digitally
read it out loud. In this way he reads Hamilton's meteor
reports, which he finds interesting.

When Lionel and Lex return to Hamilton's barn, the
ship and Hamilton himself are both gone, but Lionel's
interest is piqued enough to make him extend his stay
indefinitely – his physiotherapists can come to him.

Mad Scientist: So, it's goodbye to Dr Hamilton, the most
deranged meteor enthusiast in town. Or is it? The viewer

never sees the body, always a giveaway in science fiction. Admittedly, leaving a character's fate unresolved is not unusual in Smallville, Kansas's capital of loose ends, but in this case it could be significant. Could Dr Hamilton be set for a return, reanimated by his meteor infection? It wouldn't be unprecedented (see **17**, 'Reaper' for more undead action). His symptons as he succumbs to meteor infection are reminiscent of those suffered by Earl Jenkins in **8**, 'Jitters'.

If this *is* the character's swan song, at least it's a good one. The madness and obsession that have characterised Hamilton since his introduction have become significantly worse, and Joe Morton gleefully plays the character's derangement for every twitch and tic. Hamilton has become a very, very bad man, causing a car crash at the start of the episode, then killing the other driver from that crash to prevent the secret of the spaceship from spreading. Hamilton also seems prepared to kill Pete in the course of his quest. He has contacts in the hospital who tip him off to the story of the crashed spaceship and schmoozes Lionel in an inept, frantic manner to try and regain his funding and obtain Lex's artefact.

Down at the Farm: Jonathan and Martha insist that it is too dangerous for Clark to tell Pete his secret – it might put Pete in danger and he might not be ready for the responsibility. They are therefore alarmed when they find out that Clark has gone and done just that. At the end of the episode they welcome Pete into the family – although Jonathan is still stern about the burden Pete is taking on, warning that it won't be easy.

Another Planet: According to Hamilton, the spaceship is made of an alloy composed of elements not found on the periodic table – elements also present in the meteor rocks.

From the Pages of: See the **Secret Origin** chapter for a brief history of Pete Ross's character in the comics, and his position as keeper of Clark's secret.

Secret Identities: Andrew Jackson played Buddy in *Taken* as well as having roles in *Due South* and *Universal Soldier II: Brothers In Arms*. Michael Kopsa is the voice of Beast in *X-Men: Evolution*, and appeared in the TV version of *Carrie*. Cameron 'Cam' Cronin has had guest slots in *The X-Files* and *John Doe*.

Writers Todd Slavkin and Darren Swimmer are Executive Story Editors on *Smallville* and wrote the TV movie *Natural Selection*. Director Steve Miner comes from a horror background, having directed *House* as well as working as an assistant editor on *The Last House on the Left*. He appeared as an actor in *Halloween H20: 20 Years Later* and *Friday the Thirteenth Part 3: 3D*. As a TV director he has worked on *The Practice*, *Dawson's Creek* and *Chicago Hope*.

Music: The memorable song accompanying Clark's super-human basketball playing is 'Ordinary' by Greg Jones. Other tracks in the episode are 'Leading With My Heart' by Alice Peacock, 'Goodbye' by Stephanie Simon and 'Southbound Train' by Travis Tritt.

Trivia: Pete hums the theme tune to UFO conspiracy show *The X-Files* as he leads Clark towards the site of the crashed spaceship.

The Last Word: 'Hiding the truth only keeps people apart.' At last the underrated Sam Jones III, in the shadows for most of Season One, gets dragged centre stage and given a chance to shine as Pete Ross, Clark's oldest friend and newest confidant. Another big change to the status quo of the series, this smart move allows Pete to act as an accomplice to Clark's adventures and takes the edge off Clark's isolation (a theme now well worn to the point of tedium – how many episodes do we need to end with Clark alone and depressed?). Thankfully Jones is well up to the task of playing a more active role, and his small stature and amiable personality put the audience in an uncomfortable situation whenever he's threatened. You really feel Pete's betrayal when he finds out his friendship with Clark has been based on a lie, and root for him as he holds out against Hamilton. The final scene, where Clark and Pete play basketball in the yard of the Kent farm, is one of the series' warmest moments.

Elsewhere, it's goodbye to one recurring nemesis as Dr Hamilton jitters his way off this mortal coil (see **Mad**

Scientist above for some speculation on this point). After the death of Nixon in **22**, 'Vortex', this is another of Lex's reprehensible cronies dead and buried, cutting Lex off from his investigations into the meteors and the Kents. However, that doesn't leave Clark's secrets safe from the Luthors – far from it, now that Lionel is in town for good and seemingly determined to solve the mystery of the missing spaceship. Lionel Luthor seems to be gradually growing into a major threat for Clark and his family, a central malignant pressure within the series. With John Glover making the character compelling, charming and interesting, that's no bad thing.

Parallels run throughout 'Duplicity', as characters deceive each other, some secrets are suppressed and others are revealed. Both Lex and Lana gingerly step around parental issues that make them uncomfortable and both turn to the homely Kents when feeling unhappy in their own homes. Some friendships are strengthened while others fall apart, with both Lana and Chloe increasingly distanced from Clark. The series just keeps on changing, and all for the better. The one thing that doesn't seem to be in danger of happening in this show is stagnation – not bad for a series once mired in formula and in danger of being trapped in its own clichés!

25
Red

Production #175054
1st US Transmission Date: 15 October 2002

Writer: Jeph Loeb
Director: Jeff Woolnough
Guest Starring: Sara Downing (Jessie Brooks),
Michael Tomlinson (US marshal)
Co-starring: Garwin Sanford (Jessie's Father),
Daryl Shuttleworth (Principal), Geoff Clements, Brad Loree, Jake Moyer

Synopsis: Against the express wishes of his father, Clark blows $350 on a school class ring set with a red stone.

When Clark puts the ring on, a ripple of red energy flows through him and his behaviour begins to alter – he becomes rebellious, selfish and generally bad. As time goes on, the effects become more severe. Though he starts with minor acts of defiance – being rude to the school Principal, not studying – Clark soon moves on to more extreme behaviour. He uses his parents' credit cards to buy all the things he could never afford, starts fights in bars, and injures Jonathan when he tries to stop him.

Meanwhile there's a new love interest in Clark's life: Jessie Brooks, a new girl at Smallville High who likes the wild side. When Clark persuades Lana to go on a date with him, then takes her to a bar that serves minors, Lana isn't impressed. With Jessie present as a viable alternative, Clark chooses the bad girl over the good one, and Lana walks off in disgust. While Jessie suits the new Clark, she also has a secret – her father is on the run from his criminal former bosses, and a corrupt US marshal has been bribed to locate Mr Brooks and retrieve the disk of evidence he possesses. When Clark finds out about this he decides to claim the reward for himself so, after Jessie's father shoots the marshal dead, Clark moves in and takes the disk.

Chloe finds out that the class rings are set with worthless red meteor rocks rather than rubies. When Pete passes this information to the Kents, they realise that this must be the cause of Clark's current condition. Just as Clark has Jessie cornered, Pete and Jonathan move in, exposing Clark to a green meteor to weaken him. While Clark is down, Jonathan uses a hammer to smash the red ring.

Jessie and her father have gone back on the run. Clark is back to normal, but his relationship with Lana is severely damaged.

Speech Bubbles: Chloe: 'Nothing says school spirit more than a ring that looks like it was jacked from P Diddy.'

Pete: 'Clark Kent – chick magnet. What's wrong with this picture?'

Clark: 'It's like I have these two identities and I don't know which one is the real me.'

Small Town Boy: What starts as a small act of defiance – buying a class ring that his father doesn't want him to waste money on – spirals out of control as Clark is infected by the red meteor rock set into the ring and becomes unstable and selfish. Evil Clark begins to resemble Lex's worst aspects, and doesn't seem too removed from the rich brat Lex alludes to himself once being: in other words, this new Clark is selfish, flashy and uses his power and influence to get what he wants without any thought for others. His emulation of Lex extends to borrowing his car and, when he decides to leave home, he agrees to live with Lex in Metropolis.

On the positive side, the new Clark is confident enough to ask Lana out on a date, acting more on his feelings than he ever would have done before. However, his bad boy attitude directly contradicts what Lana liked about him, and their date falls apart when Clark wants Lana to share him with Jessie. Once the ring has been destroyed and Clark returns to normal, he tries to repair his relationship with Lana – but, because he can't explain his recent behaviour, she doesn't want his apologies.

Clark admits that his feelings of resentment in regard to the Kent farm's money problems, and the impact they have on his way of life, come from a real place. But he insists that, in spite of how he acted when under the influence of the red meteor, he understands that the love and support his family have given him is more important than money.

While under the influence, Clark uses his X-ray vision to see through Chloe and Lana's clothes.

Girl Next Door: Lana is assigned the task of showing Jessie around Smallville High, and notices the attraction between Jessie and Clark. However, Clark is insistent that he only has eyes for Lana, an overture which she, although shocked, gradually responds to. When Clark says they should be open about their feelings, Lana takes the opportunity to ask him about the day of the tornado. Clark promises to get around to that in good time, but moves the conversation back to their feelings. Lana responds to him and they kiss passionately. Unfortunately, their date ends in disaster: after Clark's appalling behaviour in wanting to share himself between Lana and Jessie and his relentless secrecy, Lana has had enough of Clark for the moment.

Not an Evil Genius: Lex is amused by the new Clark, complimenting him on his new taste in clothes, but he very quickly realises that Clark is losing the admirable qualities Lex admired in him. When Clark wants to leave home, Lex stalls him at the mansion, going off to warn Jonathan about Clark's plans.

Lex finds his office has been taken over by Lionel, who is moving in all the equipment he needs to run LuthorCorp from the mansion. Lex initially tolerates this, sympathetic to his father's disability, even though the changes interfere with his life. Clark's insolent behaviour, though, reminds Lex of his own rebellious phase, and he eventually bites back, changing his office back to the way it was. When Lex was coming to terms with his baldness as a child, Lionel offered him no mercy, challenging him to cope with his new situation. Now Lex does the same for Lionel, stopping him from feeling sorry for himself.

Bad Dad: Aside from taking over Lex's office (see **Not an Evil Genius**), Lionel has one brief run-in with the main storyline. When Lex runs off to see Jonathan, Clark is left playing billiards. Lionel walks in and Clark ends up telling him exactly how Lex resents his presence. Lionel can't believe that the Kents would raise such an impertinent son as they are good people (the full story of the relationship between the Kents and the Luthors is revealed in **28**, 'Lineage'). Lionel is present when the US marshal tries to interrogate Clark and fires off a couple of shots. Lionel is told by Clark that the marshal missed, when in fact Clark caught the bullets. Lionel is left playing with a crushed bullet, intrigued by Clark. This can't be a good sign . . .

Just the Funny Guy: Pete is already a far more vital part of the show than before. As Clark's confidant, he realises Clark is misusing his abilities early on when Clark boasts of using his X-ray vision to see through Lana and Chloe's clothes. It's Pete who passes the information about the ring from Chloe to the Kents, and it's Pete who wields the green meteor rock to control Clark at the end of the episode.

Down on the Farm: The Kent finances are still in a bad state, which isn't helped by Clark's spending spree with his parents' credit card. Clark's erratic behaviour puts his parents through the emotional wringer – they know they can't physically stop Clark from doing whatever he wants, and constantly try and reason with him. When Jonathan tries to force Clark to listen, he gets a bruising as Clark tosses him aside. It visibly hurts Jonathan to harm his own son, using the green meteor on Clark to save him.

In spite of their shaking of hands in **22**, 'Vortex', Jonathan still distrusts Lex. When Jonathan berates Clark for buying the class ring, Martha reminds him that his father didn't approve when he bought an old motorbike.

Torch Bearer: With the role of female foil split between Lana and Jessie, Chloe is left with very little to do in this episode apart from be baffled at Clark's strange behaviour. Her main involvement is to discover the secret of the class rings – Chloe doesn't like them from the start and her investigations reveal that worthless red meteor rocks are being used as ruby substitutes. Chloe obtains a refund for all the students.

Strange Visitors: The main villain of the episode is Clark turned bad by the effect of a red meteor rock. However, an external threat comes from a corrupt US marshal. Not only does the marshal not have any powers, he doesn't even get a name, making him one of the most thinly characterised enemies yet to appear in the series.

Teenage Kicks: One of the first things the red-amended Clark does is pick up a flyer for an out-of-town bar that doesn't check for IDs. Clark wants Pete to go with him and repeatedly suggests it as an alternative to studying. Eventually he goes with Lana, and ends the night with a drunken brawl. Not a bad score for debauchery.

From the Pages of: In the *Superman* comics, red kryptonite has unpredictable (and sometimes wacky) side effects, personality changes being just one. It's in the movie *Superman III* that the seeds for the use of the red rocks in 'Red' was sown – Gus Gorman (Richard Pryor) attempts to synthesise kryptonite and ends up with tobacco-tainted red kryptonite, which causes Superman to become irresponsible and evil in a very similar manner to the way the red meteors are used here. The teenage rebellion aspect, however, is the obligatory *Smallville* teen twist. The character of Jessie closely resembles the version of Gwen Stacy seen in *Ultimate Spider-Man*.

Secret Identities: Sara Downing played Courtney in a run of Season Two *Roswell* episodes, and also appeared in the movies *The Forsaken* and *Never Been Kissed*. Michael Tomlinson played an ambassador in *The West Wing* and a military doctor in director Adrian Lyne's surreal *Jacob's Ladder*. Garwin Sanford appeared in the 2000 remake of the 1971 Michael Caine classic *Get Carter*.

A consulting producer on the series, as well as writer of this episode, Jeph Loeb also wrote the movie *Teen Wolf*, and was a producer on the aborted *Buffy The Vampire Slayer* cartoon. He is best known by superhero fans as the writer of an acclaimed run on the main *Superman* comic book, as well as miniseries such as *Batman: The Long Halloween* and *Spider-Man: Blue*. Director Jeff Woolnough has also directed episodes of *Birds of Prey* and *Soul Food*.

Music: Two tracks from the charmingly named Sprung Monkey appear in this episode: 'Unexpected' and 'American Made'. Other tracks include 'Party Hard' by Andrew WK, 'Breakable' by Fisher, 'Breathe In' by Frou Frou and 'Tattoos' by Jackpot. The closing music is 'Stop Crying Your Heart Out' by Oasis.

The Last Word: 'All you have to ask yourself is . . . who is more responsible than Clark Kent?' Comics writer Jeph Loeb brings an old *Superman* staple to *Smallville*, as the green meteors are joined by their red cousins, which cause Clark to become mentally unstable rather than physically ill. It's one of the oldest stories in the books, so clichéd that comics continuity was re-written a couple of times to take the red rocks out of circulation, but here it works like a dream. 'Red' is funny, dramatic and has long-term implications for the characters

Tom Welling has tremendous fun as Clark-gone-bad, arrogantly sweeping around town, casually using his powers for kicks and taking whatever he wants. He looks cool in black leather and expensive coats too. This is a real star vehicle for Welling and, as such, some of the other characters are pushed into the background. At least Lana gets some of the limelight, although Clark and Lana's date turns out not to be particularly romantic. Just when their relationship seems to be moving forward, it takes a big leap back – but what did you expect? A smooth romantic ride?

26
Nocturne

Production #175055
1st US Transmission Date: 22 October 2002

Writers: Brian Peterson and Kelly Souders
Director: Rick Wallace
Guest Starring: Sean Faris (Byron), Gwynyth Walsh (Byron's Mother),
Richard Moll (Byron's Father)
Co-starring: Mitchell Kosterman (Sheriff Ethan Talbot),
Jonathan Sutton (Tad)

Synopsis: Lana has a secret admirer who writes poems and leaves them by her parents' grave. When Lana finally meets Byron, the poet, she is impressed with this strange young man who is home-schooled by his parents and only seems to emerge at night. When Byron suddenly runs home Lana and Clark follow, but Byron's aggressive father drives them off the family's land. Fearing that Byron is being abused, they tell Jonathan, who calls in Sheriff Ethan, only to find that Byron is officially dead. Clark and Pete break in, freeing Byron from his basement prison but, when Byron is forced into the sunlight, he undergoes a shocking transformation and turns into a monster.

Byron's parents tell the Kents that the boy was the subject of experiments to curb his antisocial behaviour. When the experiments went wrong the doctor in charge of the project faked Byron's death certificate so that his parents could care for him at home. Metron Pharmaceuticals, a branch of LuthorCorp, undertook the project.

Byron tries to take his revenge on Lionel Luthor, pulling his helicopter down as it tries to take off, but Clark manages to drag Byron down a well and into the darkness, where he reverts to being a human.

Martha gets a new job – as personal assistant to Lionel Luthor.

Speech Bubbles: Lana: 'Come on, Clark, tell me you've never watched someone from afar.'

Lex (to Lionel): 'If I find out that you have any agenda that could hurt the Kents, this amiable father–son détente will come to an abrupt end.'

'Savage' Byron (to Lana): 'They made me into someone no one can love. Not even you.'

Small Town Boy: When Lana starts receiving poems from a mystery admirer, Clark becomes jealous and overprotective to the point where, at Byron and Lana's first meeting in the graveyard, Clark knocks the poor boy out cold in a misguided attempt to protect Lana. Once he knows more about Byron, however, Clark becomes concerned more with whether the boy is being abused than what his intentions are towards Lana.

Clark has no appreciation of poetry whatsoever and is unable to see why Byron's writing impresses Lana, though he's upset that Lana would show Byron's poetry to Chloe and Pete before showing it to him. Clark gives Byron a book of limericks as a present. At the end of the episode Clark has a book of sonnets in his pocket, but he admits to Lana that poetry isn't for him. This honest answer goes a long way with Lana, leaving them on better terms.

Girl Next Door: Lana gets her first post-Whitney love interest in Byron, and the intensity of her interest seems heightened by her current feud with Clark (following on from **25**, 'Red'). Byron appeals to Lana's poetic side – as does Lex, in one particularly intriguing scene – something that neither Clark nor Whitney could ever manage. John Donne is one of Lana's favourite poets and she's visibly impressed when Lex proves to be a fellow fan. Lana also thinks that Byron is gentle, and he seems to speak straight from the heart – this appeals to Lana when compared to Clark's evasiveness.

Lana's distrust of Clark continues, with her deliberately talking to Chloe and Pete about the poetry rather than Clark. As she explains to him, Clark can't expect her to be open with him if he won't be open with her. She's not happy when Pete and Clark break Byron out of the cellar without her – Clark is keeping her out of the loop, even in regard to her own friends. Lana tries to confront the bestial Byron in the graveyard herself, and gets a bump on the head and a sprained wrist for her trouble. She later admits to Clark that, when Byron attacked her, her first thought was that Clark would know what to do. This leads her to be more conciliatory towards Clark, whose advice about Byron turned out to be correct. Their relationship is somewhat repaired from the damage caused in **25**, 'Red', but Lana still cautions Clark about hiding his true self forever – he may find he's missed out on something.

Not an Evil Genius: In a story crammed with poetry, Lex quotes John Donne to Lana in the Talon, getting on to her good side. Lex considers poetry to be all about seduction – which suggests he knows full well the effect his reading would have on Lana! He believes Byron's poetry has raised the bar in terms of the contest to win Lana's heart, implying that Clark will need to raise his game.

Lex is increasingly annoyed by Lionel's inability to hold on to personal assistants, assistants Lex is interviewing. He's even more annoyed when he wastes a whole day interviewing new candidates, only to find Lionel has hired Martha. Lex wants to know what agenda Lionel has with regard to the Kents, and tells him their current cosy relationship will end if Lionel hurts the Kents. After Lionel offers to research Byron's condition, Lex accuses him of having his priorities altered by Martha.

Lionel compares Lex's relationship with the Kents to the story of Prometheus, the son of Zeus, who tried to live among mortals as one of them. Lex can never be one of the Kents, as much as he might want to join their family.

Bad Dad: Lionel sacks Tad, one of a string of personal assistants hired by Lex and fired by Lionel. Lionel has got through four of these Ivy League sidekicks in a month, leaving Lex at the end of his tether. Lionel still uses his electronic reader, and discards it in frustration as he tries to read a copy of the *Daily Planet*. Martha is present when he does this, though, and gently takes the paper and reads the article to him. This, along with her shrewd analysis of his business tactics, causes Lionel to hire her as his latest personal assistant, saying that her honesty is a hard quality to come by. After the Byron affair is over, Martha convinces Lionel that it would be better publicity to fund Byron's treatment than cast him aside.

When Byron attacks Lionel's helicopter, Clark has to rescue him. Lionel's blindness yet again means that he has an idea that Clark is up to something incredible nearby, but has no idea exactly what. Lionel's arm is in a sling after Byron's attack, but he tells Lex that it would have been a lot worse if Martha and Clark hadn't been there. He tells Lex that Clark is an extraordinary young man.

Lionel can play the piano. After hiring Martha, Lionel plays Chopin – though he sometimes thinks Chopin lacks subtlety, he is obviously in the right mood at the time.

Just the Funny Guy: Pete helps Clark break into Byron's house. When Byron transforms into his more bestial form, he throws Pete off the porch and through the windscreen of a car. Pete ends up in hospital with a broken arm, saying the Kents should provide him with medical insurance.

Torch Bearer: Chloe is excited by the romantic attention Lana is receiving, as opposed to Clark's cynicism about the poetry and Lana's admirer. Chloe tracks down Byron's faked death certificate and finds Dr Emil Jenkins signed it. She follows Jenkins's paper trail to Metron Pharmaceuticals, where Byron was part of the project to tame youths with antisocial tendencies.

Down at the Farm: Jonathan isn't pleased when Lionel offers Martha a job, and is surprised that she doesn't turn it down immediately. Martha, however, has been thinking of going back to work for a while because the Kents need the money and she wants to use her education. Jonathan thinks farm life is getting too boring for Martha; Clark thinks Martha can look after herself with someone like

Lionel and he hasn't seen his mother this excited for a while.

Strange Visitors: Early parts of the episode are played as if Byron's father is the villain, and casting the imposing Richard Moll in the role adds to this impression. That Byron is being kept locked in the basement by his parents for his own good should come as a surprise to no one – there had to be a twist somewhere along the way – and the real threat emerges in the form of the savage Byron, the result of the drug trials he underwent under Metron Pharmaceuticals, which affected his adrenal system. This version of Byron has a pronounced brow, heavy musculature and dark eyes. His enhanced strength allows him to bring down a helicopter by hand and throw Pete and Clark about like ragdolls. This savage Byron reverts to normal Byron when dragged out of the sunlight by Clark.

Loose Ends: Everyone knows Byron hangs out in the graveyard, so why is Lana the only person to think of looking there when he's loose? Where does Byron get the coat he's wearing in the later part of his rampage?

From the Pages of: Lana refers to Clark as a 'man of steel'. The term is usually applied to Superman's great strength, but here Lana uses it to deride Clark's lack of poetic sensitivity. There's another joke about Clark not flying (see **19**, 'Crush') as he watches Martha get into the helicopter. Metron Pharmaceuticals is named after a time travelling, god-like being called Metron from the DC Comics.

Music: As well as Lionel's Chopin rendition, the tracks in this episode are 'Underneath It All' by No Doubt, 'Love Song' by Sheila Nicholls, 'Don't Ask Me' by OK Go and 'Crazy Richie' by Cactus Groove.

The score by Mark Snow is of particular note, picking up on the romantic roots of the Byron character and employing a more lush orchestral sound than usual.

Secret Identities: Sean Faris has appeared in *Pearl Harbor* and the MTV series *Undressed*. Gwynyth Walsh played Dr Timmons in *NYPD Blue* and has had roles in *Star Trek: Generations* and *Stargate SG-1*. Richard Moll has appeared in the movies *House*, *Scary Movie 2* and *Evolution*, and was the voice of Harvey Dent, a.k.a Two Face, in the *Batman* animated series. Moll also appeared in *But I'm A Cheerleader*, written by Bryan Peterson, co-writer of 'Nocturne'. Director Rick Wallace has helmed episodes of *Murder One*, *NYPD Blue*, *The Pretender* and the short-lived *Haunted*.

The Last Word: 'The imagery is a little naïve, but the meter is actually quite sophisticated.' A gothic folly on the part of all concerned, 'Nocturne' is a melodramatic bit of old nonsense that veers wildly between pseudo-poetic excess and the series' usual contemporary teen soap, never quite settling on a coherent style. The end result is a disappointing monster mish-mash of incompatible elements that nevertheless has enough good bits and decent action scenes to hold the attention.

The central metaphor of adolescent rebellion embodied as a monstrous alter ego – part Mr Hyde, part the Incredible Hulk – is a neat teen twist on a very old fantasy staple and sustains the episode well. The background to Byron's condition – that he was an antisocial youth subjected to scientific treatments to cure him – can be read as a critique of the controversial use of drugs such as Ritalin on children diagnosed with Attention Deficit Disorder. By trying to suppress his rebellious phase so brutally, the scientists turn Byron into a mood-swinging monster. It's not a subtle allegory, but at least it makes a stab at social relevance.

More interesting is the intertwining of the lives of the Kents and the Luthors, as Martha becomes Lionel's personal assistant. Both Jonathan and Lex are unhappy about this development. Could there be an alliance between these two in the offing? More interesting still is the tiniest hint of seduction as Lex quotes poetry to Lana. Now *that* would be an interesting development . . .

27
Redux

Production #227621
1st US Transmission Date: 29 October 2002

Writers: Russel Friend and Garrett Learner
Director: Chris Long
Guest Starring: Maggie Lawson (Chrissie), George Coe (William Clark),
Richard Gant (Principal Reynolds), Sarah-Jane Redmond (Aunt Nell)
Co-starring: Jesse Hutch (Troy), Fulvio Cecere (Coach),
Neil Grayston (Russell)

Synopsis: Swimming star Troy has a convulsion and nearly drowns in the Smallville High pool. When Clark pulls him out of the water, he seems to have aged prematurely and dies. Troy's girlfriend, Chrissie, doesn't seem too concerned by his death – she's more interested in organising the celebration of school, Spirit Week, and making sure the students have the best time of their lives. Spirit Week is to climax with a show at the Talon and Chrissie is putting all her energies into organising that show. The fact that Mr Reynolds, the new school Principal, can't find the records from her old school is neither here nor there.

Chrissie finds that parts of her are rapidly ageing so she sucks the life out of Russell, who is setting up the lighting for the Spirit Week show. Clark makes the connection between Chrissie and the two prematurely aged dead boys and Chloe finds out that Chrissie seems to be an eternal teen, appearing in different high school yearbooks every decade dating back to 1922. With each of her appearances comes a trio of mysterious deaths from premature ageing. Clark rescues Principal Reynolds from being Chrissie's third victim and, denied the life force she needs, Chrissie crumbles to dust.

Meanwhile, Principal Reynolds gives Clark a hard time, seemingly just because he knows Lex. Reynolds was the principal at Excelsior Prep during Lex's tenure there, and left under a cloud. When Lex talks to him, he finds out that Lionel made a deal with the board of governors at

Excelsior after Reynolds expelled Lex – Lionel made a large donation to the school, Lex was allowed back and Reynolds was let go. Reynolds didn't work again until getting the job at Smallville High.

The Kents still have money troubles, so Martha asks her father, William Clark, for help. Clark fails to heal the long-running feud between William and Jonathan but is determined to have a relationship with his grandfather.

Lana finds a photograph of her mother with a mysterious man, and suspects that he may be her father . . .

Speech Bubbles: Lex: 'In some ways you're responsible for the man I am today.' Reynolds: 'I'm not sure that's a burden I care to take on.'

Martha (to her father): 'You raised an independent daughter and you're angry because that's what you got!'

Chrissie: 'You will never be this young, this beautiful or this perfect again. But I will.'

Small Town Boy: Clark tries to play peacemaker between his father and grandfather, unsuccessfully. He also falls foul of another vein of bad blood – between Smallville High's new principal, Reynolds, and his former Excelsior Prep pupil, Lex. Reynolds accuses Clark of being a slacker with no goals, saying that a vague desire to help people isn't enough of a life plan. Reynolds sets Clark an essay on where he will be five years from now, telling Clark it's a challenge, not a punishment. Clark feels he is being persecuted for being friends with Lex – he had never even seen the inside of the principal's office until Reynolds arrived.

The feud between his father and grandfather, and the essay for Reynolds, focus Clark's mind on where his life is heading. Seeing Chrissie, a woman twisted by her desire to live in the past, gives him further reason to look to the future. By the end of the episode Clark has made a couple of decisions: firstly, in spite of all the bad blood in his family, he is going to try and develop a relationship with his grandfather, William Clark; secondly, in five years' time he'll probably be at university studying journalism. Although he doesn't want to give Chloe the satisfaction, he thinks the journalist's life is growing on him.

Girl Next Door: Lana finds photos of her mother enjoying a picnic with a strange man, dated July 1985 – a time when her parents were already married. Clark suggests Lana's mother and the mystery man were just friends, but the pose in the picture means that argument isn't very convincing. Nell's response to the photo is unhelpful – she tells Lana that her mother would never have done anything to hurt either Lana or her father. Lana is more interested in the fact that the date on the photo places it a year before she was born. She asks Lex for help and receives an envelope of information in return. Lana is nervous about opening it – her memory of her parents may be all she has left of them and the knowledge she possesses might shatter that image. When she opens the envelope, she finds that her parents filed for divorce, on the grounds of irreconcilable differences, in 1985. The Langs were separated for just over a year and Lana was born just after they got back together. The man in the photo could be her father – and he may still be alive.

Lana renovates the cinema part of the Talon in preparation for Chrissie's Spirit Week festivities.

Not an Evil Genius: Lex knows Principal Reynolds, the new principal of Smallville High, of old. When Lex feels that Reynolds is unfairly treating Clark for being his friend, and lobbies on Clark's behalf, he finds out exactly what happened to earn Reynolds' enmity (see **Bad Dad**). Lex likes Reynolds for challenging him when he was younger – he was set the same essay as Clark. The book Reynolds is reading is *The Count of Monte Cristo* and Lex sees the significance of the Principal reading a book about a man who takes revenge for an old injustice.

When Lex agrees to help Lana find out about the mystery man, he asks her to remember Pandora's Box – some boxes, once opened, can never be closed.

Bad Dad: Although Lionel doesn't appear in this episode, his presence is felt through the dialogue between Reynolds and Lex. When Lex was expelled from Excelsior Prep, Lionel's substantial donation to the school's library and the conditions placed on it have left Reynolds with an abiding hatred of the Luthors and their methods.

Just the Funny Guy: Pete mocks Clark for being in the new Principal's bad books – a first for such an innocuous student. Otherwise, Pete gets very little to do.

Torch Bearer: Chloe is flattered by Reynolds's approval of the *Torch* and her work and interviews him for the school paper. After a little digging, she finds out Reynolds didn't work after his stint at Excelsior before he re-emerged in Smallville. It's also thanks to Chloe's research that Clark finds out about Chrissie's history and other identities.

One of Chloe's sources is Chad at the Medical Examiner's office. Chad leads a lonely life – it's hard being Smallville's only goth. Chloe lent Chad some black eyeliner and Chad in return sneaks her autopsy reports.

Down at the Farm: The Kents have money trouble again and Martha makes a call that Jonathan isn't keen on her making – she asks her father, William Clark, for help. William and Jonathan have a long-running feud. A rich city lawyer, William thought Martha deserved better than Jonathan and the life of a farmer's wife – a conviction he still holds. Martha was top ten in her class at school and, according to William, could have gone to any law school she wanted. Martha says she chose the life she wanted.

When Jonathan asked William for permission to marry her, William tried to throw Jonathan out of his office, a scuffle that resulted in Jonathan hitting William. In spite of Clark's attempts to bring them together, the feud shows no sign of being resolved. William sees the financial problems on the Kent farm as proof that he was right all along. Nevertheless, William gives Clark a cheque to pass to Martha – he won't see his girl suffer.

When Clark was little, he couldn't control his powers. Jonathan and Martha kept William away from Clark because they didn't think they could trust him with the knowledge of Clark's abilities.

Mild-mannered Reporters: Chloe pins the newspaper headline about Troy's death on the Wall of Weird. The press are accepting the death as a case of rapidly onsetting progeria – a medical condition that usually sets in very gradually, causing something akin to premature ageing.

The development of Season Two: At the end of recording the first series of *Smallville*, the producers realised they didn't have time to get a full twenty-two episodes ready for air. Nonetheless, they had enough time to do principal shooting on one more episode, and decided to shoot a fairly stand-alone episode to post-produce at leisure and drop in at some point in the second season. 'Redux' is that episode. Due to the long period between the episode being shot – which took place immediately after filming wrapped on **21**, 'Tempest' – and the episode's broadcast there was plenty of time for information to leak out. From this pre-broadcast gossip, it is clear that certain plot elements in Season Two worked out differently from how they were planned at the time 'Redux' was shot. The comparison is an interesting exercise in how a television series can evolve and how plots move in unexpected directions.

According to reports, as shot, the episode had Lana telling Chrissie that she was working hard on maintaining a long-distance relationship with Whitney. References to a battle for control of LuthorCorp were also cut to fit in with the ongoing détente between Lex and Lionel. In both cases, it's easy to see why, in the hiatus between seasons, the producers decided that both these plotlines should be ditched – they're dull. In the case of Whitney and Lana, Whitney's main role in Season One is to keep Clark and Lana apart; Season Two creates conflict between the two romantic leads instead, a much more dramatic plotline that leaves Whitney completely redundant. As for the corporate battle for LuthorCorp, high finance isn't exactly a punchy subject matter for an action-based show like *Smallville*, and the détente following Lionel's accident allows the tension to simmer between father and son more effectively than having them at each other's throats.

One other addition is worth noting – in 'Redux' as broadcast, Martha isn't seen when she refers to working for Lionel. One can surmise that this plotline was another late addition to the season, and that the relevant dialogue was dubbed over the original footage at a later date. Certainly, nothing else in the episode suggests that Martha is doing a day job – she never even wears a suit.

Chloe doesn't believe any of this and is determined to get to the truth. Reynolds advises Chloe that verifying her stories will be the difference between working for the *Inquisitor* or the *Daily Planet*.

Clark decides his future may be in journalism.

Strange Visitors: Chrissie Parker, the eternal cheerleader who has spent over a century (according to her claims) as a teenager by draining the youth from three victims every decade to keep herself young. Chrissie isn't a meteor mutant – she predates 1989 by many decades – and the origin of her vampiric ability is left obscure. In US television there are three obvious sources for Chrissie's character – the villain in *Buffy The Vampire Slayer* episode 'The Witch' uses magic to recapture her cheerleading youth, while Eugene Tooms in *The X-Files* episodes 'Squeeze' and 'Tooms' has lived for over a century, emerging at regular intervals to seek the victims whose life force will keep him young. Finally, the method of draining the life force is an almost direct lift of a similar effect in the *Buffy* episode 'Inca Mummy Girl'. The notable thing that all these sources have in common is that there's a well-explained logic behind the villains' behaviour, whether it be based in science fiction or magic. Chrissie doesn't have either background and functions outside any noticeable dramatic logic. Why the ten-year cycle? How does she drain the life force – the pituitary gland (which controls ageing) is left drained, but how does she do this with a kiss? How did it all start? How come she usually drains the life from teenagers, but picks Reynolds as her victim even though he's a middle-aged man? No idea.

Go Crows: At the start of the episode, Lana and Chrissie make banners with the obligatory school motto for Spirit Week. Chrissie organises a spirit-raising demonstration of cheerleading at the Talon. Even the Talon sign gets in on the act, with the Go CROWS! slogan on the sign.

From the Pages of: Martha's parents retired to Coast City, another famous DC Comics location. During the 'Reign of the Supermen' story, Coast City (home to superhero Green Lantern) was destroyed, leaving nothing but a crater.

Secret Identities: Maggie Lawson played Alexa in a run of *Party of Five* episodes, and took on the role of famous female sleuth *Nancy Drew*. George Coe appeared in *The Mighty Ducks*, *Best Seller* and *Kramer vs Kramer*. He also played Senator Stackhouse in *The West Wing* and Byers' father in the pilot episode of *The Lone Gunmen*. Richard Gant's acting CV stretches from *The Big Lebowski* to *Godzilla*. On television he's played Bill Dornan (and other smaller roles) in *NYPD Blue* and a general in *Babylon 5*. Fulvio Cecere played Sandoval in *Dark Angel* and has had roles in the movies *Valentine*, *Best In Show*, *The Bone Collector* and *Disturbing Behavior*, as well as the TV movie version of Marvel Comics' *Generation X*. Neil Grayston played Jordan in Kristin Kreuk's *Edgemont* and played a monk in the recent *Time Tunnel* remake.

Co-writer Russel Friend wrote a number of episodes of *Roswell*, and since penning 'Redux' has moved on to become a writer and producer on *John Doe*.

Music: 'Boom, Boom, Boom' by the Outhere Brothers can be heard in the pool scene. Other tracks include 'I Feel Fine' by Riddlin Kids, 'Ivanka' by Imperial Teen and 'U Girl' by Sophie Agapios, while the episode closes with 'Somewhere Out There' by Our Lady Peace.

Trivia: Patrick Cassidy makes his first on-screen appearance in the show here – but only in the photograph which Lana finds; his first proper appearance is in **28**, 'Lineage'. Contrary to the rumours circulating in this episode's long journey to airing (see the boxout on 'The development of Season Two'), Clark doesn't wear red speedos in the swimming scene at the start of this episode – he wears shorts. Sorry, ladies.

The Last Word: 'These are the best times of our lives. Isn't that what they say?' Famously shot at the end of Season One's production block, 'Redux' doesn't fit seamlessly with the tone of Season Two. The problem is the Chrissie plot, which seems bolted together from a pile of old fantasy TV clichés, and is squeezed into a small corner of the episode. While the Reynolds plot adds some tension to Clark's school life, and the family problems for both Clark and

Lana seem to breed interesting possibilities, the 'youth-stealing' villain, though thematically appropriate, seems to do little other than provide a bit of random peril. Chrissie doesn't even have a good fight with Clark – he tosses her aside and she suddenly ages to death, then dust.

There are some worthy things about 'Redux'. The plot revolving around Lana's parentage is great, and there isn't a bad guest actor in the whole episode – the new Principal and Clark's grandfather will hopefully both return – but messy scripting and a lack of consistency make the whole trivial and lightweight, without having the bounce and humour that a less-weighty episode should have. In between the cod-gravitas of 'Nocturne' and the family tragedy of 'Lineage', a more humorous episode would have been very welcome. Unfortunately, 'Redux' is too serious to be fluffy entertainment and too nonsensical to work as drama. After recent successes, it's a disappointment.

28
Lineage

Production #175056
1st US Transmission Date: 5 November 2002

Teleplay by Kenneth Biller
Story by Alfred Gough and Miles Millar
Director: Greg Beeman
Guest Starring: Patrick Cassidy (Henry Small), Blair Brown (Rachel)
Co-starring: Mitchell Kosterman (Sheriff Ethan Talbot),
Malkolm Alberquenque (Young Clark), Angela Moore (Doctor),
Matthew Munn (Young Lex), Shelly Schiavani

Synopsis: Rachel Dunleavy arrives in Smallville, claiming to be Clark's biological mother, and won't accept the Kents' denials. She has a solid lead to base her case on – her son Lucas was adopted through Metropolis United Charities which, as established in **14**, 'Zero', only ever handled one adoption case: Clark's. When Clark finds out that Chloe has been looking into his adoption, and led Rachel to Smallville, he is incredibly angry. Chloe does give him one bit of interesting information, though – Metropolis United Charities was founded by Lionel Luthor. Rachel tells Lex that Lucas was Lionel's illegitimate offspring; Lionel forced Rachel to give the child up and banished her to a mental institution.

Rachel orders a DNA test on Clark, but Clark and Pete break into the lab and swap the sample for Pete's so that no one discovers Clark's body chemistry. Enraged by what she sees as denying her access to her son, Rachel kidnaps Lex and threatens to kill him if Lionel doesn't call a press conference to say that Clark is their son. At the press conference, Lionel announces he won't give into threats.

Rachel is about to kill an unconscious Lex with an axe when Clark rushes in, saving Lex and convincing Rachel he can't be her son. Rachel is sent to a mental institution, where no one will believe her if she tells people about Clark's abilities. Lionel tells Lex that the real Lucas died before his first birthday – but in a locket he keeps a photo of himself with a young boy, along with a lock of hair . . .

In flashback, the viewer sees the day of the meteor shower. Jonathan and Martha helped Lionel get Lex to a hospital and, in return, Lionel arranged a fake adoption for Clark. But Lionel also exacted a further price – he threatened to reveal the fake adoption if Jonathan didn't persuade the Ross brothers to go through with the sale of the Creamed Corn Factory to Lionel.

In another plotline altogether, Lana locates her mother's lover (and possibly her own biological father), environmental activist Henry Small. Henry initially doesn't want to know Lana – he has a family of his own to think about – but after she sends him a letter about herself he decides he's willing to take the tests to find out if they're related.

Speech Bubbles: Martha (to Clark): 'How can you be as fast as lightning and as slow as molasses, all at the same time?'

Clark (to Chloe): 'I'm not going to give you an exclusive on my life.'

Lana (on her first meeting with Henry): 'He hates the Talon, hates the Luthors, compared me to the Nazis, and told me never to come back again.'

Small Town Boy: Clark knows full well that Rachel's suspicions are wrong, so the mystery for him is how Rachel would come to think that Clark was her son. This leads Clark to look deeper into his adoption, demanding that his parents tell him the truth. This truth isn't one to make him happy, as he blames himself for the Rosses being cheated by Lionel. Chloe's betrayal of her promise not to look into Clark's adoption hits hard, and Clark is furious with her, saying that if she wants to find someone's mother she should track down her own (see **Torch Bearer**). In the end Clark forgives her, at least partly because he needs her help to find the kidnapped Lex, and partly because he realises she was motivated by good intentions. Clark would, as he tells Lana, love to meet his real parents. However he, of course, knows that they won't be found through looking into the phoney adoption and that no one on Earth can help him contact them.

Clark is nervous about a DNA test – he doesn't even know if he actually has DNA. Clark has a domestic use for his heat vision (see **23**, 'Heat'): toasting bread.

Girl Next Door: Lana possibly meets her biological father, Henry Small. Small is a fiery-tempered, grey-bearded environmental activist lawyer who hates everything related to the Luthors – including the Talon. Henry compares Lex's silent partnership in the Talon to the Nazis' role in Vichy France. He's shocked to meet someone who might be his daughter, the product of an affair many years before – as he tells Lana, he has a family of his own. However, after Clark tells her about Rachel, Lana realises that her approach was too direct. Clark encourages Lana not to give up, so she sends Henry a letter about herself. Henry recognises enough of himself in Lana to want to submit to a test to see if he's her father.

Not an Evil Genius: When Rachel tells Lex that Clark may be his brother, Lex seems almost meekly hopeful that it might be true. If someone as good as Clark could be Lionel's son, then that would mean there was hope for Lex. His hopes are quickly crushed and Lex continues to be betrayed by his father, who leaves him for dead when he's kidnapped by Rachel and later tells him that his half-brother Lucas is dead.

Lex parks his car in a garage bearing a LexCorp logo – the first mention of his new company in the show. The full background to the founding of LexCorp is explained properly – and belatedly – in **31**, 'Skinwalker'.

Bad Dad: Lionel was a bad husband, cheating on his wife with one of her nurses. He was an even worse lover, taking his child from its mother shortly after the birth, then banishing Rachel to a mental institute. Lionel's way of dealing with Rachel in the present is just as repulsive – he seductively whispers to her, then threatens to have her sent back to the hospital. Lionel is willing to sacrifice Lex rather than give in to Rachel, and lies to Lex about Lucas being dead – Lionel has a lock of hair and a picture of the boy in a locket. Could Lucas be the heir Lionel always wanted, brought up away from any civilising or feminine influences, entirely Lionel's creature? It's the sort of thing he would do . . .

Lionel's involvement in Clark's adoption means that he knows full well Clark came into the life of the Kents from an unusual source, and that it was around the time of the meteor shower. Lionel seems grateful for Jonathan's help in saving Lex in 1989, but went on to ask for a further price when the Ross brothers had second thoughts about selling the Creamed Corn Factory to him.

Down at the Farm: At last, the secret of Clark's adoption is revealed, and no wonder Jonathan and Martha kept it quiet. After Jonathan helped to save Lex's life, Lionel was in Jonathan's debt, a debt that Jonathan cashed in by asking for Lionel's help with the adoption of Clark. The further price, getting Jonathan to persuade the Ross brothers to sell their factory to him, means Jonathan blames everything that the Luthors have done to Smallville since – cheating people out of their land, the pollution – on himself. He had no choice but to help Lionel, to stop Lionel from revealing the illegitmacy of Clark's adoption. Jonathan stresses that Clark shouldn't blame himself; it was Jonathan's decision and he has to live with it.

Torch Bearer: Chloe is devastated when she thinks that Clark will never speak to her again and thinks that she's ruined everything by looking into his adoption. Chloe offers to give up her press card to repair things with Clark, but he knows she would never be able to do that – it's part of who she is.

Clark's line about looking for her own mother hits Chloe hard – she knows where her mother is, she also knows that she doesn't want anything to do with Chloe. Chloe's mother walked out on her and Gabe when Chloe was five (Gabe never explained why), and Chloe has never been able to stop thinking that her mother thought Chloe wasn't worth loving. This seems to be the root of Chloe's insecurity, an insecurity which leads her to be desperately grateful for any attention or affection other people show to her. Clark's rejection of her seems only to have deepened her feeling that she isn't worthy of affection.

Lana asks Chloe to do some background research on Henry Small, but Chloe has a counter suggestion – the only way to truly know the man is to meet him.

Just the Funny Guy: Pete doesn't find out about Jonathan's role in the betrayal of his family to the Luthors, which is probably just as well. Pete provides the swab to replace Clark's at the DNA lab.

Strange Visitors: Rachel Dunlevy, mentally unstable former lover of Lionel and mother to his illegitimate child, Lucas. Rachel is so determined to prove that Clark is her offspring that she's willing to kidnap Lex to pressure Lionel into admitting it. When Lionel denies her, Rachel is quite prepared to decapitate Lex in revenge. Aside from her axe-wielding, Rachel shows other obsessive signs: stalking Clark and buying a house in Smallville under the name Lucas Luthor, so that she can be close to him. Rachel is sent to a private psychiatric hospital after Clark saves Lex from her. It's presumed that, considering her mental state, no one will believe Rachel if she talks about Clark's abilities. Rachel is a rather pitiful figure and, in spite of her actions, the Kents can't help feeling sorry for her – another victim of Lionel Luthor.

Loose Ends: Has Lucas inherited his father's ruthlessness, his mother's insanity, or – God forbid – both?

From the Pages of: The house that Rachel buys, and keeps Lex prisoner in, is 1436 Blueberry Park Lane – Blueberry is a Wild West comic book character created by legendary French artist Moebius.

Music: Most of the episode is taken up with the usual rock and pop tracks – 'Yesterday' by Hef, 'Otherwise' by Morcheeba, 'Put It Off' by Pulse Ultra and '17 Years Down' by Wonderful Johnson – but Lionel introduces a bit of culture to the episode, listening to Puccini's *Madame Butterfly* in the final scene.

Secret Identities: Patrick Cassidy, debuting here as Henry Small, is half-brother to the more famous David Cassidy and brother to TV writer and producer Shaun Cassidy. He played Leslie Luckabee, illegitimate offspring of the late Lex Luthor, in *Lois & Clark: The New Adventures of Superman*'s final disastrous season. He has also appeared in *Law & Order: Special Victims Unit* and *Murphy Brown*. Blair Brown has had roles in *Altered States*, *Space Cowboys* and *Random Hearts*.

Teleplay writer and co-executive producer Kenneth Biller has a long list of writing credits on *Star Trek: Voyager*, on which he also served in various production roles, and he wrote a fun episode of *The X-Files* called 'Eve'.

The Last Word: 'Sometimes, Mom, I'm even a mystery to myself.' Bizarrely, 'Lineage' feels like the kind of episode most shows take at least five years to reach, one which delves deep into the characters' pasts, returns to the show's beginning and is filled with significant moments. It just goes to show how quickly Smallville has established itself that this episode works so well, with a tangible buzz to the 1989 scenes that really shouldn't be there for a TV pilot shown only just over a year before.

A compelling script that digs deep into the characters' desires and insecurities is enlivened by some excellent performances – all the regulars are superb, especially Welling, Mack and Rosenbaum – and some cracking direction from Greg Beeman, the series' most trusted and impressive director. Beeman excels in the flashbacks, into which he dips and from which he returns in clever tracking shots, following the gazes of Jonathan and Martha as they look into the past. The story adds further layers to the lead characters, bringing out their motivation and deepening the twisted relationship between the Kents and the Luthors.

However, no episode is perfect, and 'Lineage' has flaws: for instance the *terrible* wig poor Mitch Kosterman is lumbered with in the 1989 sequences, complete with ludicrous sideburns. There's something odd, too, in a series like this having the sale of a corn factory as one of the defining events in it's characters' lives. It's a testament to the conviction of the actors, and the strength of the script, that Jonathan's revelation still carries a lot of weight.

29
Ryan

Production #175057
1st US Transmission Date: 12 November 2002

Writer: Philip Levens
Director: Terrence O'Hara
Guest Starring: Ryan Kelley (Ryan), Martin Cummins (Dr Garner),
Sarah-Jane Redmond (Aunt Nell), William B Davis (Mayor Tate)
Co-starring: Mitchell Kosterman (Sheriff Ethan Talbot),
Mark Gibbon, Catherine Lough Haggquist (Receptionist),
Michael St John Smith (Lab Technician), Sylvesta Stuart (Orderly),
Robert Seckler (Maintenance Guy)
Music Guest Appearance by VonRay

Synopis: Ryan (from **16**, 'Stray') is being kept in a laboratory at the Summerholt Neurological Institute where scientists and his guardian, Dr Garner, are testing his psychic abilities. He's suffering from headaches and nosebleeds. Ryan escapes the test area and phones Clark, asking to be rescued. Clark installs Ryan at the Luthor Mansion overnight. At the Kent farm, Garner demands that Clark return Ryan by the following morning. The next morning the Kents are about to hand Ryan back to Dr Garner when Lex arrives with a temporary restraining order placing Ryan with the Kents. Garner threatens to have Clark arrested for kidnapping, but Lex has a counter suit ready relating to Summerholt's research practices. Ryan is free.

Ryan gets a surprise party at the Talon, and a kiss on the cheek from Lana, though he has to leave early because of his illness. While visiting Lex, Ryan passes out cold, and wakes up in hospital. Ryan already knows what is wrong with him – he has a tumour in his head which is getting bigger. He's dying. Clark refuses to accept this, and Lex finds a man who might help – Dr Thomas Burton, a cancer expert who has a radical new serum – so Clark races to stop Burton getting on a flight to Helsinki. Dr Burton operates on Ryan, but it doesn't work. Ryan gets just a few extra days. Clark takes Ryan somewhere quiet, away from the noise of people's minds – up in a balloon. Ryan dies.

Nell and Dean have decided to move to Metropolis, and want to take Lana with them. Lana arranges to stay with Chloe and her father until she finishes High School – a plan Nell reluctantly agrees to.

Lex meets with Mayor Tate to discuss the Zoning Commission holding up LexCorp's applications for expansion. Tate wants a campaign donation to oil the wheels of bureaucracy, but Lex refuses. Lex backs Tate's opponent's election campaign, preferring an honest mayor to his own immediate gain.

Speech Bubbles: Lana: 'Ryan's lucky – at least he got to choose his family.'

Clark: 'Don't go. I mean don't go to Metropolis.' Lana: 'Or what? Are you going to kidnap me too?'

Lex: 'In life the road to darkness is a journey, not a light switch.'

Small Town Boy: After receiving the call from Ryan, Clark blames himself, thinking that he must have missed some danger sign from Ryan that things were going wrong. He thinks of Ryan as a little brother and can't stand by when the Summerholt Institute's bureaucracy keeps him from finding the truth. He breaks Ryan out of Summerholt, throwing orderlies aside as they escape, and leaves him with Lex so that Jonathan and Martha aren't involved. This complicates matters – Clark can't tell Lex about Ryan's abilities – so Lex is instantly suspicious. Clark, as usual, lies and, when Lex asks how Clark got Ryan out of the Institute, he lies again, claiming he's just lucky. Clark even accuses Lex of not being interested in Ryan's welfare when Lex suggests that Ryan may have ESP abilities – even though Clark knows full well it's true.

As the seriousness of Ryan's illness is revealed, Clark finds it hard to come to terms with the idea that there's nothing he can do to help. He runs to stop Dr Burton from getting on his plane, running faster and faster, pushing himself to the limit. He even steps in front of the plane to stop it. Clark manages to get Dr Burton to operate on Ryan and is certain that the operation will work and that he's succeeded in saving Ryan. He's wrong. Ryan tells him not to be angry or sad and never to give up. Clark promises he won't.

When Ryan tells Clark that Lana is moving, Clark invites Lana around and drops hints, fishing for her to reveal all, which she eventually does. Clark is insistent that, if moving doesn't feel right, Lana shouldn't do it. Clark seems delighted by the idea of Lana and Chloe as roommates. Is this just because it means Lana won't be leaving, or the idea of the two of them in the same room?

Clark admits to Ryan that he's afraid of flying. Ryan gets Clark into a hot air balloon at the end of the episode. **Girl Next Door:** Lana enjoyed riding at the Metropolis Equestrian Center and Nell pitches her decision to move to Metropolis as an opportunity for Lana to ride there every weekend. Lana can't believe Nell has decided to move without consulting her first and feels she's being treated like Dean and Nell's luggage, to be carried along as they travel to their great new life. Lana doesn't feel ready to share the possible move with Henry Small, as he's not been confirmed as her father yet; he's not really family. After Clark says that she shouldn't accept Nell's decision if it doesn't feel right, Lana looks into child emancipation. The process could take eighteen months to complete, and with Nell as her legal guardian Lana thinks she has no choice but to go to Metropolis.

Instead, Lana arranges to live with Chloe. When Clark says that Lana will no longer be the girl next door, she suggests that Clark give his telescope to Ryan. So she knew all along . . .

Not an Evil Genius: It is finally confirmed that the fertiliser plant is now run by LexCorp, Lex's own company, which is separate from LuthorCorp or any of Lionel's interests. Lex is determined to distance himself and LexCorp from Lionel's way of doing business, so knocks back Mayor Tate's overtures for a bribe. Lex backs Tate's opponent, believing that Smallville having an honest mayor is more important than his immediate expansion plans. This seems to demonstrate that Lex can do the right thing against his own interests (or is it that Lex just won't back down?). Lex rather grandiosely compares his own conflict with Tate to Churchill's in World War II.

Lex is put in an uncomfortable position when Clark brings Ryan to the mansion for shelter – Clark has abducted a minor, regardless of his good intentions. He saves the day by coming up with a temporary restraining order to put Ryan in the Kents' custody. When Ryan becomes ill, Lex admits to Clark that, when his mother became ill, he spent time researching treatments when the best thing he could have done was spend time with her – by the time he realised this, it was too late. He wasn't with his mother when she died and Lex asks Clark not to make the same mistake.

Lex shows Ryan his collection of *Warrior Angel* comics, as mentioned in **16**, 'Stray'. Lex has two of every issue, one to keep and one to read. In the period following his mother's death, Lex found the simple good-versus-evil world in comic books reassuring. As an adult, he found out that the world was more complex than that, with only shades of grey. Lex occupies that grey space – he doesn't think in terms of moral absolutes. He believes in making compromises and getting his hands dirty – something that Lionel taught him. Lex tells

Ryan about Devilicus, Warrior Angel's arch-enemy, and how he turned to darkness without noticing, saying that the path to darkness is a journey, it doesn't just happen. Ryan tells Lex that he should remember that.

Bad Dad: Lionel doesn't appear in this episode – according to Martha, he's in Metropolis.

Mayor Tate must be bad – he claims to have been friends with Lionel since LuthorCorp first came to town. Lionel has never been cheap when it comes to donating to the Mayor's campaign fund and, as such, has never suffered from delays with the Zoning Commission.

Just the Funny Guy: Pete's mother, Judge Ross, co-signed the restraining order that put Ryan in the Kents' care. According to Ryan, Pete is afraid that he'll slip up and accidentally reveal Clark's secret and that Clark will be locked up and experimented on, just like Ryan.

Torch Bearer: Chloe has another unusual source: a guy at the phone company called Heinrich. Pete claims he's Hungarian and rides a toy scooter, but Chloe swears he's Austrian and it's a classic Vespa. Heinrich leaks Chloe details of where Ryan's phone call to Clark came from – a terrible abuse of privilege.

Down at the Farm: Jonathan accepts the police's word when they say Ryan isn't at the Summerholt Institute, and doesn't think Clark should go there. Clark's parents aren't happy when Clark kidnaps Ryan from Summerholt, especially when Dr Garner threatens to put the Kents' lives under scrutiny, an act bound to reveal Clark's secret.

Martha pretends not to like her job when she's around Jonathan, but Ryan can tell she really likes working for Lionel. Martha considers giving her job up now that she has another son to look after. She considers Ryan a gift, in the same way that Clark was. Martha has a secret, a positive one, which she is keeping from Jonathan and Clark until the time is right; Ryan promises not to tell.

Strange Visitors: Ryan, the psychic kid from **16**, 'Stray', returns when Clark rescues him from a laboratory. Left with his aunt at the end of 'Stray', Ryan ended up in the Summerholt Institute after he became ill with headaches and nosebleeds – his aunt couldn't handle the bills and Dr Garner offered to pay for his care. Ryan's aunt was happy to give him up when Garner found out about Ryan's mind-reading ability, which Garner identified as being due to a problem with Ryan's brain.

Ryan acts suitably surprised when presented with his party, even though his abilities meant he knew about it before he even entered the Talon! Ryan uses his ability to tell Clark about Pete's fears (see **Just the Funny Guy**) and Lana's upcoming move to Metropolis.

Last time Ryan was in town, he warned Clark about Lex's dark side. Before he dies, Ryan tells Clark how much Lex admires him and asks Clark to keep an eye on him. Ryan knows that Lex is standing at a crossroads (see the fall of Devilicus in **From the Pages of**).

From the Pages of: The (non-existent) comic that Lex shows Ryan, *Warrior Angel* #1, has a cover that pastiches *Action Comics* #1 – the first comic to feature Superman. Warrior Angel himself resembles Lex in a silver mask and finds sanctuary in his aerodrome, a place of safety similar to Superman's Fortress of Solitude (Clark likes the sound of it, but not the floating). Warrior Angel and his arch enemy, Devilicus, were once best friends, but became enemies when Devilicus suggested that they should conquer humanity together.

Dr Burton comes from Hub City, home of former Charlton Comics' and latterly DC Comics' superhero The Question.

Secret Identities: William B Davis played the Cigarette Smoking Man throughout *The X-Files*. Martin Cummins played Ames White in *Dark Angel*, and has also appeared in *MANTIS* and *The Outer Limits*, as well as the film *Friday the 13th Part VIII: Jason Takes Manhattan*. Catherine Lough Haggquist has also appeared in *Dark Angel* and played Wheeler in the 1996 *Doctor Who* TV movie starring Eric Roberts.

Music: The band in the Talon are VonRay, who play 'Inside Out' at Ryan's party. 'Angels and Devils' by Dishwalla can also be heard in this episode.

The Last Word: 'How would you feel, Clark, if you were uprooted and sent somewhere far away where you didn't know anyone?' Did the world need a sequel to **16**, 'Stray'? Probably not, but 'Ryan' is exactly that and, thankfully, it's a lot better than it's precursor, as Clark repeatedly gets away with every miracle he attempts – rescuing Ryan and finding the one doctor in the world who can help – before being stopped in his tracks. Clark discovers that you can't stop death and you can't save everyone. It's not an unusual lesson – Clark is told it in both **13**, 'Kinetic' and **17**, 'Reaper' – but the sheer *harshness* of killing off Ryan, an endearing little boy, hammers that message home strongly.

Yes, some of the running effects as Clark speeds to intercept Dr Burton are ropy; the fade between the *Warrior Angel* comic book cover ('A Hero Cries') and Clark looking doe-eyed in the hospital is way, way too cheesy; then there's the disappearance of the villain from the first half of the episode once the Ryan illness plot kicks in . . . but these are minor quibbles in a story that doesn't pull any emotional punches. It's not just Ryan himself who is affected by his illness. The other characters take strength from the way he faces his demons: Lana makes a stand to stay in Smallville, while Lex stands up for what he believes is right.

Elsewhere in the episode, it's farewell, Nell. Sarah-Jane Redmond was good in the role, but Nell has never been the most interesting character in the show – remember the subplot about her relationship with Jonathan? Nope, because it was dropped before it could develop beyond the hints in **1**, 'Pilot' and **10**, 'Shimmer'. Let's hope that the departure of Nell, and Lana's move to the Sullivan household, allow more opportunity to see Robert Wisden as Gabe Sullivan – Wisden is an extremely able actor, and deserves more time in the spotlight. Another guest star deserving more screen time is William B Davis, who makes Mayor Tate a distinctly different antagonist to the more famous villain he played in *The X-Files*. Tate could prove a valuable addition to *Smallville*'s supporting cast.

30
Dichotic

Production #175058
1st US Transmission Date: 19 November 2002

Writer: Mark Verheiden
Director: Craig Zisk
Special Guest Star: Jonathan Taylor Thomas (Ian Randall)
Guest Starring: Emmanuelle Vaugier (Dr Bryce),
Robert Wisden (Gabe Sullivan)
Co-starring: Serge Houde (Mr Frankle),
David Richmond-Peck (Traffic Warden)

Synopsis: Academic overacheiver Ian Randall has a special ability – he can do the work of two other students by splitting in two, a second Ian emerging from his body. When Ian finds that he's got a C rather than an A in metalwork, he takes revenge on his teacher, Mr Frankle. Clark saw the bad mark with his X-ray vision, so is the only one who knows that Ian is lying when he says he got an A on the same day that Frankle doesn't turn up for school. When Ian becomes romantically involved with both Lana and Chloe, Clark tries to warn the girls – but neither believes him. Clark lets Ian know that he knows that Mr Frankle gave him a C.

Clark and Pete investigate the metal shop, where they find Mr Frankle – dead. Ian throws a match, and the whole place goes up in flames. Ian has the perfect alibi – one of him was with Chloe the whole time. When Clark works out that Ian has been attending separate classes simultaneously, he pages Ian to arrange separate dates on behalf of Chloe and Lana. Clark watches Chloe's house while Pete watches outside the Talon, and both see an Ian – at the same time. When Lana and Chloe finally admit that they're both seeing Ian, they confront him. To protect their academic future, the two Ians fake a joint suicide note from Chloe and Lana, then drag the girls to the dam to throw them off. Clark saves the girls. One Ian falls to his death while trying to kill Lana, and the remaining Ian is knocked out. After their mutual mistrust, Clark, Lana and Chloe agree to be friends again and to be open with each other.

With Martha busy working for Lionel, Jonathan tries to fix a tractor on his own, dropping it on his leg. Martha blames herself, but Jonathan reassures her that, although he's not always comfortable with her job, he doesn't want her to give it up.

Lex is having anger-management issues. He strikes up a relationship with Dr Helen Bryce, a young ER doctor with similar rage problems who also lives in the shadow of a domineering father.

Speech Bubbles: Chloe: 'You really can't imagine that someone would choose me over Lana, can you Clark?'

Ian (to Clark): 'Lana said you send off so many mixed signals you could scramble a radar.'

Clark: 'What kind of person asks the two people he cares about to lie for him?'

Small Town Boy: Clark helps Lana move into Chloe's place, only to find that neither of the girls has time to spend with him. He soon learns the meaning of pressure himself as, when his father is injured, Clark has to do more chores. This means cancelling time with Lana, but he manages to keep up with running the farm, getting up before Jonathan and doing all the early tasks.

When Clark confronts Ian about playing Lana and Chloe off against each other, Ian says he must have learned from the master, then recounts what Chloe and Lana said about Clark. Ian thinks Clark is jealous, as do the girls. When Clark sees Ian kissing Lana, he tries to tell her Ian was supposed to be going on a date with Chloe but Lana tells him to stay out of it. Clark then tries to tell Chloe, but she's already spoken to Ian, who says he would rather be with Chloe – in spite of Lana's advances. Clark can't win.

Clark's quote (see **Speech Bubbles**) indicates blinding hypocrisy, considering the tissue of lies that is Clark's entire life . . .

Girl Next Door: Lana moves in with the Sullivans, so she is sensitive when she's seeing a guy she thinks Chloe likes – Ian. Ian and Lana bond when he helps her out with some difficult maths studying and, in return, she gives him a peer recommendation for the Luthor Scholarship. When Clark tries to tell her that Ian is seeing Chloe, Lana doesn't want to know – Ian has told her that Chloe has a crush on him, but it isn't serious. Lana can't believe it when Clark accuses Ian of murder. When she comes around to realise that Ian is playing her and Chloe, Lana is insistent that it's not just Chloe who was made a fool of – Ian played them both.

Lana is being over courteous as a new resident of the Sullivan household, doing laundry and cooking dinner. She admits that, after her parents dying and Nell leaving, she may have some issues with being abandoned.

Torch Bearer: Chloe and Ian are both Smallville High overachievers – he specialises in maths and science, she in current affairs – so they have quite a bit in common. There's an instant attraction and Chloe asks Ian for an interview, promising to be gentle with him. They talk at the Talon, and bond over the fact that they're both only children, and can't wait to experience life outside Smallville. When Clark tries to warn Chloe that Ian is already seeing Lana, she replies that Lana is into Ian but that Ian would rather be with her. Chloe understandably takes it as a slight when Clark asks if she believes that. After Ian is defeated, Chloe thinks it's a problem with her, that she attracts mutants – another example of her low self-esteem.

Chloe tells Lana she isn't a glorified guest in the Sullivan household – she lives there now and should treat it like home. Chloe lists a series of ludicrous rules for the house. She admits that, when her mother left, she feared her father would leave too, until he told her she didn't have to work to be a part of the family – she just was. The Sullivans live in Pleasant Meadows, a LuthorCorp development.

Not an Evil Genius: Lex's temper isn't improving and, after reacting violently to a parking ticket by smashing up the traffic warden's car with a golf club, Lex ends up in anger management class. Lex doesn't make the best first impression on Dr Bryce, the beautiful young emergency room doctor treating Jonathan, when he gives her details of his father's personal specialists if Jonathan needs any help – she's drily offended that Lex thinks a small-town hospital can't cope with a broken leg. It doesn't help that Lex doesn't remember a previous encounter between them, when she was a medical student in Metropolis and he was a drunk she sobered up.

Bryce initially refuses a dinner date but as they get to know each other she realises they have a lot in common. Both Lex and Dr Bryce are rebelling against their fathers – hers is Dr Stanley Bryce, a famous cosmetic surgeon whose practice Helen refused to join, coming to Smallville instead. They also have similar anger issues because of their family tensions – Lex with the traffic warden, Bryce kicking an incompetent orderly. From anger management class together they move on to dinner. There's a distinct chemistry between the two and a relationship with someone in an ethical profession could help to redeem Lex, at least for now . . .

Just the Funny Guy: Pete gets Clark to use his X-ray vision to read his grade for metalwork class through the teacher's folder. Pete laughs at Clark's usual insistence that he and Lana are just friends.

Down On The Farm: Jonathan breaks his leg trying to fix a tractor, a task he expected Martha to help him with – but Martha was delayed by her job with Lionel. Jonathan ends up in hospital but is let out with a pair of crutches and a plastercast. Martha apologises, but Jonathan is frosty with her. Martha blames herself for not being home and takes the following day off. She feels she should be where she's needed. Jonathan finally tells her not to quit her job – but that he sometimes feels the Luthors take top priority with her. He wants to work through his jealousy and Martha confirms that Jonathan and Clark always come first.

Strange Visitors: Ian Randall, the murderous academic overacheiver, whose ability to split into two doesn't just mean he gets to do double the classwork of anyone else – it means he can date Lana and Chloe at the same time. Ian needs a high grade average to get the Luthor scholarship he wants, so that he can graduate early and be in an Ivy League college within the year.

Alternative local heroes, people who distinguish themselves publically, always work well in this show, as they get to have the adoration that Clark has to avoid: in this case, the specific adoration of Lana and Chloe, who are both in awe of Ian. For his part, Ian may not even be romantically interested in the girls, they simply serve his academic purpose: Lana gets him access to Lex, while Chloe promotes him with the big article in the *Torch*. When they find out, Ian is willing to throw the girls off a dam rather than see them ruin his reputation.

Love's Young Dream: The Clark–Lana–Chloe triangle is resolved after an episode of conflict and jealousy, with all parties agreeing to be just friends. All three meet at the Talon at the end of the episode and argue through their actions. The girls apologise to Clark for not listening to his warnings but, with Clark only ever being half truthful with them, how could he expect them to trust him? Lana says they made a mistake but it was theirs to make. Clark says that he doesn't want to be treated like a jealous boyfriend as none of them have ever dated. So they decide to be simple friends – clearing the way for relationships outside of the regulars. This is a sensible story move – the love triangle was getting stale and bitter and, with Chloe and Lana now close friends living in the same house, it's hardly fair to have Clark playing them off against each other.

From the Pages of: In one particularly silly historic comic story, Superman split into two distinct people – Superman Red and Superman Blue. Splitting into two allowed Superman not to have to choose between the two loves of his life, Lois Lane and Lana Lang – instead the girls got a Superman each! This old story springs to mind when Ian does exactly what Clark cannot – spreading himself between Lana and Chloe without having to make a choice.

In metalwork class Clark makes an ornate metal 'S' to update the school logo – it just happens to be exactly the same design as Superman wears on his chest.

Trivia: The Talon sign reads TWO FOR ONE LATTE SPECIALS when Lex has his run-in with the traffic warden.

Secret Identities: Jonathan Taylor Thomas is the voice of Tyler Tucker in the cartoon *The Wild Thornberrys* and made a memorable appearance in *Ally McBeal*. His most high-profile role was the voice of the young Simba in Disney's *The Lion King*. Emmanuelle Vaugier played Susie in *40 Days and 40 Nights* and Elinor in *Wishmaster 3*. Director Craig Zisk has worked on the Tollin/Robbins comic book series *Birds of Prey* as well as *The Tick*, *Alias* and Michael Rosenbaum sitcom *Zoe, Duncan, Jack, and Jane*.

Music: Tracks heard in this episode are 'I Wish I Cared' by legendary Norwegians A-Ha, 'Settle Hills' by Dem Hills, 'Uneven Odds' by Premonition and 'In A Young Man's Mind' by the Mooney Suzuki.

The Last Word: 'Hey, girls, how about a double date?' 'Dichotic' takes on themes of the pressure, role strain and stress of modern living, while still managing to be both an engaging action fantasy and very funny. How's that for balance? All of the characters suffer from the stress of trying to do too many things at once, and only Ian has a solution – albeit a very distinct one. Jonathan Taylor Thomas isn't just a pretty face – he invests Ian with a frantic impatience, a sense that he never gets to do as much as he wants and always has somewhere else to be. He's also sufficiently charming to make it believable that he would be attractive to both Lana and Chloe, who we've seen are both dedicated to their studies. Thomas helps to make Ian one of the most entertaining and fully rounded mutants-of-the-week of the series so far; only **12**, 'Leech' provides a better teen nemesis for Clark to face off against. There's something inherently hilarious about seeing Ian date Chloe and Lana at once, dodging the difficult decision in the way that Clark never can. As Ian actually says, in playing the girls off against each other, Ian is just doing what Clark does – but successfully.

Directed with verve and confidence, 'Dichotic' manages to make the two Ians a convincing proposition – impressive, considering the difficulties inherent in trying to keep track of a story featuring duplicates. That the episode also has a subtext, and pushes along the character arcs of most of the lead characters, makes it an even greater acheivement. While not necessarily the best or most dramatic episode of *Smallville,* 'Dichotic' is easily one of the most entertaining.

31
Skinwalker

Production #175059
1st US Transmission Date: 26 November 2002

Teleplay by Brian Peterson and Kelly Souders
Story by Mark Warshaw
Director: Marita Grabiak
Guest Starring: Patrick Cassidy (Henry Small), Tamara Feldman (Kyla),
Gordon Tootoosis (Joseph Willowbrook)
Co-starring: Mitchell Kosterman (Sheriff Ethan Talbot), Rob Morton,
Michael Tiernan (Foreman)

Synopsis: LuthorCorp are building Corporate Plaza, a hi-tech office building, on a site under which runs a series of ancient Native American caves. An old Native American, Joseph Willowbrook, leads the protests against the work. Later the foreman is chased by a wolf, then killed in an accidental gasolene explosion. Joseph is arrested when a towel with the foreman's blood on it is found in his trash. Joseph is released, and Martha is menaced by a wolf.

Meanwhile, Clark becomes romantically involved with Kyla, Joseph's granddaughter, after he falls into the caves while trial biking. Kyla tells Clark about the legend of Nooman (see 'The Legend of Nooman') and Clark gets involved in Kyla and Joseph's campaign to save the caves, but when Kyla discovers Clark's powers she suspects he *is* Nooman.

Chloe finds out that the name of Kyla's tribe translates as 'skinwalkers' and that they were mythically able to transform into animals. Clark reluctantly asks Kyla if Joseph is a skinwalker. When Lionel is attacked by a wolf it is severely wounded and Clark chases it through the woods near the mansion. The wolf turns into Kyla, who was the skinwalker all along. She dies.

Lionel initially wants Lex to be his partner on the site. Lex refuses but, after seeing the caves, he offers to buy

Lionel out so that he can preserve the site. Lionel refuses and is disgusted when Lex posts bail for Joseph. When the State exercises the Historical Artefacts Amendment to save the caves, they pay Lionel far less than Lex would have, and LexCorp still gets the contract to preserve the caves.

Lana gets good news – that Henry Small is her father, and bad news – that Whitney is lost in action.

Speech Bubbles: Kyla: 'Just because something's a myth doesn't make it not true.'

Chloe (to Lana): 'Maybe we should stop falling for guys who are trying to save the world.'

Clark (on Kyla): 'For the first time in my life I feel like everything fits, like we're destined to be together.'

Small Town Boy: Clark has to convince Kyla, his new love interest, that he's 'lucky' (his favourite excuse) when he falls one hundred feet into the cave without getting a scratch. When he first looks up at Kyla with her dark hair tied back, Clark mistakes her for Lana (he later tells Lana they have a lot in common). Clark gets closer to Kyla in the barn as she shows him the constellations and where the star that Nooman is supposed to come from once was. Kyla sees him use his powers to protect her and suspects that Clark is Nooman. Their relationship develops, fuelled by Kyla wearing a bracelet that suggests she is destined to be with Nooman. Clark also begins to think that their relationship is destined.

Clark's passion for protecting the caves and defending Joseph's cause when he is arrested doesn't just come from Kyla, but from a desire that people should have the right to understand their pasts – something which he has always been denied, and which the Nooman story promises to help solve. He's passionate enough to risk getting Lex involved, even though the caves are full of clues to Clark's abilities, including the octagonal mark. However, Clark isn't blind. When the clues point to a skinwalker, one of Kyla's people, being involved in the wolf attacks, Clark confronts Kyla. He doesn't suspect Kyla herself, presuming that the attacker is Joseph. He gets a nasty shock when

Kyla turns out to be the skinwalker and dies in his arms. After she is dead Clark takes up her cause, blocking the bulldozers at the building site.

Girl Next Door: Lana finds out that Henry Small really is her father. Henry doesn't feel able to take that place in her life, but wants to earn it. Although she's not at the stage where she feels she can ask favours of Henry, Lana tells him about Kyla's cause and gets him involved. It's Henry who helps get Joseph out of jail, and manages to get a court order to briefly stop work on the site. Lana seems reticent when she enters the barn to find Clark and Kyla standing close together. She tells Chloe that she thought Clark had difficulty opening up, but that it might have been that he was just waiting for the right girl all along. Lana takes it as a compliment when Clark says that Kyla was a lot like her.

Lana has been writing to Whitney since he went away. Whitney has shared more of his feelings in his letters since they broke up than when they were together. Lana is understandably worried when he stops writing back. She can't believe it when she finds out that Whitney has disappeared – as with when she found out about her father, the first person she runs to in a crisis is Clark.

Not an Evil Genius: Lex rejects Lionel's offer to let Lex come in as a partner on the office park project. Lex initially refuses to post bail for Joseph when asked by Clark, and instantly identifies Clark's enthusiasm as being due to Kyla. When Clark talks to Lex about destiny, Lex points out he's the wrong person to ask – he's been trying to escape his destiny for his entire life. But when Lex sees the octagonal gap in the caves, he takes an interest in preserving the site, realising that it holds the key not just to some ancient history, but also to the mysteries he's been trying to solve himself. Lex arranges the bail for Joseph and offers to buy the project from Lionel so that he can preserve the caves. When Lionel refuses, Lex backs the preservation of the caves by the state and bags the contract for the preservation in the process.

Lionel explicitly states the business developments that have taken place since **21**, 'Tempest' – Lex went through with the employee buyout of the plant, and has used it as the foundation of his own business empire. This is a useful explanation as, up to this episode, it's never been directly stated what happened.

Bad Dad: Lionel acts proud of Lex's independence, and suggests they join forces on his building project, claiming it's a sentimental gesture. Lex reminds Lionel that he equates sentimentality with vulnerability. Lionel is not happy when Lex posts bail for Joseph – it only deepens the public relations nightmare the project is becoming. When Lex offers to buy Lionel out of the office project so that the caves can be preserved, Lionel instantly realises that Lex hasn't turned activist but that there's value in that land. Lionel is determined to find out what Lex's discovery is.

Lionel compares Martha to his late wife – they have the same honesty, a quality Lionel has missed. He approves of Martha's plan to make a condolence call to the dead foreman's family – he doesn't want to seem uncaring. There's something seductive in the way that Lionel talks to Martha, a respect and compassion he doesn't show to anyone else.

Torch Bearer: Chloe doesn't know what to make of Clark's relationship with Kyla, or his new-found activist streak. She does some digging into Kyla's tribe and finds out about them being skinwalkers. Chloe tries to convince Clark that this legend might be true, but he doesn't believe her – ironic, considering the speed with which he swallowed the Nooman story.

Just the Funny Guy: Pete and Clark go trial biking together – until Clark falls through a hole into the caves.

Down at the Farm: Jonathan and Martha are worried about Clark getting too involved with Kyla and her grandfather, fearing that he'll reveal too much of himself because he thinks the story of Nooman holds the key to his origins. There's also the little matter of Martha's role as Lionel's executive assistant – Martha can see the importance of the office development to the local economy and this puts her in a difficult position when Clark becomes more involved with the protest. She then has to act in her official capacity as a representative of LuthorCorp. Finally, Martha backs the protestors, risking her job to stand with Clark as he blocks the bulldozers.

Strange Visitors: Kyla the wolf girl, or 'skinwalker', is not just the primary threat in the episode, but also the first superpowered love interest for Clark. Kyla's people were the result of interbreeding between a visitor from the stars and a human woman five hundred years ago. They brought green rocks which gave Kyla's people the ability to change shape. Kyla herself admits that she accepts that Clark is Nooman so easily because she feels different herself. Kyla believes in destiny and that the bracelet she wears marks her out as being destined to be with Nooman. (After Kyla's death, Joseph gives the bracelet to Clark to give to the girl he finally ends up with, allowing that prophecy perhaps to still be fulfilled.) Kyla says that she never intended to seriously harm anyone in her campaign of terror (indeed, the death of the foreman is an accident, caused when he fires a flare off and it lands in gasolene). As she dies, Kyla calls Clark 'Nooman'.

The Legend of Nooman: The legend of Nooman is a mixture of Clark's origins and the standards of the Superman tale and, as such, drops some hints about possible future storylines. The legend states that Nooman will come from the stars in a rain of fire, will have powers similar to those Clark possesses and will go on to protect the entire world. Nooman is a descendant of a previous alien visitor, who was the father of Kyla's people. This first visitor from the stars brought green rocks with him, which caused changes in people and the first skinwalkers to appear. This first visitor returned to the stars five centuries ago, promising that Nooman would follow him.

Nooman will have a friend, Sagat, who will turn against him. Together, according to Kyla, they will make a balance between good and evil. The woman who Nooman is destined to be with is illustrated with a design similar to Kyla's bracelet (though the green stone at the centre of the design could also be Lana's necklace).

Another Planet: The cave paintings incorporate an octagonal-shaped indentation similar to the lock on Clark's spaceship. The language in the caves is the same as that on the piece of metal Jonathan pulled out of the ship (see **1**, 'Pilot'). Kyla's grandfather can't translate it – it isn't a written language used by his people and Joseph has only seen individual symbols used in decoration rather than as text.

Love's Young Dream: With the air cleared in the Clark–Lana–Chloe axis at the end of **30**, 'Dichotic', the leads are free to pursue other options – which is exactly what Clark does with Kyla. When Lex asks what happened to Clark's infatuation with Lana, Clark says it's a different feeling with someone who returns his affections.

From the Pages of: Nooman, the prophesied hero of Kyla's people, who has powers similar to Clark's, is drawn in the cave paintings as blue with a stylised 'S' on his chest. Sound familiar?

Secret Identities: Gordon Tootoosis played a shamen in *The X-Files*, a chief in *Auf Wiedersehen, Pet* and a governor in *Reindeer Games* – just a few roles on his distinguished CV. Director Marita Grabiak has shot episodes of *Angel*, *Firefly* and *ER*.

Music: Clark and Pete's trial biking is accompanied by The Vines playing 'Outtatheway'. Other tracks include 'Don't Know Why' performed by Norah Jones, 'The Game of Love' by Santana with Michelle Branch, 'Psycho Ballerina' by Jackpot and 'Wave Goodbye' by Steadman.

The Last Word: 'It's amazing how quickly a light can go out.' It's a classic story: the hero falls for a girl he shares an adventurous spirit with, but her adventurous spirit leans towards the bad side of the tracks. The girl, on the brink of redemption, dies tragically. A classic heroic narrative, and it works as well here as it ever has. Breaking away from the usual love triangles, Clark gets a romantic relationship with someone who has a lot in common with him and who has a similar hidden life. That Kyla dies is inevitable, but it still has an impact.

The environmentally friendly themes of the episode are hackneyed but at least play well into the wider small-town-versus-big-city concerns of the series. As time goes on, it seems the *Smallville* production team are more and more willing to go beyond their initial adolescent tensions and take on wider issues. Bringing in questions of history and the preservation of monuments and the conflict between these aims and immediate economic needs, adds a level of maturity to the series, one which is welcome.

That this history lesson takes in alien visitors lays the groundwork for future storylines. Were Kyla's people the only tribe to be visited by aliens? And just how does this relate to Clark? That these clues are in Lex's hands as well adds another possible spin to this interesting development.

On the surface a simple tale of boy meets wolf-girl, 'Skinwalker' has, like the best of this series, hidden depths.

Forthcoming Episodes

At the time of writing, the second season is set to continue with:

Confirmed as reappearing midway through the season are Lana's ex, Whitney Fordman (Eric Johnson) and shape-shifter Tina Greer from **4**, 'X-Ray'. Rumours state that a number of classic *Superman* characters will appear through the rest of the season, including Maggie Sawyer of the Metropolis Police Department's Special Crimes Unit (SCU), and possibly future *Daily Planet* editor Perry White. Lois Lane and Bruce Wayne are still future possibilities, although the latter is unlikely to appear soon due to reluctance on the part of Warner Bros to have a major film franchise in a TV project. Expect the *Smallville* production team to get their way on this one if the series' success continues!

Smallville on the Page: Novels and Comic Strips

Printed incarnations of a series are a vital support network for any franchise. When George Lucas started to boost interest again in *Star Wars* in the 90s, he did so initially by launching a trilogy of novels; books have kept *Doctor Who* fans stocked up with new adventures in the years since the television series ended; all versions of *Star Trek* live on in print. In the world of comics, the role that the *Aliens* and *Predator* comics have played in keeping the spirit of the films alive cannot be underestimated, while the writers and actors behind *Buffy the Vampire Slayer* and *Angel* frequently contribute stories to the spin-off comics, relishing the freedom the medium allows. Printed spin-offs are not just a ready source of easy income for the licence holders, they give fans something to tide them over between episodes and they maintain a brand's presence on shop shelves – a proliferation of merchandise keeps the name in the public eye and suggests commercial success of a property.

In other words, books and comics aren't just cash-in merchandise, they fulfil an important role in turning a property from a success into a phenomenon. *Smallville* spin-offs have been approached with a degree of caution, with some time elapsing before the first books and comics arrived. Aside from 'Elemental', the *TV Guide* comic strip, none of the stories below appeared before the start of the second season of the show. However, with the television show rolling into a second year with even more success than before, a healthy publishing schedule has now developed and looks set to keep running for the foreseeable future.

Novels from Aspect Warner Books Inc (USA) and Orbit Books (UK)

Strange Visitors

by Roger Stern
Published: September 2002

Synopsis: Having discovered a meteorite elsewhere, faith healer Donald Jacobi comes to town, promising amazing healing powers from the meteor rocks. When an accident with a laser and a meteor rock does actually cure cancer sufferer Stuart Harrison, Jacobi goes from being a con man to a true believer. But not everyone is happy with his findings . . .

Notes: In his author's notes Stern states that this story is set between **14**, 'Zero' and **15**, 'Nicodemus'. Virtually every recurring character from the show appears at some point in the book, including Roger Nixon and Professor Hamilton. In a very cute scene, Hamilton tells Lex that the meteor rocks contain large quantities of the element Krypton. Continuity references abound, as the characters repeatedly think and talk about the events of earlier episodes.

Lex has a CB radio headset in his car and wears a false beard at one point.

Secret Identities: Roger Stern is well known for his writing work on the various *Superman* comics, which led to him novelising *The Death and Life of Superman*, the long story arc that killed Superman and eventually resurrected him. Stern's novelisation made the *New York Times* bestseller list.

The Last Word: An inauspicious start to the range, *Strange Visitors* lacks any substance of plot and displays some woefully unsubtle writing techniques. The story never really kicks in and most of the book is spent with various characters discussing or thinking about their personal histories. There's a certain logic to recapping what has gone before for the benefit of new readers, but when it's done in a manner this cack-handed and overblown it does more harm than good. Does the reader really need chunks of novelised scenes from the pilot dropped in as Clark's reminiscences? Shouldn't the 'meteor healer' plot have more to it than two set pieces, only one of which really constitutes an action scene? Worst of all, the characters frequently don't sound like themselves, a cardinal sin in this kind of book. Some of them are treated well – Lionel Luthor in particular is excellently handled, mainly one suspects because he's very similar to the comic book version of Lex – but others get lumbered with bizarre info-dumps and stilted dialogue.

Stern wears his knowledge on his sleeve too much – do readers really need a long lecture on the history of *The Three Stooges*? It doesn't clarify anything about the characters, and has no thematic relation to the plot (compare and contrast with the beautiful use of *Cyrano de Bergerac* in the young-adult novel **See No Evil**).

Strange Visitors is rarely completely awful, but is frequently mediocre. It eventually builds up to being quite readable, especially in the scenes with Jacobi and his sidekick, Wolfe, but then ends with a couple of pedestrian action scenes. Underwhelming.

Dragon

by Alan Grant
Published: November 2002

Synopsis: Biker Ray Dansk has just been released from jail, where he's been doing time for murder. Returning to his home town of Smallville, Ray hides out in an old cave. The cave is tainted with meteors and Ray begins to resemble the dragon tatooed on his chest, physically transforming as he seeks to take revenge on those who testified against him. Meanwhile, both Clark and Lana visit the shop owned by old Miss Mayfern, who serves them mysterious green tea. Both get their secret wishes fulfilled – Lana's desire to swap

Whitney for Clark becomes real, while Clark becomes the normal kid he always wanted to be . . .

Notes: Chloe jokes that, with all the weirdness going on, they could film *The X-Files* there. *Smallville* is, of course, shot in Vancouver – the same place they filmed the first five seasons of *The X-Files*. Whitney's surname is Ellsworth rather than Fordman (see **Arrival**) – clearly the writers of these novels were given out-of-date character outlines to work from. There's a reference to Ray being a 'ghost rider' – *Ghost Rider* is a supernatural biker comic published by Marvel and is frequently tipped to become a movie.

Secret Identities: Scottish comics writer Alan Grant has worked on many strips for the UK's *2000 AD* and has also written a large number of *Batman* comics.

The Last Word: A big step up from *Strange Visitors*, *Dragon* is flawed but interesting. The writing style is brisk and efficient, while all the regular characters seem like the ones seen on TV – a vital element in any tie-in book. There are some unusual quirks, including a near-death experience scene for Pete that hardly fits into the series' usual science fiction approach, and a series of references to the Luthor Mansion's past in Scotland that seem like a gratuitous homage to the author's homeland. However, for the most part, *Dragon* is readable and pacy, an efficient action yarn that feels like it could be an episode of the show. By the end the logic of the storyline seems to be increasingly fuzzy, but that's not unusual in the TV series; in a novel it seems more jarring, but it at least fits with the tone of the show.

Hauntings

by Nancy Holder
Published: January 2003

Synopsis: Clark and Lana meet Ginger, whose scientist father died in an experiment years before. Together they try and solve the mystery of the ghosts haunting Ginger's new home, and how they relate to the glowing green presence in the cornfields . . .

Notes: The book claims the fertiliser plant was built by LuthorCorp in the mid 1980s. Either that's a typo, or Holder hasn't actually seen the show: Lionel signed the deal to build the plant in 1989, back in **1**: 'Pilot'. As the 1989 date is all over the series, it's hard to see how the author got this wrong. Holder gives some extra detail to the events of **1**: 'Pilot': in that episode, Lex apparently drove his Porsche into Clark and off the Old Mill Bridge, which is on the Carlin Road (named, one presumes, after former DC Comics *Superman* editor Mike Carlin). In another basic error, Clark is in the room as Lex and Hamilton openly work on a meteor-related experiment – as Lex kept his involvement with Hamilton and his private researches into the meteors secret from everyone, but *especially* Clark, this rings incredibly false.

Secret Identities: Nancy Holder is the author of several *Buffy The Vampire Slayer* and *Angel* novels, as well as tie-in books for *Sabrina the Teenage Witch* and *Highlander*.

The Last Word: A straight ghost story with the barest sliver of meteor activity to fit it into the *Smallville* format, *Hauntings* manages to sustain itself through most of the novel's length, only to collapse completely with a denouement that fails to justify anything that came before. There's no clever twist, no attempt to tie the supernatural goings-on into the series' usual science fiction/superhero logic. A story about people becoming ghosts after being involved with the meteors would have been fun; a ghost story with a few references to the meteors 'boosting' the power of the spectres isn't. The prologue to the book suggests that the experiments of Ginger's parents may have some connection and that there may be a pseudo-scientific explanation to what has happened but, apart from a sappy climax where Ginger's father appears out of the afterlife, there's no connection between Ginger's personal tragedy and the hauntings than a very loose theme of coming to terms with the dead.

It's a shame that basic plotting and a failure to get to grips with the series' tone so elude Holder as she nails most of the characters' concerns and voices and produces decent

prose for the majority of the book. There are enough
continuity references to suggest Holder has at least read
synopses of the episodes, but little sense of the series'
premise. One can't help feeling, considering the author's
CV, that this is a retooled *Buffy* or *Angel* novel proposal. In
one of those series, which both deal in the supernatural and
are better suited to more spiritual themes, it would have
been fine. As a *Smallville* novel *Hauntings* just doesn't work.

Whodunnit

by Dean Wesley Smith
Published: March 2003

Synopsis: Clark and Lex team up to unravel a mystery
involving the brutal murder of a family and the abduction
of Lionel Luthor.
Secret Identities: Dean Wesley Smith is the author or
co-author of numerous *Star Trek* novels.

Young-Adult Novels from Little, Brown and Company (USA), Atom Books (UK)

#1 Arrival

by Michael Teitelbaum
Published: October 2002

Synopsis: Novelisation of the pilot episode, including some
scenes deleted from the broadcast version. See **1**, 'Pilot' for
more story info . . .
Notes: This novelisation seems to be based on an early
version of the script, including many deleted scenes (some
that are included on the DVD of the episode, some that
are not) and details not seen before. Some of these clash
radically with the series – Whitney's surname is different,
Lionel is considerably older and there's an explanation for

Clark's adoption that doesn't match the mystery-shrouded business referred to in **14**, 'Zero'. The plotline with Lex giving Lana's necklace to Clark from **2**, 'Metamorphosis' is folded into the last chapter allowing Teitelbaum to cleverly tie up that plot thread.

Secret Identities: Michael Teitelbaum is the author of tie-in books for *Samurai Jack*, *Pokémon* and *Batman Beyond*, and is also responsible for that classic of world literature, the *Paula Abdul Poster Book*!

The Last Word: An efficient novelisation of the first episode of the show, *Arrival* takes the action from the screen and gives it a little more detail. Some of the details jar with what we know from the series but, aside from an overuse of comic book sound effects in the action scenes, this is a fair, if uninspiring, bit of writing.

#2 See No Evil

by Cherie Bennett and Jeff Gottesfeld
Published: October 2002

Synopsis: Clark gets thrust into the acting world as he becomes the last-minute lead in a school production of *Cyrano de Bergerac*. Clark's leading lady, school diva Dawn Mills, uses a meteor rock to make herself invisible and begins to take violent revenge on her rivals. When Clark fails to take enough of an interest in her, Dawn decides to take Lana out of the picture . . .

Notes: Meteor-induced invisibility was a plot device in **10**, 'Shimmer'. Clark demonstrates another remarkable ability – a super-memory that allows him to memorise the play without even trying.

Secret Identities: The authors wrote **8**, 'Jitters' for television, but are also renowned writers of books and plays for young adults. Their *Teen Angels* series of books is being developed into a drama for the WB (the same network who broadcast *Smallville*).

The Last Word: Now this is more like it! As you would expect from a novel written by writers from the TV series,

See No Evil effectively captures the spirit, characters and mood of the show. The plot has the simple hooks of a Season One episode, right down to the Clark-left-alone ending, but gains extra depth from the echoes of *Cyrano* in the regular characters' lives – of particular note are a superb variation on the fencing-and-insults scene from the play, with Lex deriding his own baldness, and a lovely sequence where Lana helps Clark rehearse the play's balcony scene. The prose style is simple and punchy, but never condescending, functioning as a decent teen novel as well as a TV tie-in. Highly recommended, this is a story that would have been worthy of airtime as part of the TV show, and makes for the best print spin-off so far.

#3 Flight

by Cherie Bennett and Jeff Gottesfeld
Published: December 2002

Synopsis: Clark's fear of flying is put to the test when Pete and Lana persuade him to go skydiving with them. Clark takes on a job at the local pizza parlour and meets a young girl, Tia, who has a possessive father and an unusual trait – green wings growing from her back. A series of robberies happen over town, with green feathers found at the scene, and Clark helps Tia learn to fly while trying to get to the truth about her criminal family.

Notes: There's a slightly inept attempt to fit this story into Season Two continuity – Whitney is referred to as being on leave from the army, but Lionel still has his sight. These two facts are completely contradictory. Chloe discusses Tia's missing mother, but she never refers to her own mother having left home when she was little (see **28**, 'Lineage').

The Last Word: Another great book by Bennett and Gottesfeld, who once again show the authors of the 'adult' range how it's done. While the central plot is slim – there's never any doubt who the villains are and the confrontation with them is rapidly resolved – the book has character and emotion by the bucketload. Tia Haines, and the staff of the pizza parlour, are all welcome new characters, while the regulars are portrayed with uncanny accuracy. Yet again, the authors balance their knowledge of the series with their abilties as writers of fiction for young adults to create another enjoyable book. Of particular note is the way they give the characters inner lives – unnecessary on TV, but vital in a novel. Most memorable of these character moments is the final scene, where Clark skydives for the first time. This hint of his superheroic future is alone worth the price of the book, and is beautifully executed.

#4 Animal Rage

by David Cody Weiss and Bobbi JG Weiss
Published: February 2003

Synopsis: An animal-rights activist, Heather, gains the ability to shape shift into animal form after coming into contact with the meteor rocks.
Secret Identities: David Cody Weiss and Bobbi JG Weiss are co-authors of a number of books tieing into *Sabrina the Teenage Witch*.

#5 Speed

by Cherie Bennett and Jeff Gottesfeld
Published: April 2003

Synopsis: When a series of racist attacks plague the town, Clark has to deal with a hate-fuelled attacker who has superspeed abilities.

#6 Secrets

by Suzan Colon
Published: June 2003

Synopsis: Lex develops a mutual attraction to Clark's Spanish teacher, Lilia. Unfortunately, not only does Clark have a crush on the same teacher, but he suspects she can read minds . . .

Secret Identities: Suzan Colon has written a number of *Batman* books, including a photo-book adaptation of Akiva Goldsman's dreadful script for Joel Schumacher's *Batman & Robin*.

Comic Strips

Elemental

Published in *TV Guide* 8–14 December 2001

Story: Alfred Gough and Miles Millar
Script: Martin Pasko
Art: Terry Dodson (pencils), Rachel Dodson (inks),
Alex Sinclair (colours)

Synopsis: Lex is throwing a party when Jacob Snell, a kid with a grudge against the Luthors, uses his power to control the weather to attack them. Jacob loses control of his power, though, and is left without his memory. Lex is suspicious that Clark always seems to be around when such freak events occur.
Secret Identities: Martin Pasko's comic writing includes *Dr Fate* and *Blackhawk*. Terry and Rachel Dodson have devoted their artistic abilities to Kevin Smith's comic *Spider-Man/Black Cat: The Evil That Men Do*.
The Last Word: To describe 'Elemental' as 'slight' would be to attribute to it depths it doesn't possess. Little more than a brief pastiche of the Season One formula, the story is nonetheless a cute oddity for fans and a clever way of promoting the series to *TV Guide* readers. The Dodsons' art is nice enough, but doesn't really convey the characters very well.

Raptor

Published in *Smallville: The Comic #1*

Writer: Mark Verheiden (special thanks to Ben Verheiden)
Art: Roy Allan Martinez (artist), Trish Mulvihill (colourist),
Digital Chameleon (colour separations)

Synopsis: Embittered teenager Greg Fox tries to attack Lex with an explosive. When the explosion blasts fragments of meteor and fossil into Greg's body, he begins to undergo a transformation into a half-dinosaur creature. Clark has to save both Lana and Lex from the beast . . .

Secret Identities: Artist Roy Allan Martinez has worked on Wildstorm's *Grifter* and DC Comics' *Wonder Woman*. Trish Mulvihill has been nominated for comics' prestigious Eisner award for her colours on *Wonder Woman* and *100 Bullets*. Digital Chameleon are a company working on digital colours across the comic book industry.

The Last Word: An obvious attempt to do a story that would be difficult to pull off on TV, 'Raptor' has little more to offer than a monster beyond the reach of a television budget. The script is functional and in a clever device uses Chloe as a narrator, but the storyline is too pedestrian. Greg, like so many meteor mutants, is thinly motivated and shallow. While Roy Allan Martinez's art is highly intricate, that intricacy and realism makes the poor likenesses of the regulars less forgiveable – not capturing the characters is acceptable when the art style is more simplistic, but here the characters just look *wrong*. Future strips would benefit from a bolder approach than this pseudo-realism, as demonstrated by the other strip in the comic . . .

Exile and the Kingdom

Published in *Smallville: The Comic #1*

Writer: Michael Green
Art: John Paul Leon (artist), Melissa Edwards (colourist and separations)

Synopsis: Lex muses on the changes in his life since he came to Smallville, and on how he no longer wants to be part of the big-city lifestyle he left behind.

Secret Identities: John Paul Leon has drawn *RoboCop: Prime Suspect*, *Static* (and *Static Shock*), *Challengers of the Unknown*, *New X-Men* and a *Superman: The Man of Steel* annual. Melissa Edwards has worked on *Tattered Banners* and *Disavowed*.

The Last Word: By far the better of the two strips in DC Comics' first *Smallville* comic, 'Exile and the Kingdom' is a pleasant surprise from writer Michael Green, whose TV scripts have tended towards the formulaic. Here he delivers a touching insight into Lex, who believes that living in Smallville is allowing him to change for the better. John Paul Leon's likenesses of the characters are not precise, but the boldness of his linework more than makes up for any inaccuracies. A good script, lush artwork . . . what more could you want?

Afterword: A Year and a Half in Kansas

First seasons of an American television show are an amazing learning curve. Once a pilot has been accepted and a series approved, production has to be stepped up in a matter of a few months, throwing the production team into the hectic process of creating twenty-odd hours of television drama. During the course of that first year a series will hopefully find both an audience and its creative feet, often developing into something other than the producers had originally intended. The sheer speed with which that quantity of television air time can chew through stories and ideas can produce unexpected results – a series can mine its original premise for ideas within a very short period of time, at which point it has to evolve or face creative death.

By these standards, *Smallville*'s first season seems to have had a reasonably controlled evolution. A number of interviews with the creative team show that the repetitive nature of the initial 'mutant-of-the-week' stories was entirely intentional, creating a comfortable formula to allow an audience to build, at the same time giving a constant restatement of the series' ideas and characters. As the series progresses and becomes more confident in its ratings position, the creators allow themselves more sustained story arcs and less emphasis on simple action stories. Season Two sees the production team expand their storytelling repertoire even further, creating a mesh of ongoing character conflicts and subplots through the first ten episodes of year two. Having found its feet in its first year, the show now has the confidence to expand beyond formula, to let its characters and storylines grow. There are still a few places the series could go – a super-powered nemesis that takes more than one episode to despatch

would prove an interesting innovation and would provide
a larger threat for Clark to face off with.

The character dynamics of a series will inevitably only
prove their worth once a series is on the air. Two
storylines, though, seem well planned from the outset – the
developing relationship between Clark and Lana and the
friendship between Clark and Lex. Both ingeniously twist
in the middle of the season, taking material that threatened
to topple over due to its lack of closure and sending it
spinning in a fresh direction.

The love triangle between Clark, Lana and Whitney
dominates early episodes, providing a core romantic focus
that's vital for a new television drama. However, these
'will-they, won't-they' relationships can either become
tiresome or can be too easily resolved, causing audiences
to switch off. Whitney's family troubles cause Clark and
Lana's relationship to cool down as common decency
forces them not to crush Whitney's spirit while he's
suffering this personal crisis. The tension between Clark
and Lana remains, but is unspoken and incapable of being
fulfilled. It's a neat device to avoid the pitfalls of such key
romances. By the end of the season the ensemble are
well-enough established for the series not to be tied to a
central romance, allowing Clark to date Chloe and Whitney to grow beyond his original arch-nemesis status into a
fuller human being. Ironically, **21**, 'Tempest' and **22**,
'Vortex' dissolve much of this in two episodes: Whitney
departs, to be dumped by Lana a few episodes later; Clark
and Chloe rapidly break up; and enough cold water is
thrown on Clark's relationships with both Lana and Chloe
in the first few episodes of Season Two to put the series on
a completely different track. It's a clear signal that the
production team aren't too worried about having to
include a regular dose of teen romance, and that the series
is about far more than love triangles and sexual tension.

Clark and Lex's friendship goes through a similar arc to
the Clark–Lana–Whitney axis, although the tension between them comes from a rather different source: Lex's
lingering suspicions about Clark's heroic rescue of Lex

from his sinking Porsche. Someone as intelligent and as insatiable for knowledge as Lex couldn't ignore the signs that something is up with his new friend and the investigation into the accident causes a thread of tension to run through their relationship for the first half of the season. **12**, 'Leech', where Lex sees a powerless Clark at the same time as he gets the results of the investigation back, is an incredible exercise in plot convenience, but successfully manages to redirect Lex's attention away from any suspicions he has about Clark. Lex's protective attitude towards Clark's family causes him to suppress the findings of his investigation, as well as dismissing them himself. The remains of that investigation lead to the climactic events of **21**, 'Tempest', which threaten to expose Clark to the world by revealing his Kryptonian origins via his reactivated spaceship. This whole arc seems meticulously planned and provides a dramatic spine for the first season. Perhaps realising the limitations of having Lex constantly on Clark's trail, the production team set a different course in Season Two, focussing Lex's interest on his new business developments and passing Lex's former interest in Clark's oddness on to Lionel and, more intriguingly, Lana. What was once a source of tension between Clark and Lex – the fact that Clark performs seemingly inexplicable rescues – becomes one of the secrets that stop Lana getting close to Clark.

Other developments within the series seem more ad hoc, based on the growing evidence of the strength of the cast. Allison Mack is instantly sympathetic as Chloe, and her fast-talking approach to the character makes her a great vehicle for jokes and exposition. As such, Chloe quickly becomes a dominant member of the supporting cast throughout the first season: the character adds depth to any scene with Clark, communicating her affection for him through some sharp non-verbal acting. Just look at the number of times Chloe makes doe eyes at Clark when he's not looking or her obvious discomfort when he obsesses over Lana. This prominent use of the character has been widely accepted by fans of the show, with dedicated Chloe websites and even a campaign for a Chloe action figure! In Season Two we see a shift in Chloe's character as she tries to distance herself from Clark and she falls out of the limelight for a while, before emerging as a friend and confidante for Lana. As Lana's feelings have frequently been mysterious in Season One – ostensibly so as not to reveal how much of an interest she has in Clark – having Chloe around becomes a useful device to tap into Lana's psyche, and thereby deepen the character.

Unfortunately, with Lex, Lana and Chloe all proving fascinating characters in a scene with Clark, something has had to give. In this case Sam Jones III's portrayal of Pete Ross – ostensibly Clark's best friend – has been sidelined for much of the year. It's no fault of the charming Jones that there's been little room for Pete in the stories, and towards the end of the season efforts have been made to give him a stronger presence in episodes such as 'Nicodemus' and 'Drone'. Pete's building resentment of Lex is a useful character trait, but more was needed for him to truly stand out. In **24**, 'Duplicity', the third episode of Season Two, Pete gets that promised new direction, discovering Clark's secret and becoming a partner in Clark's superheroic activities.

As well as Pete being sidelined, Season One also saw Martha (Annette O'Toole) frequently being little more than a referee between Jonathan and Clark's father–son conflicts; O'Toole was another casualty of the relationship between two actors (Schneider and Welling) sparking on screen and thus being brought to the fore. Season Two sees a new role for Martha as she becomes personal assistant to Lionel Luthor. The conflict between Martha's urban upbringing and rural adulthood have been hinted at in the past and putting Martha in a professional role relating to the Luthors puts her at the forefront of the LuthorCorp storylines, as well as close to the heart of the Lex–Lionel conflict.

Lionel Luthor himself is another character who has taken a larger role in Season Two, after the character's prominence grew through Season One. As Lionel, John

Glover has proved to be another paternal asset to the series and his verbal sparring with Lex has allowed both actors to cut loose. Realising the effectiveness of the Glover–Rosenbaum dynamic in bringing out Lex's darker characteristics, the production team hired Glover as a regular cast member for the second season, blinding Lionel to create a degree of sympathy for him as he twists his way into the life of Smallville's residents. Lionel is aware that there's more to Clark than meets the eye – not that he can see the boy himself – and **28**, 'Lineage' reveals that Lionel knows full well that the adoption of Clark is a sham. After all, he organised it. Lionel is the greatest imaginable threat to Clark's secret – he knows Clark appeared on the day of the meteor shower, he knows the adoption is a fraud, and he knows about Dr Hamilton's research. Could Lionel be the large-scale nemesis necessary to provide a recurring threat through a number of episodes? Should he get his hands on some meteor-rock contact lenses, you can bet on it . . .

There's one card the production team still have up their sleeves that they have yet to play. In spite of flirting with the possibility of opening up the secrets of the spaceship that brought Clark to Earth, **22**, 'Vortex' sees the ship deactivated with no great revelations. For now, Clark's alien heritage remains a secret. But in **31**, 'Skinwalker' there is the tale of another visitor from the stars, many centuries ago, who arrived from the sky like Clark and had similar powers. To what extent have Clark's people been involved in human history and what does that have to do with Clark being sent to Earth? Could there be other members of Clark's race seen in the show? It's certainly just one of many exciting possibilities for a show that has established itself both in creative terms and in the ratings in the course of a season and a half on the air. With a solid basis like this to build on, the sky might not even be a limitation.

Credits and Thanks

I am gratefully indebted to the following people and sources whose knowledge I have tapped for this book.

Les Daniels' *Superman: The Complete History* is an essential purchase for anyone interested in reading up on the character, and is beautifully designed by Chip Kidd.

www.kryptonsite.com has repeatedly proven to be the most up to date source of news on *Smallville* and is highly recommended as a resource. www.tvtome.com is an excellent source of general television information and www.imdb.com is similarly useful for credit information.

Thanks to Allan Bednar, Graeme Burk, Greg McElhaton, Lance Parkin, Eddie Robson and Jim Smith for their insights and background knowledge. Any accuracies that may have slipped into this book are entirely due to these gentlemen. Thanks to Jon de Burgh Miller for sorting out my computer during the writing of this book. Without the help of Scott Andrews, the updates for the second season would not have been possible – cheers, Scott.

Apologies to Vanessa Hill, Sarah Archibald and anyone else who I may have failed to keep in touch with while writing the book.